REPARATIVE MEDIA

Distribution Matters

Edited by Joshua Braun and Ramon Lobato

The Distribution Matters series publishes original scholarship on the social impact of media distribution networks. Drawing widely from the fields of communication history, cultural studies, and media industry studies, books in this series ask questions about how and why distribution matters to civic life and popular culture.

Emily West, *Buy Now: How Amazon Branded Convenience and Normalized Monopoly*

Robin Steedman, *Creative Hustling: Women Making and Distributing Films from Nairobi*

Anne Kaun and Fredrik Stiernstedt, *Prison Media: Incarceration and the Infrastructures of Work and Technology*

Lee McGuigan, *Selling the American People: Advertising, Optimization, and the Origins of Adtech*

Jennifer Holt, *Cloud Policy: A History of Regulating Pipelines, Platforms, and Data*

Aymar Jèan Escoffery, *Reparative Media: Cultivating Stories and Platforms to Heal Our Culture*

REPARATIVE MEDIA

CULTIVATING STORIES AND PLATFORMS TO HEAL OUR CULTURE

AYMAR JÈAN ESCOFFERY

The MIT Press
Cambridge, Massachusetts
London, England

The MIT Press
Massachusetts Institute of Technology
77 Massachusetts Avenue, Cambridge, MA 02139
mitpress.mit.edu

This publication has been supported by the MIT Press Grant Program for Diverse Voices.

The MIT Press would like to thank the anonymous peer reviewers who provided comments on drafts of this book. The generous work of academic experts is essential for establishing the authority and quality of our publications. We acknowledge with gratitude the contributions of these otherwise uncredited readers.

This book was set in ITC Stone Serif Std and ITC Stone Sans Std by New Best-set Typesetters Ltd. Printed and bound in the United States of America.

Library of Congress Cataloging-in-Publication Data is available.

ISBN: 978-0-262-55326-1

10 9 8 7 6 5 4 3 2 1

EU Authorised Representative: Easy Access System Europe, Mustamäe tee 50, 10621 Tallinn, Estonia | Email: gpsr.requests@easproject.com

CONTENTS

ACKNOWLEDGING WHO I COME FROM: HEALING OVER CENTURIES

Reparative Media is about healing ourselves, our communities, and our cultural systems, how stories are technologies for repair at each level, told through my story of cocreating a streaming media platform by and for storytellers surviving multiple systems of harm. On this journey, I learned that practicing repair seeds reparations. We think of reparations as people getting money for being harmed, but it is so much more than that. It is about cultivating new ways of being, new stories and infrastructures that can heal, informed by our ancestries. Reparations provoke questions best answered in story. Who are you and how have you been harmed? What are you owed? So I start this book by acknowledging my ancestral intelligences, not only the stories of who I come from and who owes me but also, more importantly, who I owe for helping me heal.

Professionally, I'm known as AJ. Family, friends, and community know me as Aymar (uh-MAR; the "y" is silent, and if you don't know how to pronounce it, call me AJ!). I am the Black queer son of Caribbean immigrants, most recently Jamaica and St. Lucia. My parents immigrated to the South Bronx, New York City in the 1970s. My mother, Pam, and my father, Francis, met in New York, but I was raised in a mostly white and Asian American gentrifying New Jersey suburb, where my grandmother, born Barbara Escoffery, moved to care for a client. I never lost sight of New York. (It will come up later in the book.) My mother loves fashion and worked at Macy's Herald Square until I was a teenager. I have vivid memories of visiting New York City in the 1990s, especially on Thanksgiving when my mother took us to march in the Macy's Parade. I thought she was the coolest person ever and dreamed of living the New York City fantasy. But my mother faced a glass ceiling as a Black woman in fashion in the 1990s and eventually left Macy's to become a middle school teacher and then a principal of a school in Harlem. Although he never went to college, my father worked his way from janitor to the facilities manager for dozens of Bronx public schools. He worked two jobs to support our family, spending several nights each week in Columbia University Hospital's boiler room. I am immensely indebted to my parents, who sacrificed so I could have the life that inspired this book.

I grew up surrounded by intelligent, ambitious, caring Black women who anchored me in love and inspired me to enter academia. My mother's mother was a second mother to me. She drove my brother and I to school every day and made us breakfast and dinner every weekday. Fleeing a terrible marriage to a Kingston-based entrepreneur, my grandmother left Jamaica for the US with only her kids and a sixth-grade education. The US needed immigrants to care for aging Americans, so she spent her life as a domestic worker caring for seniors, using home-cooked meals and conversation to help them live longer than doctors' diagnoses. Caretaking may not have come naturally to my grandmother. She grew up a trickster. She loves to recount her childhood hijinks in Jamaica, pranking neighbors who flocked to her grandmother's home looking for food and shelter. Although she was not a natural caretaker, she learned to be a great one, an important lesson for me. She cultivated her caretaking skills not only for her senior clients but also her neighbors: She befriended our town's white sheriff and cooked dinner for his kid too (his wife could not cook, which taught me to appreciate my grandmother's culinary art!). She raised three daughters and one son, my uncle Mickey, all of whom grew up to be independent and relatively successful, especially in the field of education. My grandmother lives with my auntie Marcia, a computer science professor who has been studying artificial intelligence for over two decades. My auntie Roxan lives several towns over. She was the cool auntie, a teacher, and eventually a principal who loves arts, crafts, and . . . genealogy.

My aunties Roxan and Marcia's research into our family tree was indispensable as I started to write this book and wondered about who I came from, my relationship to slavery and colonialism. My auntie has been researching the family tree long before Ancestry.com made it easier. Since the 1990s, she has been visiting every family funeral she can and asking everyone about what they know, performing grassroots research. Her first important source was my grandmother's aunt Dorcas Escoffery, who, when I was twelve, became the first person in my immediate life to pass away. Aunt Dorcas lived with my grandmother in her living room, and I saw her every day. A bourgeois daughter of the Jamaican upper class and seventy-plus years my senior, Aunt Dorcas and I did not have much to discuss, but she was always interested in my day, told me I was smart, and encouraged me to keep applying myself in school. I believe my auntie would have been proud that I grew up to be a professor who organizes racialized people toward liberation, as the Escofferys have been organizers and entrepreneurs as well as adventurers and migrants seeking freedom on Caribbean shoals.

By 2021, in the depths of the pandemic and the death of my aunty Olive, I finally accepted my aunt Roxan's offer to learn about our history, and she had a lot to say. With Aunt Dorcas's help, she traced my maternal line to the 1700s. Sitting in my grandmother's home was a woman whose great grandfather had memories of the Haitian Revolution and campaigned for abolition in Jamaica. From Dorcas, Roxan learned of my most infamous ancestor, a man named John Escoffery, my grandmother's great grandfather, a shopkeeper in Kingston. There is more research on John Escoffery than anyone else in my family because he was enmeshed in an important case in Jamaica preceding the abolition of slavery on the island. In the Lecesne-Escoffery case of the 1820s, colonizers accused Louis Celeste Lecesne and John Escoffery of campaigning for the abolition of slavery. The colonial white government pursued their deportation, claiming they were not citizens of the British Empire because they were secretly born in Haiti. Colonists feared postrevolutionary Haitian migrants, believing the Haitian Revolution would inspire others across the Caribbean.

My ancestor might have been organizing, but according to my research, not for the full abolition of slavery, though it might have helped. Instead, he was organizing the "free people of color" of Jamaica—often mulatto or mixed people who owned land and slaves themselves—to be able to have the same rights as white people (e.g., inherit estates and serve on juries). "There was . . . little likelihood of [free people of color] uniting with slaves in a plot against the whites, as the people had long emphasized their superiority over the slaves and in return were generally disliked by the slave population," scholar Gad Heuman wrote.[1] Still, my ancestor's actions were seen as a threat to Jamaica's racial order, and he and Lecesne were deported to England.

In England, their case caught the attention of abolitionists working to end slavery across the British Empire. Dr. Stephen Lushington, a member of the British Parliament, abolitionist, and lawyer, took up their case, only to realize that Escoffery and Lecesne were not ideal figureheads for abolition since both owned property and slaves themselves. Lushington followed through anyway, "determined to prove their innocence and by implication that of the free coloreds involved in the campaign for full civil rights."[2] He won, and the deportation order was rescinded with restitution paid to Lecesne and Escoffery. The case, though complex, had significant implications as it "proved to be an important development for the coloreds."[3] Scholar Gad Heuman notes how soon after the case in 1829, the Crown issued an order declaring free people of color legal equals to whites in St. Lucia, where my father's side of the family comes from, and did the same in Trinidad months later. Two years later was the Great Jamaican Slave Revolt, and the British Parliament abolished slavery in 1833.

I am an abolitionist working toward the liberation of all Black, Indigenous, and racialized people. As you will see in this book, I have spent years working to heal systems. I do this work to heal harms I did not commit—the exclusion of my people and communities from ownership over their stories and platforms in media and technology—but I am also working to heal the harms in my own family. The Escoffery case reveals how the Jamaican side of my family privileged land-owning, lighter-skinned Black people over those who were enslaved. Indeed, my grandmother told me that although she married a dark-skinned man, she would not have been able to if her grandmother had been alive to see it. My grandmother's grandmother was nevertheless famously generous to her Black Jamaican community, who came out in the hundreds to celebrate her at her funeral. My grandmother resisted her family's prejudices, healing our legacy of discrimination. I have my own work to do ensuring that my efforts toward the abolition of harmful systems do not exclude people with fewer privileges than I have.

Looking at my entire family tree offers a nuanced view of reparations. I see how clean, master narratives that culminate in clear victories are impossible: the connections to slavery but also slave owners; the presence of colorism and people of all shades; our class privilege compared to the shifting reality of anti-Blackness in the Americas; the complex nature of harm, from the Jewish lines in my family who fled the Inquisition in Europe to their privileged mulatto descendants who fled after the Haitian

Revolution only to own slaves themselves. Those who believe reparations in the United States can somehow be limited to "American descendants of slavery," excluding Indigenous people and recent Black immigrants, lack an appreciation for the complexity of history and genealogy. I am a US American and a descendant of slavery. My family tree includes numerous dead-ends, ones my aunt has spent decades trying to fill but likely will not because records were rarely kept of the lives of slaves. Yet like many American descendants of slavery, I am also a descendant of slave owners, who themselves campaigned for the rights of who we now call Black people and whose actions contributed to the abolition of slavery.

History shows us that reparation is a never-ending process, not a goal to be won or a tranche of scarce resources to be divided among competing factions. I have seen this in my own life, not just of ancestors I will never know, because I grew up in a violent home that eventually started to heal. Throughout it all, I identified so closely with my mother, who raised me the first four years of my life with the help of the other mothers in her family. I remember trying to intervene in and mediate the harm she experienced. From an early age, I was called to promote peace and resolve conflict. If you listen closely to arguments between people who love each other, over years and years, you start to realize that people repeat the same fight. You learn about triggers and the ways people can avoid fighting. You learn what people need to hear to heal, that harm and healing are dialogic, a never-ending back-and-forth. Of course, I always failed. Parents rarely heed their children's advice. As I got older and shed my anger at both my parents for not accepting me as queer, I loosened my grip on resentment and acknowledged the intergenerational traumas they healed. My father gave me intimate knowledge that people, particularly men, can heal. My fierce, ambitious mother taught me faith in love despite pain and the knowledge that Black women often derive their strength from incredible vulnerability.

It took me decades to realize my parents were healing and many more years to start the process of healing my own post-traumatic responses: the way I freeze or fawn when presented with conflict between people I care about and the ways I internalize others' critiques of me, especially if those critiques are based on my gender, as my early experiences with Black men were violent and people in the white neighborhood I grew up in treated me as a threat, as unworthy of attention, or as a strange, miraculously intelligent being in defiance of stereotypes. I have spent years learning not to fear myself and acknowledge my inherent value. Finding that peace and love within will be a lifelong process.

I know I may never fully recover, but in trying, I practice a daily form of personal reparation that shows how complex, difficult, and necessary it is to work to heal our systems and histories with as much care and commitment as we do ourselves.

My history shapes who I am, the mistakes I made researching this book, and the unique contributions I bring to this work and the intellectual history of reparations. Working to organize diverse artists, who as a profession are notoriously self-focused, is not for those with outsized egos or who cannot endure conflict. There were a few times while conducting this study when I was asked or encouraged to "pick sides" in situations with *conflict* but no clear *harm*. My inability to do so was sometimes met with skepticism, even anger, but I came to realize that I could not choose sides because I had in my own life seen how conflict is complex but can be resolved over time if we commit to each other. I drew on my ability to endure conflict, however fragile, and to trust that repair and healing are possible because I have seen it in my own family. I bring to it an openness to being held accountable as a Black man because I too have been harmed by Black men. I am not flawless, but I commit to consistently trying to do better, knowing the powerful effects of self-work. I bring to this work a deep love for the community of people who believe in me and the chosen family who inspire me, because I know how critical we are to healing each other—and the systems we all struggle to survive or thrive in.

You have known me as AJ or Aymar Jèan *Christian*, but this name has always felt incomplete. It represents my complex relationship with my father and mother, yet it lacks my maternal grandmother and my connection to this lineage of fighting for justice. This book is published under the name AJ or Aymar Jèan *Escoffery* to honor how essential my grandmother and auntie have been to who I have become, while removing the trauma of homophobia I experienced in the Christian church. My grandmother told me that had it not been for Jamaica's patriarchal laws, she would have immigrated to the US with her birth name Escoffery. If she had, I likely would have used this name as I was experimenting with changing it in my early twenties, partly in reaction to my Christian parents spurning me after coming out. Queer people have always chosen their names to expand traditional notions of blood family, and Aymar Jèan Escoffery feels like the name I was born to have.

I'm acknowledging who I come from and the ancestral intelligences that inform how I live.

Queer people have long practiced cultivating family outside of our blood lines, allowing us to imagine liberation outside of traditional systems and family structures. My chosen ancestors have better track records in the struggle for liberation. I claim intellectual ancestors like Stuart Hall, father of the study of race in media; Audre Lorde, the great artist and theorist of queer solidarity; and W. E. B. Du Bois, the father of sociology in the US. In my creative practice I claim ancestors like Ellis Haizlip, queer creator of the first unapologetically Black-produced nationally syndicated TV show in the US, *Soul!*, which deeply inspired OTV. But I also come from living greats who inspired the work of this book, like Oprah Winfrey, who I grew up watching as she produced her show in Chicago and gave America a taste of the city's soul, and Issa Rae, who most directly inspired the creation of OTV after I interviewed her and watched her develop and distribute the work of Black creators in Los Angeles.

This book owes its existence to a generation of artists who helped create the platform at its foundation and taught me a lot about healing and repair. I am most heavily indebted to Elijah McKinnon and Stephanie Jeter, who took a chance on a kooky Black professor with disorderly hair and mediocre style and helped found OTV | Open Television. After them came Chris Walker and then Sarah Minnie, Jenna Anast, and Rebba Amaris, who supplied OTV with labor much more valuable than they were initially paid. To the original OTV Studio team led by Stephanie and including Julie Keck and Oscar Dang, you are my heroes. Beyond the OTV teams were hundreds of artists who helped us help them achieve their creative visions. Many of them are named in this book and in the companion website, but I owe special gratitude to Sam Bailey, who was the first artist to reach out to me, created our first series, and cocreated our most popular series. Without her, I'm not sure this book would exist. OTV would have shuttered without legal consultation from Mikhael Bortz, Joseph Voss, and Thomas McDonough. We also desperately needed funding, and I am forever in debt to the funders who offered OTV its first grants: Pop Culture Collaborative's Bridgit Antoinette Evans and Tracy Van Slyke, and the Field Foundation's president Angelique Williams-Power with program officers Tempestt Hazel, Tracie

Hall, and Lolly Bowean. Later, they were joined by incredibly trusting program officers who funded OTV's general operations, including F. Javier Torres and Robert Smith at Surdna and Jen Humke and Kathy Im at MacArthur. I also must thank Voqal, who through Chicago Filmmakers was the largest funder of OTV productions after the artists and their communities.

Community-based projects are highly networked endeavors, and there are too many people to thank here, but I will try and inevitably fail. Chicago adopted OTV as its own, and so many people invited us into their spaces to show our work in the early years. I benefited from other community-based projects that helped me get to know artists and the city: the Chicago Home Theater Festival, where I served as a host and producer thanks to Irina Zadov, Laley Lippard, and Blake Russell; Honey Pot Performance, thanks to Meida McNeal, Abra Johnson, Felicia Holman, Aisha Jean-Baptiste, and Jo de Presser; Kristiana Rae Colón, Damon Williams, Jennifer Pagán, Jenna Anast, Kwamena Jackson, Najee Searcy, and the many other founding members of #LetUsBreathe; Lauren Ash, Nick Alder, and Rae Chardonnay of Party Noire; Jane Beachy, Joe Varisco, Will Von Vogt, and Bindu Poroori of Salonathon; and Chances Dances, thanks to Aay Preston-Myint, Latham Zearfoss, Rita Bacon, Justin Mitchell, Jacquelyn Carmen Guerrero, and many others. In our early years, OTV needed hosts to host us, including Angelica Ross, Preston Jones, Kiam Junio, Ife Olatunji, Sydney Stoudmire, Henry Chang, Andrew Mausert-Mooney, Kera MacKenzie, Thavary Krouch, Ann Meisinger, Christy LeMaster, January Parkos Arnall, and many more. My neighbor and Youth Empowerment Performance Project founder Bonsai Bermudez, my friend Kamilah Rashied, and icon Jen Delos Reyes were powerful shoulders to lean on. The Chicago film community embraced OTV, particularly Eugene Park and the team at Full Spectrum Features; Angie Gaffney, Nicole Bernardi-Reis, and the Independent Film Alliance; Anthony Kaufman and the team at the Chicago International Film Festival; Troy Pryor and Creative Cypher; and Riese Rubin and Chicago Filmmakers. The Chicago press that OTV earned was invaluable as the national press ignored us, so I must thank *NewCity* publishers Brian and Jan Hieggelke and writer Ray Pride; *Windy City Times* and *Chicago Reader* publisher Tracy Baim and writer Brianna Wellen; and *Chicago Tribune*'s Britt Julious, Sadé Carpenter, and Nina Metz.

Finally, I do this work in the memory of artists and community leaders who have transitioned, particularly Shervin Bain, cocreator of the hilarious

Low Strung on OTV; J. J. Ingraham, who supported OTV's Sundance partnership and for-profit; Aerin Cooper, who comforted me on the set of our first talk show; Orb Box and Beverly Joy Bundles, who brought me joy; and icons of abolition Malik Alim and my cousin Botham Jean.

As a project intervening an exclusive industry, OTV and our artists were supported by so many executives who helped further our mission of systemic transformation. I owe a particular debt to the late Max Saines, an agent who introduced me to dozens of executives in Hollywood. I was deeply inspired by meetings and connections with Christine Davila (WarnerMedia, Ojalá), Emily Upton-Davis (Hulu), Nick Austin (Sony), Makiah Green (Netflix, MACRO), Sara Rastogi (ColorCreative), Alex Dao, Laura Turner Garrison, and Alana Mayo. Particular thanks goes to Karim Ahmad and his team at the Sundance Institute, including Amber Epinosa-Jones and Moi Santos, for partnering with OTV, and Lilly Wachowski for her generous offering of space and creative development. Finally, special thanks to Jonathan "Jono" Friedman and Bad Robot president Brian Weinstein for their invaluable advice at a critical juncture in this study.

This is an academic book funded by university resources and inspired by scholar-mentors. Thank you to my editors at the MIT Press—Justin Kehoe, Ramon Lobato, and Josh Braun—for their careful feedback, as well as Ideas on Fire for additional editing, indexing, and formatting. At Northwestern University, I could not have completed this work without Dean Barbara O'Keefe, who hired and retained me; my chairs Ellen Wartella and Leslie DeChurch; my department mentor Pablo Boczkowski; and my friendtor Dean E. Patrick Johnson, a fearless advocate who chaired the OTV board, supported by Yvonne Welbon, C. Riley Snorton, and Allie Mullen. I must thank the faculty of the Department of Communication Studies for their faith in me. Over forty undergraduate, master's, and PhD students supported the work in this book. Most important was Chelsea Peterson-Salahuddin, who performed consistent analysis of my qualitative data for several years, whose writing is included in brief sections of the book. In addition, master's and PhD students Nicole Morse, Mark Díaz, Marwa Tahboub, Kemi Adeyemi, Erique Zhang, Kelly Boner, Aalisha Sheth, Scott Cambo, Daniel Dvorkin, and Oscar Dang were invaluable. Many undergrads were very helpful, but I particularly thank Rey Tang, Ahlaam Yasmin, Aisha Hauser, Bill Pahutski, Sheyda Tribble, Sean Magner, and Sarah Turner for data analysis, production, editing, and development support. Lastly, the incredible staff at Northwestern held this project together: JaTaune Bosby, Jordan Dues, Sharron Shepard, Debbie Fair, Joy Stoyanova, Marysia Galent, Kasia Zieleniucha, and Madeleine Agaton. In addition, Northwestern's Sexualities Project led by Steven Epstein and Héctor Carrillo provided invaluable funding early on.

I would not be who I am without the great mentors and peers I have in academia, including Katherine Sender, John Jackson, Lisa Henderson, Henry Jenkins, and Joseph Turow, who offered recommendations and advice at key moments. I have been blessed with so many more who helped shape my ideas and career trajectory, including Moya Bailey, Sasha Costanza-Chock, Josh Kun, Paula Chakravartty, Vicki Mayer, Mary Gray, Adrienne Shaw, Jess King, Sarah Banet-Weiser, TJ Billard, Derek Johnson, Brooke Duffy, David Craig, Ramzi Fawaz, Alfred Martin, Kristen Warner, Devorah Heitner, Anjali Vats, André Brock, Rachel Kuo, Sarah Jackson, Kara Keeling, Lori Lopez, Lisa Nakamura, Srividya Ramasubramanian, Annie Sullivan, Lauren Herold, Safiya Noble, Zama Dube, Charlton McIlwain, and the rest of the Critical Race and Digital Studies Community.

My ideas were shaped as much by spiritual healers as academic theorists. Opening myself to other ways of knowing and being was critical to managing the complexities of a research project that expanded my ideas of family, friends, community, work, creative energy, and home. I could not have done this work without Chani Nicholas, without whom I would have never had the perspective to manage OTV. It took an army of healers to protect and heal this tender vessel, including Devin Niecy, Dorian Ortega, Tara Nikita, Naimonu James, Jasmine Barber, Leucas Miller, Jade Perry, Edwin Alvarez, Aya-Nikole Cook, Marie-France Collin, Adam Elenbaas, Rick Levine, Maya Green, Blake Butler, Diana Rose Harper, and Jon Ong.

Finally, my heart. Thank you to the people who hold me close and never let me go. In addition to blood family discussed earlier, I thank my brother Mikhail for reminding me who I am. My chosen kin madison moore, Yanru Chen, Khadijah Costley White, Heidi Khaled, and Brett Bumgarner never let me forget or dim my shine. To my loves Milo Vieland and Karl Swinehart, you have inspired me more than you'll ever truly know, and to my rock, my best friend, who brings me joy, holds space for my pain and healing daily, Derek Lee McPhatter, I owe you everything, my heart, my life, and undying devotion.

* * *

Every creator quoted or discussed at length in this book reviewed the manuscript and consented to its publication after receiving a letter with offerings, which can be reviewed here: reparative.media/book/offerings-for-consent.

Parts of this book have been previously published in the following:

Christian, Aymar Jean, and Chelsea Peterson-Salahuddin. "Rage Against the Streaming Studio System: Worker Resistance to Hollywood's Networked Era." *Information, Communication & Society* 26, no. 5 (2023): 923–940.

Christian, Aymar Jean, Faithe Day, Mark Díaz, and Chelsea Peterson-Salahuddin. "Platforming Intersectionality: Networked Solidarity and the Limits of Corporate Social Media." *Social Media and Society* 6, no. 3 (2020): 1–12.

Christian, Aymar Jean, and Khadijah White. "Organic Representation as Cultural Reparation." *Journal of Cinema & Media Studies* 60, no. 1 (2020): 143–147.

Christian, Aymar Jean. "Beyond Branding: The Value of Intersectionality on Streaming TV Channels." *Television & New Media* 21, no. 5 (2020): 457–474.

Christian, Aymar Jean. "Expanding Production Value: The Culture and Scale of Television and New Media." *Critical Studies in Television* 14, no. 2 (2019): 255–267.

Christian, Aymar Jean. "Chicago Renaissance Redux: Black Cultural Production and the Social Practice Art of Television." In *Local TV: Communities, Histories, Aesthetics*, edited by Annie Sullivan and Lauren Herold. University of Georgia Press, forthcoming.

Christian, Aymar Jean. "Organic Research: Cultivating Knowledge with Our Communities." In *Public Scholarship in Communication Studies*, edited by Silvio Waisbord and Thomas J. Billard. University of Illinois Press, 2024.

INTRODUCTION: HEALING SYSTEMS

We are more connected than ever.

So why has it felt like our cultural divisions, our deepest collective wounds, are intensifying?

Hate and violence are rising even as popular film and TV stories have never been more inclusive. Political division and mental health crises are intensifying even as social media platforms are distributing diverse perspectives and healing strategies. Lies and propaganda are proliferating online even as access to knowledge has never been higher.

Why? In the United States, our cultural systems—media, technology, and information—are perpetuating harms. Large corporations have been platforming ideologies that promote hate and ignorance. They serve us films, television series, and advertisements inspiring desires for individual fantasies over collective well-being. The ways these systems serve us stories and information limit our ability to heal ourselves, our communities, and our planet.

Our culture is an ecosystem. Yet corporations control too much land for harvesting our attention, connections, knowledge, and data. They serve us culture and information as fast food: monoculturally farmed and then quickly packaged, produced, and distributed for us to binge for entertainment. We know that the fast-food industry benefits from unethical and unsustainable production and distribution practices. We eat plastic in our food, produced on farms that harm the soil and animals, served to us by underpaid workers who lack collective bargaining rights. Food is then served in homogenous fast-food chains, spaces people must pay to access.

Similarly, large media and tech institutions distribute most of the culture we consume. They decide who gets to produce stories and how. They prefer to serve stories and information that are fast and globally consumable over what is slow, locally diverse, and sustainable.[1]

Of course, not all film, television, and social media is unhealthy. I subscribe to more media and tech platforms than most. I once loved a good binge! For most of my life, my happy place has been eating copious amounts of sweet things and watching hours of television. It helped me cope with being a closeted queer kid surrounded by violence. Media can offer powerful pleasures and tools for healing ourselves and cultivating bonds. But despite the temporary pleasure of eating cookies with milk or coffee, as I aged, I started to realize how harmful this was to my mental, emotional, and physical health and how mindful I needed to be about how much I consumed.

Is binging television and social media helping our culture? The many writers, scholars, and leaders in media and tech I spoke to while researching this book tell me the answer is no. They doubt that our cultural systems are designed to cultivate the richest ingredients for an edifying, diverse cultural diet. They doubt that these systems can nourish our deepest desires to feel connected through and beyond our pain.

The problem is our systems, not all the people working in them or even perhaps the technologies themselves. As Donella Meadows explains, "A system is a set of things—people, cells, molecules, or whatever—interconnected in such a way that they produce their own pattern of behavior over time. . . . The system, to a large extent, causes its own behavior."[2] There are plenty of people who want to "do good" but struggle to do so because of processes beyond their control. They tell me that corporate goals are not aligned with what they believe is best for the culture, what we need to heal our divisions and cultivate interdependence or solidarity. They are struggling to change generations of practices designed to extract as much as possible from our cultural environment while giving as little back in return. They admit we could benefit from "decommodifying" media and technology, regulating them as community-run public utilities or supporting cooperatively owned platforms.[3] Power in media is too concentrated, disincentivizing care for the collective.

Can we cultivate a better system? When we view culture as an ecosystem, we see that diversity,[4] interdependence, and sustainability are key to our collective thriving. Healing our collective wounds—racism, misogyny, xenophobia, homophobia, classism, ableism, and other forms of hate—requires a specific method of repair: *redistributing* power more equitably to the historically disempowered. Many people think that this is divisive. I have seen firsthand it is not. Changing how we distribute stories and information might shift the power dynamics that make so-called "diversity and equity" efforts problematic. We might make *everyone's* life better.

Our culture needs *organic* ways to serve communities stories and cultivate the knowledge generated from the process. Diversity is organic, and what is organic can heal. The reparative approach is to culture what regenerative farming is to agriculture. Regenerative farming values biodiversity and an Indigenous approach to working in deep relationship with specific, local environments, thereby repairing the harm corporate agribusiness has done.[5] It challenges the idea that land is private property because ecosystems develop interdependently. We have allowed corporations to own too much our culture via *intellectual* property, be it seeds for farming, stories for film and television, or algorithms for social media. Reparative or community-based research and development (R&D) can help show us how to heal the cultural environment that media and tech corporations exploit for profit.

Reparative Media imagines this community-driven process as a cookout: spaces where we all own and share organically crafted and ancestry-informed nourishment. This book offers a story and framework for storytellers, scholars, organizers, and funders trying to start or sustain such projects. I hope this book opens the ways you see, use, and consume media and technology. I hope it inspires you to act to repair what has been exploited. *Reparative Media* is not a "how to." It asks questions about how we can heal our cultural environment and offers some preliminary answers based on my research and personal experience.

This book explores reparative media through the story of researching and developing OTV | Open Television. You can think of OTV as a distributor like Netflix but independent, locally rooted, and powered by intersectionality. OTV's app serves films and series by creators who identify with multiple communities historically marginalized by systems, or intersectionality. Unlike Netflix, it was curated by community instead of algorithms, with stories greenlit and owned by creators instead of executives, backed more by story- versus numbers-based data.

OTV is a collective effort. The idea emerged from my first book, *Open TV*, and I take credit for the specific labor I performed to build its foundation, described in the second chapter. Yet OTV would not exist without my cofounder Elijah McKinnon, who I elevated to executive director in 2020, and a founding team including Stephanie Jeter and Chris Walker, with dozens of others (figure 0.1). Elijah came to me as an expert in marketing and recent graduate from art school and started as head of marketing and design. A Black nonbinary polymath, Elijah offered an incredible range of talents and services to the organization in its founding years, including creating OTV's brand image, website, social media and style guide; producing most of our local events; creating, directing, and producing scripted, unscripted, music, and live video series; and consulting creators on marketing their series. Stephanie was OTV's first head of production, and I met her years before Elijah. A meticulous, visionary director, Stephanie was one of the few Black women I knew who had consistent experience working for both studio and indie film and television. I relied on her expertise to consult creators on production questions I could not answer, and she advised many of our early creators, helping them avoid common mistakes; she also produced several programs. Chris Walker curated our social media channels, coproduced events, wrote newsletters, and maintained our website before taking over as head of marketing when Elijah became an executive director. This team led dozens of writers, directors, actors, and multidisciplinary storytellers in making reparative media.

In this book the word "I" will be used as judiciously as possible, written mostly to clarify that this story is from my perspective. To work collectively, I had to decenter myself as the founder, head researcher, and "development executive," those who decide what stories get funded in Hollywood. This book is about storytellers, and they all have different stories about this period. Throughout the book, you will meet the many people, organizations, and institutions who worked in "radical kinship" to cultivate a cultural ecosystem nourishing of communities historically deprived because of how they identify.[6]

Reparative Media is the "behind the scenes" of the making of what you see in figure 0.2 (watchable online), from my perspective. Watch the twenty-minute super cut of OTV's programs from 2015 to 2020 at the link in the caption to figure 0.2. For me, it is as strong an argument as the rest of this book for the power of intersectionality to cultivate stories and platforms

FIGURE 0.1
Storytellers and the OTV team at OTV Tonight at the Museum of Contemporary Art Chicago, the fourth season premiere of original programming in 2019. Clockwise from top left: *Brujos* star Justin Mitchell aka DJ Hijo Pródigo, *Brown Girls* writer Fatimah Asghar, *Damaged Goods* creator Vincent Martell, *Brown Girls* director Sam Bailey, OTV head of community Jenna Anast, OTV intern Ahlaam Yasmin, *FOBia* creator Priya Mohanty, moderator Eva Saha Daniel, *Brujos* star Isaac Gomez, producer Karla Huffman, Aymar Jèan Escoffery, OTV Studio consultant Oscar Dang, OTV head of exhibition Chris Walker, OTV head of production Stephanie Jeter, OTV cofounder Elijah McKinnon, *Brujos* codirector Reshmi Hazra-Rustebakke, and *The Right Swipe* director Justin Casselle with writer-actors Juli Del Prete and Kyra Jones. Credit: Ally Almore.

FIGURE 0.2
Watch "The Evolution of OTV 2015–2020": vimeo.com/madelab/otv-evolution.

to heal our culture. It shows how creative and community-based practice generates theory. Stories are theories. You must engage them to understand my argument. In the online version of this book, you can click on any show and learn more about it. OTV storytellers show how liberated, multifaceted (if imperfect) media could be if we cultivated stories from the grassroots and distributed them via small, locally focused digital platforms.

Our work challenges Hollywood and Silicon Valley's extractive, exclusionary, and occasionally divisive practices. It takes the fear and mystery out of intersectionality. It is possible to cultivate channels that represent more of this country and world, even if only from a "second city" and with few resources. It also shows what riches lie deep in the matrices of cultural marginalization. This is what TV and social media should look and feel like, in my humble opinion. Stories are more connective, sincere, and healing when funded, produced, distributed, and exhibited by and with communities surviving systemic harm.

How did we cultivate a reparative streaming platform? To get on OTV, a creator only needed to be based in Chicago and developing a story that centered multiple forms of systemic harm (racism, sexism, etc.). I met with nearly everyone who requested a meeting and asked why they were telling their story. Requiring storytellers to engage intersectionality cultivated fertile ground for solidarity to grow. Otherwise, it was an open invitation.

Every project fit in one of three verticals: (1) *Open TV Presents*, pilots, short films, video art; (2) *Open TV Originals*, series we premiered; or (3) *Open TV Re-Presents*, series we rereleased or syndicated. Each vertical served as a critique of corporate platforms: (1) we released pilots to challenge the history of Hollywood's gatekeeping; (2) we premiered original series nonexclusively, allowing creators to republish their stories on multiple platforms to challenge Hollywood's exclusivity; and (3) we syndicated videos from bigger platforms that underpay most creators to challenge Silicon Valley's devaluation of diverse, complex stories. To test the value of local, in-person versus online engagement, we screened almost every project in our home city of Chicago. At screenings, creators received community feedback (or "notes," as Hollywood executives say), nurturing deeper, more meaningful connections among storytellers and their communities. After each season or "cycle," I interviewed every creator and OTV team member to understand their challenges and innovations, which helped us program the next cycle more ethically and sustainably, as well as generate research for this book.

What do reparative stories look like? Consider Karan Sunil's *Code-Switched*, a comedy drama series that follows the interconnected lives of five South Asian American Chicagoans. Inspired by his own experience as an Indian American, Karan drew from Chicago's deep well of comedians to tell a story that recasts the classic US sitcom and resists the ways Brown people are stereotyped or rendered invisible. As he stated at OTV's premiere event at the Museum of Contemporary Art (MCA) Chicago: "I grew up watching a lot of TV with my dad. We'd sit there and watch Kramer and *Seinfeld* and be like, 'where we at?' Then we do see us and it's like the dude that solves the code right before the big explosion." An important innovation for Karan was casting different types of South Asian people to resist stereotypes: "The South Asian demographic is like billions of people. I personally don't think America understands South Asians. They just look at brown and they're scared. There's so many different kinds, but at the same time, we are very fractured as well: Muslim and Hindus, Indians and Pakistanis, Sri Lankans."

Code-Switched highlights both cultural differences and solidarities among first-generation millennials in the diaspora. OTV screened the pilot one week after Karan wrapped production, which, like most OTV projects, he completely financed and organized: hiring cast, crew, and editors. We paid $2,000 to distribute the series on our online platform and exhibit it in Chicago. We also offered advice and consultation on production and marketing throughout the process. The community feedback we collected at the screening was helpful for him as a storyteller, both the written notes he received from the post-screening survey and the laughter in the theater. Karan told me he used the Facebook livestream and post-screening demographic data to see if his writing was resonating and to show stakeholders in Hollywood that a pan-South Asian show could have broad appeal. Two years later, after premiering the full series on YouTube to tens of thousands of fans one day after it premiered on OTV, Karan sold *Code-Switched* to Hulu. Here we see how critical our local focus and openness to distributing fresh stories unfiltered by executive notes was in supporting the creation and widespread reception of an original comedy about solidarity.

Solidarity emerged as a key theme in most stories distributed by OTV, as you will read in chapter 3. Our two most popular series, *Brown Girls* and *Brujos*, present clear examples of how intersectionality brings different people together and challenges systemic oppression. *Brujos* creator Ricardo Gamboa, a nonbinary writer-actor-director who would go on to write and produce for Showtime's *The Chi*, wrote the series to critique the fantasy genre's limited view of race, sexuality, and history. In *Brujos*, three Latinx witches fight the descendants of "New World Colonizers," represented as ruthlessly ambitious, somewhat nerdy white businessmen who deviously devour people of color and their magic. The series supernaturally evokes the corporation's history of global colonization and white supremacy. The three brujos must band together to stop them, despite their differences, and eventually they enlist other Black, Asian, trans, and women-identified witches in their quest for liberation. Through humor and horror, the ambitious series depicts solidarity as necessary to resist the extractive nature of corporate power. As someone who grew up on Chicago's predominantly Black and Latinx South Side, home to Cook County Jail, the third largest system in the country, Ricardo's obsession with the question of freedom from oppressive systems is inspired by lived experience.

By contrast, *Brown Girls* represents solidarity through the mundane, everyday dramas of two friends, a Black woman and queer Muslim woman.[7] Written by poet Fatimah Asghar, who would go on to write for Disney+'s *Ms. Marvel*, and director Sam Bailey, who would eventually direct Disney+'s *Ironheart* and Netflix's *Dear White People*, *Brown Girls* revels in the small moments of discovering and asserting one's identity, needs, and friendships. With music from Jamila Woods's lilting album *HEAVN*, itself an ode to Black feminist healing and activism, the dramedy became a hit and HBO pickup by showing two women of different identities supporting each other through very different culturally specific struggles, including sexism, homophobia, and Islamophobia. Both qualitative/quantitative and online/offline responses to these shows, explored in chapter 4, offer ample evidence for intersectionality as a productive and healing framework for solidarity and connection across cultural differences.

OTV intervenes in the media system as one of the few television distribution channels owned by Black queer, trans, and femme people, serving complex stories that defy easy categorization. This form of "intersectional distribution" is virtually nonexistent in Hollywood and Silicon Valley because it resists corporate methods for easy extraction. Corporations historically prefer to target by single identity categories, place stories in clear genres, or distribute short simple narratives that spread fast on social media platforms. Market segmentation, segregation, or automated classification makes it easier to identify us and sell us products. In the cable era, this meant dividing us by age (e.g., MTV), race (e.g., Black Entertainment Television [BET]), sexuality (e.g., Logo), gender (e.g., Lifetime), or ethnicity (e.g., El Rey). In the streaming era, they use algorithms to sort and segregate us in more sophisticated ways: Creators who commit to genres like true crime or adult comedy (e.g., Netflix) or who make short, simple narratives that speak to clear identities (e.g., TikTok) are more likely to find viewers. By contrast, OTV creators produced narratives that defy easy categorization by cultural identity or story format. Through intersectionality, storytellers who wanted to work with us were inspired to think across and outside their own experience, to consciously engage and expand their understanding of community. Organically, without rules or consultants, we never released anything that our community said was hateful or stereotypical.

We are reimagining social media "platforms." Platforms are tools for serving stories and information: whether Netflix serving film and TV, Instagram serving photos and videos, or thought leaders sharing knowledge on any app. Platforms are technologies for distribution that "facilitate, aggregate, monetize, and govern interactions between end-users and content and service providers."[8] OTV now has an app (figure 0.3), but we take a more expansive view of the word "platform." Before the internet, platforms were spaces for hosting community engagement: "a raised floor or stage used by

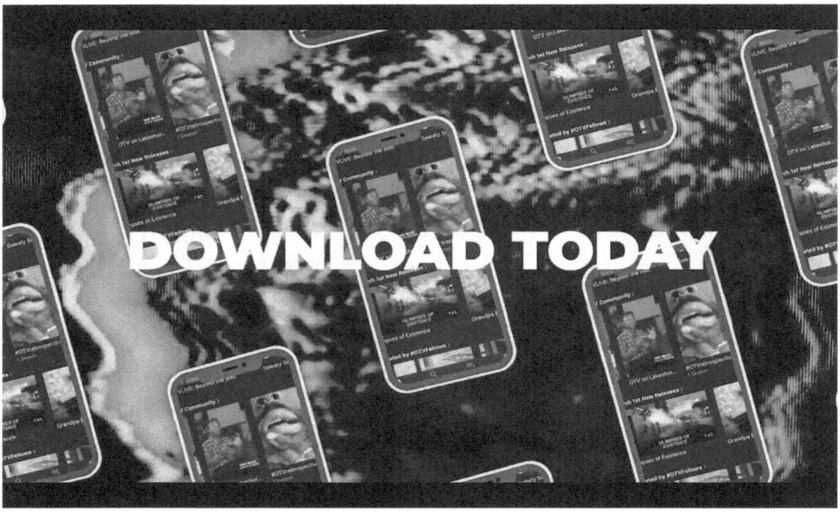

FIGURE 0.3
Still from the trailer for OTV's app. Credit: OTV.

public speakers or performers so that they can be seen by their audience."[9] In a digital world, it's easier to platform stories, ideas, creators, and communities. Too easy. As Tarleton Gillespie writes, social media platforms "offer to merely host . . . The platform would like to fall away, become invisible."[10] Our work shows that ethical platforming is never invisible. Hosts must be in relationship with who they invite and intimately address power, culture, and harm as a form of care. OTV did this by connecting digital community locally, starting with Chicago, whose history of segregation inhibits cross-cultural community building while enabling intra-community solidarity. The tech industry has its own harmful, segregationist distribution practices as it manages our connections globally "at scale." Most social media platforms prefer to simplify distribution using keywords or proxies for the identities that separate us from each other—difference as marketing tool.

By contrast, in one of the most segregated, over-policed cities in the United States, OTV hosted over fifty screenings and events in Chicago, and not one lacked representation across identity lines. We covered all three sides of the city—north, south, and west. In post-screening surveys and through ethnographic observation, we saw there is broad desire to embrace cultural differences. Unable to cultivate big data, we scaled our data to understand specific local dynamics, revealing what big data strategies miss. These local, real connections are even more important as big data supports the creation of "large language models," giving birth to artificial intelligence (AI), human-simulated culture and information. We still used tech, old and new: projectors, laptops, social media for raising awareness, digital videos for trailers, email, specific lighting, chairs, and even the occasional use of video editing software for screening projects that were not yet finished! But the real technology was managing the relationships between storytellers and communities, designing spaces for engagement and connection. This is the difference between grassroots versus big data hosting or platforming.

Our experiment challenged legacies of data neutrality and extraction common in both corporate tech and university research, both in Chicago[11] as well as in the humanities[12] and social sciences. This book is about a research project in Chicago grappling with the legacies and current realities of universities as extractive and exclusionary institutions.[13] Academics still privilege theories and generalizable "objective" data that can be applied across contexts and history to secure broad impact. We drop into communities, study their problems, publish our findings as quickly as possible, rack up citations, and move on. I argue that this framework can limit the depth of our understanding and disservices the communities we study. Community-based research resists generalizability. It favors specificity and interdependence, the kind of data best developed in solidarity with our participants—or collaborators.

OTV is not separate from institutions that power media, technology, and knowledge systems. Our work nourished the whole ecosystem, even extractive corporations. In fact, as you saw with *Code-Switched*, *Brown Girls*, and *Brujos*, OTV helped pave a path for creators to sell their intellectual property and work in Hollywood. OTV creators received development deals and gigs at Hulu, HBO, Showtime, Netflix, WarnerMedia, and more; nominations and wins at the Emmys, Webbys, Streamys, Tellys, Gothams, and more; and screenings at the Tribeca Film Festival, Chicago International Film Festival, Brooklyn Museum, and dozens more. We also helped them amass followings on social media platforms. What we learned generated knowledge published in university-approved peer-reviewed journals and books.

To some, our work reeks of corporate co-optation of community labor. There's some truth to that, which I address in the final chapter. Reparative practices must survive a harsh cultural ecosystem dominated by corporate media, tech, and research. Sustainable reparative projects have the impossible task of securing resources and attention in an environment where most people are focused on what is most visible and powerful, where cultural and economic capital are concentrated. OTV's budget and audience are fractions of fractions of Netflix's or YouTube's. We struggled to earn the attention of our communities, limiting our ability to raise revenue and pay storytellers. Unable to live off OTV payments, creators had no choice but to work in Hollywood or build large social media followings, even though many told me they preferred Chicago to Los Angeles.

Healing and repair are messy. Throughout this book, I will use these words somewhat interchangeably, but they are different in specific, nuanced ways.

Healing is the nonlinear, never-ending process of recognizing harm and working to reverse its effects. Systemic healing unfolds unevenly over generations. On an individual level, healing is something our bodies are always doing or trying to do. Our bodies are constantly beset by pathogens even if we rarely feel the impact.

Repair is the specific medicine, the everyday process of using natural tools to address harm. I use the word *reparative* to describe this practice of intervening to support personal, communal, and systemic healing. "Reparation . . . is concerned with building the just world to come. But its more specific role concerns *how* we get there," Olúfẹ́mi Táíwò writes.[14] *Reparative* describes how we can act within and outside of harmful systems to minimize harm and cultivate healing systems. It is a daily practice.

Reparations are systemic healing. Ultimately, we need *cultural reparations*: historical accountability for what Khadijah White describes as *extraction, exclusion,* and *distortion* in culture industries and concrete steps toward repair in the form of redistributing capital and power, a full accounting of which is beyond the scope of this book.[15] State-sanctioned reparations for material harms like incarceration, slavery, and housing discrimination will take generations, though already in process in states like California or Illinois and cities like Evanston or San Francisco for descendants of slavery and colonization. Cultural reparations for discrimination in art, media, and tech are far behind.

Even if reparations never come, reparative practices still nourish our communities and the culture at large. This is about the daily, unglamorous, never-ending, ever-changing work of repair that is the necessary precondition to any sustainable form of reparations. adrienne maree brown, a leading voice for media practitioners and community organizers in the digital age, believes we can engage in this process of repair through what she calls an *emergent strategy*: "the way small actions and connections create complex systems, patterns that become ecosystems and societies. . . . Emergent strategy is how we intentionally change in ways that grow our capacity to embody the just and liberated worlds we long for."[16] Using the metaphor of flocking birds, brown foregrounds a theory of cultural repair as organic, reflecting a broader turn toward healing ecologies among Black feminist writers.[17] We can also look to Eve Sedgewick's "reparative reading" as an early intervention into the violence of literary theory; Ruha Benjamin's viral justice as a framework on healing strategies amid information inequalities; Meredith Clark's notion of reparative journalism; Apryl Williams and Chelsea Peterson-Salahuddin's urge to integrate reparative, restorative, and transformative justice frameworks to algorithmic content moderation or policing; and a range of new books from Black, queer, trans, and disabled intellectuals on harm and repair.[18]

Now is the time to nurture the world we need. This work is hard, but there can be incredible joy in reparative acts! Healing can be painful, but for me, working to repair media through tech was the most rewarding and surprising journey of my life. It helped me expand my community, chosen family, and my sense of self. My healing journey was not only difficult meetings and intense labor. It was also doing yoga with our audience at the MCA Chicago, twerking with Black folks at the after-party in Humboldt Park, kiki's with drag queens and performance artists, and enjoying poetry, music, dance, and other art forms surrounded by people I love and respect. I blossomed into the best version of myself doing this work. Practicing what André Brock calls the "libidinal economy"—we resisted the "deficit models" people ascribe to Black media and tech and forged "a space for mundanity, banality, and the celebration of making it through another day."[19] Of course, libidinal exchanges also carry risk and threats of harm. Ramzi Fawaz and Lisa Henderson argue that these relations are both "demanding"[20] and "anarchic."[21] I saw this firsthand.

We have all been harmed or will be. We must try to repair it even if "full health" is rarely or never achieved[22]—and even if past harms continue to affect our (cultural) climate in ways that make healing more difficult. Many scholars, particularly in Black studies, believe the scale of harm is beyond repair, that there is nothing to repair to, that we are socially and culturally dead, that neither for-profit nor nonprofit organizations can repair.[23] The only response to this theory is to critique systems with no hope of healing them, to resign ourselves to the end of the world, or to do whatever we please with what little breath we have. In our resignation we forget that corporate capitalism and settler colonialism on the scale we know it has not always existed and is an anachronism in the history of this planet. We forget that we have legacies for reparative approaches. It is not new. Black and Indigenous ecologists have long advocated for intersectionality and community-based practice as a framework for repairing generations of land misuse through enslavement and resource extraction.[24] Communities maintaining these practices are alive today and actively working to heal systemic harms and plant the seeds for a different future. So many people are already doing this work of bridging ancestral with digital strategies for cultural ecosystemic repair.

It is not the job of people who have been harmed to heal their oppressors. But if we want to heal, those with the deepest wounds should shape the process. Our work benefits everyone, so those with more power and privilege have a responsibility to offer support and resources. We do not live in a reparative media ecosystem, but OTV showed me we have the tools to cultivate it. Intersectionality, Indigeneity, and solidarity must structure this long process of healing. Realizing we *all* are healing from systems of oppression is critical. Localizing and decommodifying our platforms, cultivating meaningful stories and knowledge, is the next step. Digital technologies can amplify these efforts. Community-based research can hold us accountable to our impact. Our ancestral intelligences offer frameworks, stories, and protocols to help us nurture reparative practices.

THE COOKOUT: SERVING SOULFUL MEDIA WITH ANCESTRAL INTELLIGENCE

I understand reparative media through a practice that has nourished my family and community for generations: the cookout, an ancestral way of distributing culture at the local level. Growing up, my parents loved to host cookouts. As Caribbean immigrants who stumbled into an upper-middle-class Jersey suburb by way of the Bronx, our cookouts bridged family divides across class, geography, and nationality. By inviting both sides of the family and our neighbors, we cultivated a platform for making and consuming culture outside corporate spaces: cooking Caribbean and Black American food, eating, and dancing to reggae and soca that we rarely heard on corporate radio. Our cookouts were not conflict-free—there is always tension when people come together. But our love, as unmanufactured as our food, fertilized soil for nurturing bonds.

The cookout reminds us that culture is best served organically, in community, with love and solidarity. The cookout is about distribution: Hosts serve what they cook using recipes and gathering practices sourced from generations of knowledge. It is *re*distributive: Anyone invited to the cookout can also produce a dish or something else to share, and they get more in return. If you're not going to bring anything, at least bring generous vibes! The cookout is for family, extended family, and neighbors. It is diverse but organically so. It is semi-public, showing the importance of carefully drawn, porous borders for social engagement.

Distribution is power in culture. It shows us how story development (inviting) and production (cooking) are connected to exhibition (hosting) and the knowledge generated from the process (cultivation). Distribution is something we all do but seldom control: You do it every time you watch a studio film and share your thoughts on a social media platform. Generally, corporations control distribution in our culture. At the cookout, distribution is a collective, decentralized process, where value is equitably distributed (figure 0.4). Experimenting with community-based distribution offers insights into how we might repair inequalities resulting from corporate power.

Hosting a diverse but majority Black cookout, OTV served the cinematic equivalent of *soul food*. We continued Chicago's legacy of community-created stories and platforms, its deep tradition of *soul*—from *Soul Train* to soul music, art, poetry, theater, journalism, and even vegetarian food. Soul food is best served locally, cooked by our families, mamas, aunties, or local restaurants. I'll never eat better soul food than my late Aunty Olive's, who transitioned as I was finishing this book. Corporate chains cannot match it because her recipes, her ways of producing, were passed down for generations, culturally specific, and serially served in intimate contexts surrounded by love.

Soul food is the product of perseverance and solidarity, a product of the colonization of Africa and the Americas. It integrates multiple cultural

REPARATIVE SYSTEMS

Reparative systems redistribute the value we generate as we cultivate our cultural ecosystem.

FIGURE 0.4
Reparative systems: The supply chain as a cookout.

DEVELOPMENT / INVITING

Development involves creating and pitching stories for studios or platforms to purchase or cultivate. For corporations, a story has to meet the platform's needs for brand identity, critical acclaim, and/or audience. At the cookout, development involves inviting people to cook dishes or contribute to collective nourishment. Invitees' connection to community or tradition matter more than the host's image or desires.

PRODUCTION / COOKING

Cooking is at the heart of the cookout, just as stories are at the heart of our cultures. We are what we make and consume. For corporations, story production works best when standardized to speed the process of creation. At the cookout, we take our time, making as much as we can with what we have with whomever will help us. The goal is connection.

DISTRIBUTION / SERVING

The cookout is a space for distributing food to community, just as platforms are spaces for distributing stories to audiences. Corporate platforms distribute to increase growth and profit. The cookout distributes only as much as necessary to include the people who are representative of its community. The goal is equitable over profitable representation.

EXHIBITION / HOSTING

Hosts anchor cookouts as platforms for community engagement. The host knows what rituals, ingredients, and information will cultivate a sense of community and solidarity: a sense that we're all in this together. Corporate social media platforms struggle to cultivate solidarity and healing environments as they focus on profiting from the work of invitees and increasing the scale of our interactions over the quality of our connections.

RESEARCH / CULTIVATING

The cookout is about how we nurture each other, and we can always do it better. Everyday hosts conduct organic forms of research on their programming. Simply, they ask. We debrief, often in groups, about how things went and make changes. Corporate hosts are inaccessible. Their processes for cultivating data are opaque. They are not accountable to their guests, unlike cookout hosts. Cookout hosts know they are accountable to guests and must check in with who they invited.

FIGURE 0.4 (continued)

traditions, from Africa, Europe, and Indigenous North America. Enslaved Black people were given scraps from masters, sought council from Indigenous Americans, and mastered seasoning to maximize flavor, using the healthiest ingredients they could.[25] Scholar and James Beard awardee Adrian Miller writes of its complex ancestral roots: "All of soul food's dominant themes are there . . . the low social status of blacks, racial stigma, resourcefulness, ingenuity, and communal spirit."[26] Some shame soul food as cheap and unhealthy, but it is a deeply collective and creative practice that has helped generations survive incalculable oppression. It shows how Black culinary arts critiques corporate production and distribution:

> Big agribusiness and the food-processing industry would have us believe that their modern hybrid and GMO crops and cheap processed foods are the only way to feed the world. Yet here was proof that a family of poor African Americans—because of their ingenuity, work ethic, and spirit—could eat better than most upper-middle-class Americans do today. Sure, it was a lot of work, but in many families throughout history, the joy of a beautiful meal has always been worth the work of getting the food to the table. I argue all the time that labors of eating well are a far more worthy use of time than most of what we do these days, whether it's watching reality TV or getting caught up in the latest Internet gossip.[27]

Just like soul food, OTV's stories may appear low budget to those of us raised on corporate media, but each project took an incredible amount of work, time, and care: *slow media as soulful slow food*. Most Black Americans have been raised on slow/soul food. But in the US today, most of us are not raised on slow/soul media or technology, so we struggle to cultivate a taste for community-based making. US Americans have never experienced a diverse, noncorporate media system designed to cultivate stories and platforms as healing, flavorful, creative, homespun, and communal as soul food.

Seeing media through the cookout provokes questions about how we make and release healing, soulful stories. As shown in the figure above, communities ask these questions to ensure that the cookout is as restorative and connective as possible.

Who is invited, what are they cooking, and how? (*chapter 3 on story development and production*)

Who is hosting and where? (*chapter 4 on exhibition and community engagement*)

How do we do it better next time? (*chapter 2 on research and knowledge creation*)

To heal our culture, we should answer these questions by centering the needs of those most harmed—versus centering profit—and working to equitably redistribute—versus extract—value. These questions frame this book. In the next chapter, I use them to discuss historical and contemporary examples of reparative media, and the rest of the book uses OTV to show in-depth how our project responded to the need to serve soulful media.

Ancestral intelligences like the cookout transform polluting extraction into healing cultivation. In any ecosystem, harm is inevitable, but nature evolves ongoing, never-ending processes for healing: When forests burn, water nourishes new life, and when living beings die, fungi transform death back to life.[28] In cultural ecosystems, artists and storytellers are natural healers, equitably distributing power in diverse, competitive environments. Art and storytelling are ancestral technologies for surviving and thriving in our environment, for distributing information through culture. Potawatomi botanist Robin Wall Kimmerer makes this argument convincingly in *Braiding Sweetgrass*, showing how Indigenous communities developed sustainable, life-nourishing science by communing with diverse ecosystems and encoding knowledge through story and myth, knowledge that Western scientists took generations to understand.[29] We have always told stories to understand how to navigate social and environmental conditions necessary for survival, but as a culture, we massively undervalue the labor of storytelling.

The cookout teaches us how to develop *reparative systems* that can slowly, locally transform the cultural ecosystem that corporations extract from for fast, scalable capital accumulation. Reparative systems differ from corporate *extractive systems* in how they redistribute labor and value more equitably and sustainably. Each extractive system is rooted in a specific city but has global impact: a cookout too big to host with care. The relationship between power and place is hard to overstate in media and tech. It has been nearly impossible to generate value in film/TV without living near Hollywood or in tech without Silicon Valley, two of the most expensive places to live in the world.

Reparative story and community development exposes the root causes of harm in our cultural climate and cultivates a more abundant culture. In the next section we excavate these roots and expose how media and tech perpetuate harm. Many scholars argue that this harm is rooted in the corporation as the primary way we distribute capital.

EXTRACTIVE SYSTEMS SERVING PLASTIC CULTURE

What would an equitable, sustainable US cultural ecosystem feel like? It's hard to imagine. Corporations dominate the distribution of goods in our global economy, from food to media and technology. They consistently deliver useful or pleasurable products for us to consume, particularly in the US. With a dwindling public media infrastructure and tiny public tech infrastructure, the US heavily relies on corporations to deliver stories and information.[30] It's easy to focus on the presumed benefits of corporate capitalism: jobs and products, "but even the most beneficial growth leads to ecological and human costs if its tendencies toward systematically distorted development are left unmediated and unchecked."[31] Over the last few decades, the United States has struggled to regulate our media and tech industries, preferring they regulate themselves. They now own more of our stories, technologies for distributing those stories, and the knowledge and wealth cultivated from this process: "The media system is increasingly consolidated. Two to four corporations dominate in each sector, limiting the diversity and democratic potential of cultural production."[32] Echoing critiques from Robert McChesney, Todd Gitlin, Victor Pickard, and many others, Thomas Tufte calls this a global "crisis of development," which is fundamentally a "crisis of participation and inclusion."[33]

Corporations extract capital from the distribution of culture and information (figure 0.5).[34] With a center of power in Hollywood, the US *media system* thrives on limiting the supply of stories to harness millions of peoples' desire for entertainment. Media conglomerates offer few opportunities for storytellers to profit from or "cook" their stories, which executives view as intellectual property. Centered in Silicon Valley, the US *technological system* supports extractive hosting by platforms that own our data and shape our connections. Tech platforms target communities on a global scale without being transparent about what they are learning or how they are using our data. This troubling relationship between ownership of data, intellectual property, and mediated sociocultural experiences is more concerning with the emergence of AI. The *university system* also survives on an unequal division of labor and knowledge distribution. Research universities prioritize knowledge generated as quickly as possible under artificial time constraints to maintain the value and scarcity of job security via tenure.

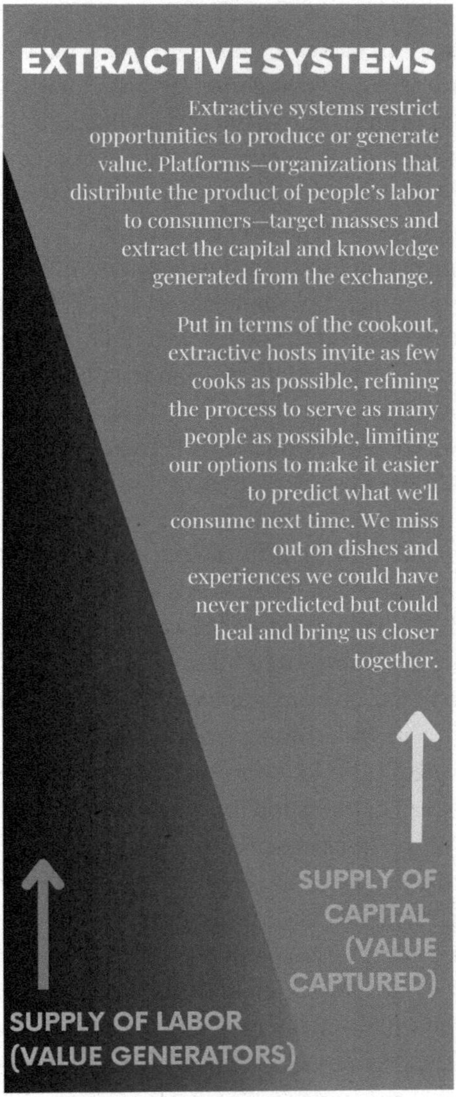

FIGURE 0.5
Extractive systems: How platforms extract value from producers and communities.

Of course, corporations are large and complex. They distribute a lot of stories and information, some of which are pleasurable and even healing. Many are also part of bigger conglomerates developing products and services outside of the culture sector or host many departments with differing standards for research and employment. Some good can come from this. Overall, however, I argue that these systems are not ideal for cultivating the stories and platforms we need to heal our culture.

The power of media and tech corporations has waxed and waned since the dramatic rise of industrial capitalism in the 1800s and postindustrial capitalism since the mid-1900s. What has remained the same is the roots of the corporation in colonization, the extraction of the earth's resources, and the unequal redistribution of the capital generated. The modern global corporation, advanced by the Dutch during their empire in the 1600s, facilitated the slave trade and exploitation of the earth's natural resources.[35] Working closely with the government and military, the corporate model spread throughout Europe and to the colonies as an efficient way to generate value from trading these resources on a global scale.

Corporate activities expanded from exploiting *physical* to *intellectual property* (IP) accelerating from the nineteenth to the twentieth century. IP is foundational to media and tech companies, from copyrighted films and series to patented algorithms and platform functions. During the rise of industrialization, media and tech corporations became key institutions for facilitating the trade of cultural and information products and the preservation of empire. This included distributing stereotypical narratives of colonized and oppressed people from which we are still healing. We see media and tech assisting empire in everything from the use of radio to facilitate communication between Europe and its colonies around the turn of the twentieth century to the development of the internet to preserve US information sovereignty and global supremacy in the decades preceding the twenty-first century. Like physical property, IP has always been unequally owned and culturally constructed: "Intellectual property is a racialized concept, which obscures whiteness and racial power through the mobilization of national feelings of hope, optimism, and pride, as well as fear, anxiety, and protectiveness," Anjali Vats writes.

Social and cultural control is deeply embedded in media and technology. Paula Chakravartty, Miriyam Aouragh, and many others have traced the emergence of the US as an empire to the rise of its dominance in media and information:[36] "Self-presenting as open forums for democratic communication, information and entertainment, corporations have become platforms for *plastically packaged cultural products*, polluting our cultural environment."[37] From purportedly "objective" newspapers that spread the US government's false claims to justify war to the sanitized version of American culture on broadcast television throughout the twentieth century, media has been a tool to justify the subjugation of people for its entire history. Any liberation from these subtle forms of control must come from intersectional, community media.

Corporate media power has been peaking in the early twenty-first century. Despite bringing some more competition and choice, digital technologies have arguably allowed US media and tech companies to reconsolidate power as they did throughout the twentieth century.[38] A small number of corporations largely decide what stories we see and don't see, whether through human executives or algorithmic decision-making. Corporate power is not in representation (what we see) but rather in distribution (harder to see): control over labor, IP, and the means to serve consumers. From video game developers and movie studios to social media and AI platforms, corporate media/tech power is suppressing the value of culture work, marginalizing community-based businesses, limiting access to communities, and making it incredibly challenging for firms outside the corporate system to compete. Most of us can only name a handful of TV channels or social media/AI platforms, which gives these platforms incredible power over who they hire and what they show us.

Few dispute the supremacy of these few corporations, though there are different perspectives on their power. Tanner Mirrlees frames the debate as one between "cultural imperialism," which views these largely US-based corporations as infiltrating cultures, and "cultural globalization," advanced by scholars like Marwan Kraidy, who views cultural flows as more locally/nationally contextual, where state actors, audiences, and producers cocreate and sometimes resist dominant narratives.[39] I lean toward cultural imperialism because I prioritize relations between power and property, over which producers and audiences have less control, however hard they try.

In Hollywood, we are seeing the slow, unsteady rise of what I call the Streaming Studio System: media conglomerates owning series and films (IP), owning the studios that produce those stories, and owning the channels for distributing and exhibiting our stories through their own apps (Disney+,

Netflix, etc.).[40] Studio power over storytellers and audiences is strengthening despite the perennial shifts in the market. Over the last twenty years, government regulators have supported strengthening corporate control over media, allowing cable and internet provider Comcast to purchase studio and distributor NBC, Disney to purchase Fox, Discovery to merge with WarnerMedia, and Viacom to merge again with CBS.[41] By the early 2020s, most streamers owned massive billion-dollar "franchise lands":[42] Marvel, Pixar, and *Star Wars* (Disney); DC Comics and *A Song of Ice & Fire* (Warner); *Star Trek* (Paramount); *Lord of the Rings* (Amazon); the books of Ann Rice (AMC); *Law & Order*, *One Chicago*, and *Real Housewives*, among others from NBC's library (Peacock). The rise of streaming coincided with what Shawna Kidman calls the "franchise era," where "value came from studio-owned intellectual property, not from the contributions of individual artists or workers."[43] These stories and their characters remain among the most valuable forms of IP (film, series, merchandise, games, theme park rides, etc.).

Streaming massively increased the number of new TV series, starting with Netflix's entry into the market in 2012 and peaking at over two thousand total series in 2022.[44] Diversity increased too, putting new representations behind paywalls. This was exciting to see, but whether this benefited our culture is up for debate. The wave of stories decreased the value of each individual story to the corporations serving them. Executives have had less time to listen to pitches, offer feedback, and consider what they were serving the collective. These platforms may be misrepresenting Black and other communities, especially compared to the healing and connective stories on OTV. In an analysis of trailers on identity-focused playlists in 2022, my lab found that platforms disproportionately promote trauma or stories about exceptionally gifted people overcoming trauma, with only a small percentage promoting joy or complex stories of everyday people experiencing joy and pain.[45] However, inaccurate representation goes beyond stereotypes or what Kristen Warner calls "plastic representations" of various "minorities."[46] There is certainly evidence for that, as recent studies have found with Black, Asian American, Muslim, and immigrant stories on corporate film and television.[47] But media companies may be misrepresenting a range of issues beyond cultural identity. For example, the University of Southern California's (USC) Norman Lear Center has found that climate change is woefully underrepresented in film and television.[48] Researchers also found that the way death is represented is grossly out of step with people's everyday lived experience: The vast plurality of TV deaths are violent, whereas most people die of illness.[49] How might these representations affect our perception of the scale of harm and possibility for healing in our society?

The Streaming Studio System is also harming the workers who write and produce these stories. Concentrated power is worsening conditions in what was already incredibly stressful work.[50] Worker stories indicate widespread mental and physical harm, from verbal abuse by executives to long hours and working while sick.[51] Writers and actors in Hollywood went on strike in 2023 as streaming suppressed wages and opportunities, their shows downsized and canceled, and as AI threatened their livelihood, making the strike the first labor action with AI on the negotiating table. The greatest rise in TV series in US history coincided with massive decreases in payment, job stability, and working conditions: "It's funny how pay in Hollywood started going down when diversity numbers started going up. . . . It's a very worrying correlation," said veteran actor Parvesh Cheena, who makes an appearance in Karan Sunil's *Code-Switched*.[52] Racialized storytellers denied ownership of their stories for generations feel the effects of this system deeply. In Hollywood, our identities and stories are trends, at the whim of capitalism's boom and bust cycles. It took seventy years of television for Indigenous peoples to have their first primetime TV sitcoms—*Reservation Dogs* for FX on Hulu and *Rutherford Falls* on Peacock—and both superbly written series were canceled after just a few seasons. In reparative media, by contrast, creators are owners of their stories and their communities critical stakeholders in their thriving.

Netflix is paradigmatic of the Streaming Studio System. It owns, distributes, and exhibits most of its stories, including films, series, and video games. Throughout its first decade in original programming, Netflix marketed itself as reforming the old Hollywood system, bringing more diverse and global stories.[53] This was more than hype. Netflix built production hubs in Latin America, Asia, Europe, and more recently Africa, progressively globalizing TV. Ramon Lobato exhaustively chronicles this ambitious effort to represent the world in ways that complicate claims to its global supremacy in this first decade, mirroring Kraidy's theory of cultural globalization: "It does not evenly envelop the world. It has wide reach but narrow impact . . . full of gaps, that come into contact unevenly with local and national surfaces."[54] Yet it is undeniable that Netflix, with over 250 million subscribers, is the largest distributor of film and television in the world, making it the most at stake in debates about the politics of representation. That these stories are algorithmically curated presents vexing questions around diversity: "While there is greater diversity being presented on the surface, the question remains whether this results in sustained engagement with what is being watched," Olivia Khoo writes in her analysis of how Netflix serves its programming.[55] With ownership of its stories and exclusive distribution rights around the world, Netflix faces decreasing competition or pressure to represent culture's many intersections. Indeed, reports suggest its use of data is ambivalent and "post-demographics," using data to confirm executive biases as often as challenge them.[56] One study of the foundations of its algorithm exposed cultural tensions: "from 'great works' to more tepid forms, from personal to prepersonal renderings of cultural identity, and from a court of human appeal to an algorithmic one."[57] Ten years into its programming initiative, Netflix chief Ted Sarandos revealed the company's ambitions to colonize TV for everyone: "We want to be HBO and CBS and BBC and all those different networks around the world that entertain people. . . . We're currently programming for about 650 million people around the world."[58] Mareike Jenner writes that Netflix is creating a culturally superficial "transnational middlebrow": "Visibility politics is common to middlebrow television . . . allowing for signifiers of changing attitudes toward race, gender, or ability, without changes to the way narratives are constructed."[59] By contrast, what we see through OTV is how our grassroots approach yields complex, specific, uncensored stories encouraging deep identification and engagement.

Rooted in Silicon Valley, tech conglomerates have grown much more powerful than their Southern California peers by buying competitors and extracting value from our stories and data.[60] Social media platforms use our engagement with stories and images from writers and artists to develop automated decision-making tools to sell us ads, refine large language models, and ultimately develop AI.[61] Social media platforms have emerged as critical technologies for communities around the world to understand themselves and others: tools for cultural connection and identity development.[62] There are many studies on how social media cultivates connection. This is true within communities that share similar identities, as we see in the emerging body of work about Black communities online. We also have scholarship on online solidarity building. Activists resist identity segmentation, as we see cis and trans Black women "hashtag activists" and Black-Asian solidarities that emerged during the pandemic.[63]

Still, most platforms automate cultural distribution, discriminating between who is seen and valued and who is not.[64] These platforms can extract from the most problematic elements of our culture. A group of researchers working for Google found that "large datasets based on texts from the Internet overrepresent hegemonic viewpoints and encode biases potentially damaging to marginalized populations."[65] Developing algorithmic systems for "prioritizing, classifying, associating, and filtering information" ultimately challenges Indigenous ways of knowing, where humans cocreate knowledge in harmony with our ecosystems.[66]

This mass extraction of data warps the original dreams of the web, from a countercultural global community to corporate cyberculture.[67] The early years of web 1.0 and 2.0 saw the cultivation of community.[68] Every platform started with intimate groups of users who supported and sustained each other, from chat rooms in the 1990s,[69] to YouTube or Twitter in the 2000s,[70] to even TikTok or Vine in the 2010s. Each one eventually grew past a point where conversation and connection could happen organically, putting pressure on creators to be authentic to communities too large to engage sincerely.[71] In my first book I described these early periods as "open" to show what kinds of production and engagement were possible within broader cycles of openness and corporate control.[72] Eventually, companies like Google pressed quickly to make platforms like YouTube profitable, focusing on scaling capital rather than community, spreadability over story quality, and status over meaningful connections.[73] Indeed, many tech companies, from Google to Netflix, have been accused of widespread censorship to maintain a presence in authoritarian countries.[74] In our reparative media work, by contrast, we valued community-led moderation and held ourselves accountable to the most vulnerable people in the places we hosted.

Digital community has become the largest space for communal interaction, but we are on stolen land. We struggle to know and influence the rules of engagement and the borders that platforms police. Social platforms have a trust problem. They do not prioritize culturally rich, nuanced storytelling that sincerely represents local conditions or culturally specific forms of marginalization or expression. Sareeta Amrute argues that this is because platforms have not invested in trust and safety teams who can learn complex social issues, local languages, and idioms.[75] But the problem goes deeper than that. The underlying infrastructures of algorithmically driven platforms prioritize the rapid circulation of that which can be quickly seen and understood, what simply confirms or offends our cultural preconceptions.[76] Platforms value culture and information using statistically driven algorithms that sort, segregate, or systematize our interactions: surveillance and border policing of networked neighborhoods.

Unsurprisingly, these dynamics can reinforce embedded inequalities: "Google's dominant narratives reflect the kinds of hegemonic frameworks and notions that are often resisted by women and people of color," writes Safiya Noble in her foundational study of its search algorithm, among the most sophisticated in the 2010s.[77] Ruha Benjamin describes the current networked environment as the "New Jim Code."[78] Wendy Chun agrees, arguing that "predictive data analytics for Internet users work—if and when they do—not by treating every Internet user like a unique snowflake, but rather by segregating users into 'neighborhoods.'"[79] That harm can emerge from these statistical practices should not be surprising. Chun and other scholars like Tukufu Zuberi have shown how eugenics spurred the creation of statistics: the use of science to justify racial stratification and thus economic and cultural inequality.[80] On corporate platforms, we can see race as a technology, a tool for reproducing cultural inequalities, supported by statistics.[81] Meanwhile, OTV's locally and intersectionally focused distribution practices consistently resisted identity simplification and bridged divides, potentially repairing the harms of real-world and networked segregation, as discussed at length in chapters 3 and 4.

Scholars are essential to making sense of these cultural harms, but we too can harm. University researchers believe our data is less extractive than corporate entities, yet we often fail to recognize how our institutional practices have historically benefited from extraction. Acknowledging this might push us to do our work differently. In his exhaustive history of the university, Craig Steven Wilder finds close relationships between the university and the material and cultural subjugation of Black and Indigenous people through colonization: "European powers deployed colleges to help defend and regulate their colonial possessions and they turned to African slavery and the African slave trade to fund these efforts."[82] This continued well into the nineteenth century. My own neighborhood on Chicago's South Side was the original site of the University of Chicago, whose land was donated by Stephen A. Douglas, owner of a violent slave plantation in Mississippi, who used its profits to purchase the university's land and place himself as its first president of the board of trustees.[83] Today, many other universities, from Georgetown to the University of California, are offering reparations, formally recognizing their relationship to slavery and the colonization of Indigenous peoples.[84] Of course, universities took steps to repair this history in the mid-twentieth century, where student-led movements led to the creation of what Roderick Ferguson calls "the interdisciplines" of American, Black, Latina/Chicana, Indigenous, gender, and queer studies.[85] Ferguson acknowledges the value produced by these fields while also showing how the university and the state used them as "grand enticements" to "offset the possibility for future ruptures," a form of social/cultural control.[86] In response, scholars are encouraging us to go beyond the university's capture of our knowledge, reject fantasies of uplift, and leverage the university's grand enticements to cultivate knowledge outside of it in collaboration with those excluded.[87] Yet many of us are overproducing theory and underproducing practice, the kind of experiments that take time and care to manifest, generating hyper-specific data but deeper impact.

Research universities generally do not value data that serves communities as much as theory that serves academics.[88] Thoughtful people—within and outside the corporate university—are acting to change these dynamics. As a university-based scholar, I saw how community-led experiments can show us alternative ways to cultivate knowledge and how risky this work can be. Research has tremendous power to offer meaningful solutions to the world's problems, but it is going too fast. CVs from young scholars at top institutions are getting longer and longer. I'm guilty of this myself! The university system requires that we produce this knowledge to gain status in the system, with tenure as the pinnacle of value. For me, creating knowledge outside of the university threatened the value of my labor in the university system but was the most rewarding thing I have ever done. To refuse the university's capture of all our knowledge production is to engage fugitivity, what Stefano Harney and Fred Moten call the undercommons: "The undercommons in some ways tries to escape from critique . . . *retreating . . . into the external world.*"[89] Refusing to stop at critiquing harm and instead experimenting with repair liberates our knowledge from exclusively benefiting ourselves and our institutions.

Repair thrives in durable, flexible, and community-accountable systems outside of extractive institutions. Any form of reparation should give those historically disempowered ownership over our data, knowledge, and stories: the time, freedom—ultimately, the power—to represent ourselves organically and sustainably.

Intersectionality shows us the power of representing the multiple, intersecting ways that systems have harmed communities. In the next section I argue that intersectionality is also foundational to repairing harms.

THE HEALING POWER OF INTERSECTIONALITY

Our stories are critical data for understanding systemic harm and healing. My own experience navigating the systems of racism, misogyny, and homophobia deeply informs my work. I grew up in the 1980s and 1990s amid a surge of Black representation on film and television. TV—and cookies—offered comfort and escape from household trauma. TV was how I came to understand myself as a Black American, born of Caribbean immigrants and raised in a multicultural suburb of New York City. I loved series like *In Living Color*, *Fresh Prince of Bel-Air*, *Martin*, and more, all led by Black men.[90] Of course, I also loved comedies produced and led by Black women like *Living Single*, *Moesha*, and *Sister, Sister*, whose women were more compelling than the men in my opinion. But Black men on TV were my primary examples of what I could hope to be as an adult.[91]

As I slowly came to understand myself as queer, I noticed the often-limiting ways media portrayed Black masculinity: in binary opposition to women, rarely embracing love between men, or showing how expansively men express gender.[92] Black men on screen were "real cool," strangers to their desires, aggressive if not violent both emotionally and physically, and helpless against governments and systems. If not, they were unrealistically perfect fathers or partners who did not seem to exist in the world I lived in. As a soft, empathic, and nerdy Black child, I developed a dysphoric relationship to normative Black masculinity.[93] As I grew older, I realized women and trans people of all races, even my own, were also wary of me, a result of stereotypes but also real traumatic experiences. Black men have been harming our kin as our environments have harmed us, inhibiting our ability to love ourselves and others. bell hooks wrote at the time: "Sadly, the real truth, which is a taboo to speak, is that this is a culture that does not love black males. . . . And that especially most black men do not love themselves. How could they, how could they be expected to love surrounded by so much envy, desire, hate?[94]" My insecurity was rooted in my inability to identify with normative Black masculinity: emotionally detached, aggressive, and power-hungry at most, or in firm opposition to femininity at least. I felt a stranger to myself when I was treated as if I was those things anyway: incapable of care, tenderness, and empathy, let alone feminism and solidarity. Were it possible to take pride in who I was, I could have done more to dispel these myths in my everyday life and assert different forms of Black masculinity that might change the people and culture around me. This is what I mean when I say harm to the cultural ecosystem affects us all: It limits how *all* of us see ourselves and each other, no matter what power or privilege we hold.

I wish I could say media healed me, but representations of queer Black men almost never emerged in my formative years. When out Black gays emerged on Black sitcoms—nearly the only genre Black people could lead before *Scandal* and *Empire* in the 2010s—they were relegated to storylines where they come out and then disappear, because corporations and executive producers presumed Black audiences were homophobic.[95] The lesson from media was clear: My life did not matter.

I started to heal—queer—my relationship to Black masculinity through friends, my partners, and ultimately the community I cultivated. I intentionally sought queer and trans kinship when I arrived in Chicago in 2012 and was immediately struck by how liberating and gender-diverse our lives can be in ways I'd never seen on television. Seeing, dancing, and communing with brave queer and trans people of color learning to love themselves outside the binaries of race, gender, and sexuality empowered me to the do the same.

Through OTV, I wanted to show the reparative power of intersectionality that I was experiencing in my community at the local level. I wanted to heal myself and help others do the same.

Intersectionality offers a theoretical framework for healing systems. It reveals how race, gender, sexuality, and other identities intersect with each other and powerful institutions. It is not an equation or rule,[96] but it helps us be specific about where to locate our social, cultural, and political pains. It is a framework for engaging with the world to transform one's environment equitably and sustainably.[97] We have the term intersectionality because scholar Kimberlé Crenshaw surveyed her field of the law and found its environment oppressive to Black women surviving the intersecting systems of racism and sexism. The law simply could not recognize, interpret, or value their stories and experiences, limiting its democratic potential and compelling us to reimagine the entire system: "For feminist theory and antiracist policy discourse to embrace the experiences and concerns of Black women, the entire framework that has been used as a basis for translating 'women's experience' or 'the Black experience' into concrete policy demands must be rethought and recast," Crenshaw wrote.[98]

Around the same time, bell hooks surveyed the field of media, becoming a leading scholar integrating intersectionality into media studies by critiquing films, music, and television through her own position as a Black woman.[99] Following her legacy, Moya Bailey coined the term "misogynoir" to describe the specific forms of harm that Black women encounter and resist, drawing on Patricia Hill Collins's notion of "controlling images" and hooks's call for complex counternarratives.[100] Significantly, Bailey explicitly connects Black women's media representations to other forms of harm in society, solidifying the relationship between intersectionality and healing: "Negative images and narratives do more than affect the self-esteem of the populations depicted. Misogynoiristic caricatures *materially* impact the lives of Black women by justifying poor treatment throughout all areas of society and throughout US history."[101] Still, Bailey shows how Black women do not simply accept these representations but create everything from social media campaigns to independent web series to repair them.

Similarly, we can clearly see the healing power of intersectionality in some of OTV's pilots and short films. In Rebba Amaris's OTV pilot/short film *Conspiracy Theorist*, a Black woman navigates a PhD program and her disintegrating mental health as she is portrayed as "crazy" by mentors and peers for criticizing theories that do not integrate race or gender. As a former PhD student, Rebba was intimately familiar with how Black women are often seen as conspiracy theorists for questioning academic theory and culture. She told me that "rather than avoid action," she "embraced [TV] as a dialectical tool for constructive argumentation." On OTV, Rebba was "granted the liberty as a developing artist to discover her practice on her own terms." The brilliant, surreal pilot asks whether Black women can heal in a world that questions their perception of reality—reminding us how important valuing experience is to understanding intersectionality. Scholar-artist Marshall Green poses similar questions in his film *Triggers*, a visual poem told through vogue and modern dance, jazz, and a letter to his younger pre-transition self. Marshall refuses the binary of gender transition as a transmasculine adult, embracing the dissensus of knowing what it was to be a little Black girl, now a grown Black man healing from patriarchy and state-sponsored racial violence.

Intersectionality inspires stories as theories to show how systems harm. But recognizing the complexity of harm compels us to *act* to repair, including organizing or telling stories. Through OTV, our creators practiced intersectionality as a *theory of social action*, as Patricia Hill Collins argues.[102] Like healing, intersectionality cannot be understood only in theory. It requires practice. Collins uses the example of Ida B. Wells, who published specific, local stories of lynchings to show how theorists of intersectionality reveal it by *feeling* or noticing systemic oppression and *acting* to change systems: "The meaning of a particular social theory lies not in just in its words but also in how its ideas are created and used. . . . Western social theories have long been placed in service to various systems of domination. It is important not just to read what theories say but also to understand how social theories work within society."[103] Academia and other fields have been slow to embrace intersectionality because of this rigor—social critique *and* action—and its refusal of Western theory's love of generalizability in favor of specific interventions in service of local communities.

In this way, intersectionality is kin to Indigenous theory. Intersectionality inspires a collective process of understanding through action how to honor communal experiences and ecosystems. Indigenous theory inspires us to understand our community's relationship to the land we occupy, our impact on it, and our history with it. Linda Tuhiwai Smith writes, "Indigenous research is a humble and humbling activity," inviting those with power and privilege to transfer power to those who have had land, knowledge, and culture stolen from them.[104] To heal, we must first acknowledge that our lands were stolen, colonized by capitalism, fueled by racism, patriarchy, and other forms of cultural hate and division.

Intersectionality is organic, whereas corporate colonial capitalism is plastic and extractive. Colonizing Indigenous land for private property has caused material pollution, from plastic in our oceans to pollutants in our air. As Max Liboiron writes, "Pollution is best understood as the violence of colonial land relations rather than environmental damage, which is a symptom of violence."[105] Yet we are less aware of how the colonization of *intellectual* property produces *cultural* pollution or damage: how a small number of corporations profit from the production of big-budget film/TV stories and big data-driven platforms, polluting our culture and challenging deep, intimate, cross-cultural connections.[106]

Capitalism has also separated us from our environment and each other through its unequal distribution of resources. In his constructive view of reparations, Olúfẹ́mi Táíwò pushes us to repair not only colonization's *material/environmental* effects but also the effects of the unequal *distribution* of *social/cultural* capital: "Distribution is key to understanding the fundamental workings of society. . . . Distributive justice encompasses all these dimensions of how we parcel out the benefits and burdens of social cooperation [e.g., levels of prestige, access to social networks]."[107] For me, the process of distributing stories for repair was as social and cultural as it was material, conducted at the local level. Without responding to the needs of my immediate local community in Chicago, unseated territory of the Council of Three Fires (Ojibwe, Odama, Potawatomi), among many other tribes, I could not have healed myself. So much rich cultural diversity may never have emerged, cultivating radical new bonds and ways of being, in addition to generating economic, cultural, and social capital.

Developing stories that centered intersectionality in Chicago deepened and widened my perspective on how profoundly Hollywood, Silicon Valley, and academia perpetuate harm by extracting from my communities while also offering an organic path to reparation. Rooting ourselves in our localities helps us see and address culture's exclusions and harms more specifically and sincerely. At the local level, we can more easily identify and compost big "-isms." This is an ongoing, never-ending process of listening, taking accountability, revising, contesting, and changing. Through OTV, we can see how to use intersectionality to experiment with healing systems through reparative R&D.

REPARATIVE R&D: SERVING ORGANIC CULTURE

My collaborators, community, and I cultivated (re)distributive infrastructures: a media and tech-based cookout. I structured OTV | Open Television as an experiment in distributing—or *serving*—film/TV, social media, and knowledge in ways that organically amplify the power of those most marginalized by systems. Distribution structures community organizing. It encourages us to give something (knowledge, resources, connections) and use what we take (at best, the right to redistribute what people create at no cost to them) to benefit others. In *reparative R&D*, the less you take and the more you give, the more value you can create and the more repair you can distribute. Those who believe that repair is impossible simply have not taken the time to understand the power and practice of distribution: how culture is made, how systems work, how everyday people respond, and how we as scholars can engage these tensions.

Reparative R&D is the slow, messy process of uncovering and understanding how harm happens and how to distribute healing collectively. Reparative research necessarily includes development and vice versa, or as Ernest Boyer writes, "moving from theory to practice, and from practice back to theory, which in fact makes theory . . . more authentic."[108] Understanding how systems harm and how communities resist shapes practice, and what we learn from practice deepens our knowledge of systems.

Reparative R&D embraces conflict and dissensus, understanding difference creates meaning. We know from nature that conflict and pain are necessary for growth and ecological transformation. We see our interdependence, moving beyond dependent and independent variables to track how we resist and produce relations through and outside systems not designed for us. Reparative R&D must be designed to learn from and adapt to what is happening in the ecosystem while allowing for change, decentralizing control, power, and ownership.

A reparative approach requires researchers to take a step back and allow others who have been harmed by systems to lead. In this I was very inspired by the Design Justice Network. Sasha Costanza-Chock, a steering committee member of the Design Justice Network, argues that "design justice rethinks design processes, centers people who are normally marginalized by design, and uses collaborative, creative practices to address the deepest challenges our communities face."[109] We benefit from opening our studies to change and vulnerability.

Our reparative R&D process asked how we could subvert corporate distribution by sharing power over IP—our stories and data. As seen in figure 0.4, reparative R&D supports both the development (inviting) of systemically disempowered storytellers and the production (cooking) of their stories, while researching how stories perform after they have been distributed. It ideally supports the development of platforms (hosting) to release those stories and cultivates knowledge by asking audiences or the community how they feel about what they saw, informing how we serve stories the next time.

By employing a range of methods, my team and I deepened our understanding of the limits and possibilities of this grassroots distribution structure. The most important data was my experience of this process and my relationships with collaborators, collected using the traditional anthropological method of field notetaking. But (auto)ethnography is only the first step.

To support story research, between 2015 and 2021, I conducted 132 official interviews with creators, including 10 exit interviews with OTV team members and 58 "exit" interviews with creator teams who released programs on OTV, a majority of the roughly 80 films, pilots, series, and other types of programs we helped develop and distribute in that period.[110] These led to seven annual public reports that I wrote on the organization's development,[111] eight reports on how creators and community members were receiving OTV,[112] and four peer-reviewed academic articles, in addition to half a dozen other scholarly papers. I visited or directly participated in the production of 14 different films, pilots, and series, combining participant observation with participatory action; I earned director, producer, or executive producer credit on 10 projects, but there were many others my team and I helped without official credit. Over the years, the organization also developed 10 internal databases to offer creators more support in production. We tracked directors, producers, editors, designers (costume, hair, makeup), musicians/composers, cinematographers/photographers, sound, production assistants, locations, and writers. We also developed five databases to help creators find local and national resources to support their projects, including writing/directing opportunities (130), funding opportunities (56), fellowship/award/grant opportunities (50), stock footage (17), and remote production (7 sources Sarah Minnie developed to assist filmmakers during the pandemic).

To research the platform's hosting practices, we screened those programs 52 times in Chicago, conducting 72 surveys for community feedback, including surveys about other OTV programs like our mentorship/training offerings.[113] Each screening also served as a deeply embodied case study of how to exhibit these kinds of works in unique, culturally specific, and interdisciplinary ways. We tracked where these programs showed up in exhibitions outside of OTV—99 times from 2015 to 2019, from the Brooklyn

Museum and Tribeca Film Festival to the National Museum of Mexican Art and Outfest—and how many press outlets covered the programs—over 250 times from 2015 to 2020, including *Time*, *Elle*, *The New York Times*, *Out*, and BET. Online, our exhibition efforts yielded over 1 million cumulative plays on our videos on Vimeo and hundreds of thousands of engagements on Facebook, Instagram, Tumblr, and Twitter.

Following the growth of OTV, I conducted four trips for meetings in Hollywood with writers/executive producers, studios, networks, agencies, and management companies, resulting in field notes from over three dozen meetings with companies like HBO, Netflix, WarnerMedia, 3Arts, and more. You will read more about these in the conclusion in what is the first study of the "general meeting," the most common type of meeting in Hollywood about which there is virtually no scholarship. I say more about these meetings and how they provoked me to consider the deep interconnectedness of our systems.

HOW TO READ *REPARATIVE MEDIA*

Reparative Media uses OTV to show how this organic R&D process can heal systemic harm in the production of story through media, community through technology, and knowledge through research. It begins with the overview of my theory of this process and ends with a deeper discussion of the many ways conflict and harm can manifest in ourselves, our communities, and our organizations.

Most of this book focuses on one project, though I will include other historical examples of reparative media throughout. However, the first chapter, "The Cookout," shares other examples of reparative media through the lens of the cookout. When hosts plan a cookout, they organically ask themselves a series of questions to make sure the event serves their community. These questions—like "who's cooking" (production) and "where are we hosting" (exhibition)—ground us in how to develop reparative media. The chapter draws on historical and contemporary examples in media and tech to show how community leaders, entrepreneurs, journalists, scholars, and artists have responded to these questions to heal systemic harms.

The rest of the book is structured around how the OTV team, creators, and community leaders responded to the questions we asked while planning our cookout.

The second chapter, "Reparative Research," explores how scholars cultivate knowledge and theory. Scholars teach leaders in media and technology, but what are we teaching—and what are we not? "Reparative Research" explores the possibilities and limits of an organic approach to cultivating knowledge in the university system. In this chapter, I share lessons from running OTV as a community-based research project for five years and identify some core tenets of reparative research: understanding who you are as a researcher, methodological flexibility, mutual benefit, open-access data, and decentralizing power. Reparative research can only grow in a conducive environment. Each study should be rooted in a specific place or community, informed by and responsive to harm, and cultivating diverse resources to repair it.

In chapter 3, "Reparative Stories," I explore what a reparative approach to "cooking" film and television stories can teach Hollywood about how to heal their legacy of producing harmful narratives of raced, gendered, and classed people. This chapter focuses on how OTV's pilots, series, and films were developed and produced, the stories of the dozens of creators we supported. In this chapter I critique how shows are developed in Hollywood and the challenges to inclusion. Then I offer an overview of how intersectionality informed the history of social practice artmaking in Chicago, independent film/TV, and social media production in ways that repair historical exclusions. The bulk of the chapter reveals the core tenets of reparative story development: creator ownership of IP, community-based financing, cultural over technical "production value," and creator-centered distribution. In the conclusion I explore the struggles of indie production, including harm/conflict and lack of resources, and how OTV is evolving to better support creators in telling stories.

Chapter 4, "Reparative Platforms," defines what I mean by community and shows how social media platforms could benefit from an organic approach to "hosting" community through an analysis of OTV's online and Chicago-based exhibitions. Healing social media and emergent AI platforms requires taking seriously the work of developing community across identity lines. I draw on local, Indigenous, and emergent Black feminist practices of care, site specificity, and restorative justice to understand what needs to happen to repair our culture through technology. This chapter contrasts data from case studies of how OTV projects circulated on social media to how projects circulated in the city of Chicago, and in cities around the country and world. I show the value of local/in real life versus global/digital exhibition and how intersectionality supports solidarity locally and on social media. I identify the core tenets of reparative platform development: cultivating local exhibitions, using intersectionality to disrupt segregationist algorithms, and developing care-centered agreements for digital engagement.

Finally, in chapter 5, "Practicing Reparations," I conclude with a meditation on reparations as an individual, interpersonal, communal, and systemic practice. I tell stories of interpersonal, intra-community, and intercommunity harm and conflict around OTV and how both the organization and I are addressing them. Then I discuss the creation of OTV's nonprofit and for-profit entities and the barriers to reparation in the nonprofit and corporate industrial complexes. I challenge the conversation that is currently too tightly focused on people getting *material* needs like land, investment, housing, and healthcare. These are so important, but they are not sustainable without a *cultural* shift, a shift in *how we understand ourselves and others*, a shift in how systems work both materially and immaterially.

Culture is how we understand our lives and our environments. The process of cultivating culture—how we make and serve it—should also be healing. Technology alone cannot heal our souls, psyches, and cultures. Stories heal. Communities heal. Artists or storytellers are cultural healers. Their stories are essential technologies for serving cultural knowledge, and grassroots distribution guided by intersectionality is a key and underused method for systemic repair. As Favianna Rodriguez, artist, activist, and founder of the Center for Cultural Power, says, "Stories change people, and people change systems."[114]

We can change cultural systems, healing colonized fields and ourselves. We can reform existing systems and build new ones at the same time. We can see the fields of media, technology, and research as sites for our own cultural cookouts. But we must start locally. We must share our knowledge. We must create culture collectively and distribute it equitably. Reparations is not something we have to wait for to heal the wounds of the past. We cannot wait. The world is at stake, and state-led reparations require systems to administer them. We can cultivate the world we need, right now, wherever we are, whatever we are doing.

1 THE COOKOUT: SERVING SOULFUL MEDIA

> The challenge that the cultural worker faces . . . is that the tools of my trade are colonized. The creative imagination has been colonized. The global screen has been colonized. And the audience—readers and viewers—is in bondage to an industry. It has the money, the will, the muscle, and the propaganda machine oiled up to keep us all locked up in a delusional system—as to even what America is.
>
> —Toni Cade Bambara[1]

> Rarely, if ever, are any of us healed in isolation. Healing is an act of communion.
>
> —bell hooks[2]

Who's invited to the cookout?

"The Cookout" is a Black cultural practice where families and communities gather, eat, and enjoy each other's company. We imagine the cookout as an outdoor activity, as seen in the film *The Cookout*, one of Lionsgate's first films targeting the Black community that would help them become a major studio. Because the cookout is outside, it blurs public and private. It may be hosted at someone's home, but in theory, anyone can roll up. You don't have to be Black. It is not a private dinner, so guests can bring a friend, lover, family member, even a coworker. There's room for more. It's abundant.

The cookout is a contested space—families and communities have factions. Search for "the cookout" on X or Google, and you see people asking, "who *isn't* invited to the cookout" or "who *can't* come to the cookout?" Our cookout discourse is very negative. Black folks fear someone will show up who has an issue with the host, the family, or the community at large—or who puts the wrong ingredient in the potato salad! As Black people, the question of who is *not* invited is a fun question for us to talk about because it allows us to play with identity politics in a way that invites joy into difficult situations. But some confuse the cookout for what Dave Chappelle famously dramatized as the "racial draft," where different races trade members of their race for people of other races who are more "down" for their cause: a competition for the best ally.[3] Or others use the system of "cards," where you can lose your "Black card" for violations against the race, a way to police who gets to identify as us.

Our focus on who is *not* invited to the cookout is a form of community protection and survival. We understand community through the lens of policing and competition because capitalism and state violence deeply shape our experiences.

Reparative systems focus on who *is* invited to the cookout. It resists competition and border policing, but not everyone is invited. Reparative media flourishes in smaller, local ecosystems, where we can all know each other and see our impact on the environment and each other. The cookout can't be for everybody, or it loses the intimacy necessary for deep connection. It is an appropriate allegory for reparative work because it is not fully private or public, mostly local but welcoming of people from other places. It does not promote the competition of the racial draft or the policing of race card systems, but it acknowledges the importance of protection and care in cultivating the environments we need to thrive. Instead, anyone theoretically has an invite to the cookout until their actions cause the invitation to be rescinded. Still, they might have the opportunity to be invited again should they demonstrate through action an awareness of the harm they caused: Next time, leave the sugar out of the grits, and we'll be good!

When we ask who is and is not invited to the cookout, we are talking about the politics of distribution at the *grassroots*, or community level. Distributors are the hosts, tasked with deciding who gets invited and served. The invitation is the first step in a complex process of cultivation. Hosts are responsible for (1) inviting chefs who *produce* or cook food, (2) developing spaces for *serving* food and other forms of entertainment, (3) hosting spaces to *exhibit* these joyful offerings for those who want to come together to consume it, (4) and assessing the process to *cultivate* the knowledge to do it better the next time. This grassroots process of R&D, of distributing what nourishes and recycling what doesn't, is critical to ecosystemic sustainability. A key problem with our cultural ecosystem, particularly in the US, is that we've ceded control of platforms to corporations that extract profit and property over reinvesting what they take for nourishment, connection, and knowledge. The cookout is grassroots because it is about nurturing the seeds of connection in hyperlocal, biodiverse soil—the more diverse the ecosystem, the more fertile the soil, the deeper and more interconnected the roots, and the more resilient the ecosystem.

Community media exemplify the cookout ethos. This is not new. We have ancestries of community media around the world, particularly in countries outside the US grappling with legacies of colonization. In later chapters I explore the histories of public and public access media, independent film, and video collectives and their relationship to repairing our cultural wounds. But, briefly, in his foundational study of community media, Kevin Howley finds examples of community media in radio, print, television, and film in the US and around the world, building on the work of scholars and producers like DeeDee Halleck, Deirdre Boyle, and Clemencia Rodriguez.[4] Howley defines community media as anti-mainstream "grassroots or locally oriented media access initiatives" that resist global power and assert local culture and agency.[5] We can hear resonances of the cookout in his argument for why community media is both popular and strategic: "popular in that these initiatives are responses to the *felt need* of local populations to create media systems that are relevant to their everyday lives; strategic in that these efforts are purposeful assertions of collective identity and local autonomy in the era marked by the unprecedented concentrations of media ownership."[6]

Similarly, Faye Ginsburg defines Indigenous (Aboriginal Australian) media as "reproducing and transforming cultural identity among people who have experienced massive political, geographic, and economic disruption."[7] Research on community media consistently highlights collaborative production and distribution processes that are decidedly anti-corporate, anti-commercial, and participatory.[8] We might think of this as "alternative media" focused on social and cultural change,[9] or as Chris Atton writes, "the deliberate decentralization and relinquishment of control of the processes of reproduction and distribution."[10] Atton highlights "open copyright" and "open distribution" as key tenets of alternative media in ways that mirror the cookout's decentralization of cooking and hosting.[11]

Yet my cookout framework highlights a critical gap in the history of community media in the United States: the lack of consistent entertainment distribution platforms run and owned by Black, Brown, and Indigenous women, trans, and queer people.[12] Most research on community platforms owned by racialized people across intersectionalities are outside the US in places where governments have been more proactive about media equity. Most of these efforts focus on documentary and journalism, rarely entertainment or narrative television/video.[13] Moreover, projects are often run by people not from the communities represented; quite often, this looks like white people documenting people of color or "empowering" them with access to recording technology. Christina Dunbar-Hester highlights these tensions in her study of the low-power radio movement, though she notes how activists intentionally grappled with race and class inequalities in ways that look different from corporate "DEI" initiatives.[14] Simply put, queer, trans, women, and people of color have had fewer invitations to the alternative community media cookout, let alone been granted the power and access to host their own. This has profound implications for how healing media can be in the US, home to incredible diversity and many of the world's largest media and tech conglomerates.

The cookout is about *communities representing themselves* through *joy*. Entertainment is as critical to community building and learning as journalism or documentary.[15] In the US, we have some history of Black-produced television, particularly in the 1960s and 1970s, and queer-produced television starting in the 1980s, but with rare exception, these communities did not own or run the stations that distributed their work (see chapter 3). Because they lacked ownership over distribution, they were subjected to censorship or struggled to cultivate lasting community relationships and revenue. Funders' fears about oppressed peoples' free expression through mass media often led producers to choose "safe" forms of delivering information through documentary or journalism, avoiding the creativity of comedy, drama, video art, and so forth. Without control over distribution or the funding to entertain, diverse and community-minded producers and distributors have found it challenging to sustain and develop the reparative media work most exciting to their communities. This has harmed our cultural ecosystem.

This is why we created OTV. In the digital age, the lower cost of production and distribution coupled with the increase in diverse communities engaging each other through entertainment shows the need for community-run platforms. OTV | Open Television is not the only one by far, and it is not wholly new. However, in its focus on intersectionality guiding distribution, it is rare, perhaps singular. Yet I agree with Clemencia Rodriguez and others that researchers of alternative, radical, or citizens' media need to avoid "reinventing the wheel."[16] This chapter uses the cookout to connect OTV to its contemporary and ancestral peers, while further explaining why the cookout is a productive framework for organizing reparative media projects.

Framing reparative media through the cookout prompts critical questions of the processes by which media, tech, and knowledge institutions serve us culture (figure 1.1):

Development: Who is *invited* and how?
Production: Who is *cooking* and what?
Distribution: Who is *serving* and why?

FIGURE 1.1
The cookout as an equitable system.

Exhibition: Who is *hosting* and where?

Research: How do we understand and *cultivate* community better next time?

Each of these questions relates to an aspect of researching and developing a healing culture through media. The rest of the book answers these questions, focusing specifically on OTV.

WHO IS INVITED AND HOW?

As they say in Chicago, "Who all gonna be there?" If you can't cook, that's OK! Your invitation is based on what you bring to the table. Maybe you're an extrovert and help guests introduce themselves. Or maybe you're friendly with local officials and law enforcement, so you offer some protection. If you are not bringing something tangible of value, especially if you are a guest of a guest, the least you can do is not crush the vibe. Better still, help the host!

When we ask who's invited to the cookout, we are really asking if the people attending care about us, *how* the platform (the cookout) is developing a hospitable container for our connection. Corporate media are not primarily designed to care about the people they invite to their platforms. They are designed for profit, or value extraction. They generally develop and distribute the biggest stories (Hollywood) or the most stories (Silicon Valley) to attract as many people as possible to make as much money as possible. While it is important to have platforms for everybody, platforms need democratically regulated protocols for who they invite. Society does not care for everyone equally, based on how they identify and what they bring to the table. US governments have struggled to regulate media and hold it to the standards of democratic representation. The consequence is that for most of our media history, corporate media has not been for everybody. When they have tried, corporations eventually rescind the invitation (chapter 3) or offer an inhospitable vibe (chapter 4).

The history of US film and television features cycles of inclusion and exclusion for people who are so rarely invited to bring their gifts to the table, solely because of their race, ethnicity, gender, sexuality, class, and other identity markers. Either storytellers are excluded or their inclusion temporary or circumscribed. The Hollywood system retains its power by keeping artists stressed about their status within it. It depletes storytellers' imagination—a soft form of mental incarceration—and makes it harder to take care of themselves. The limited capacity to dream, to tell stories with freedom, is a hidden cost of the system that we never see. Much of what we see is what corporations believe will *hit* and *trend*: the stories that make it through their tight supply chains—invitations limited. Many generations of storytellers died prematurely awaiting invitations. This makes for a bland party, but for most people in the US, it's all we've ever known, so we don't even know there's a healthier party offering more flavor and connection.

Most US social media platforms have open invitations for anyone to participate but then use machines to moderate and control who is seen and heard, often amplifying people who harm. To be sure, moderating a discussion among millions, if not billions, of people, is a complex endeavor and difficult to generalize, as Tarleton Gillespie argues.[17] Yet the consequences of inaccurate moderation are likely felt more deeply by communities that have been historically silenced. LGBTQ+ users across platforms have publicly decried takedowns of their speech, censored merely for expressing who they are. For example, Oliver Haimson found stark differences in moderation. Conservative participants' content removals from platforms often involved harmful speech removed according to site guidelines to create safe spaces, but transgender and Black participants were censored largely for sharing their own story despite following platform policies.[18] For years, Black YouTubers complained about rising challenges to their visibility, causing YouTube to respond with a funded program. Black TikTok users went on "strike" for the same reason and because of widespread appropriation of their talents by other users.[19]

In our local communities, we are much better at curating the room and managing power dynamics. "Micro media" outlets invite communities to find the information and entertainment they need while inviting caring outsiders who want to learn and connect.[20] Historically, US "ethnic media" from the Black press to immigrant-led journalism serves as a countervailing force against corporate misrepresentations of their communities. Sharing information in culturally specific ways invites readers and consumers to participate in civic discourse, necessary for community survival and participation.[21] This is changing, for the worse. Miya Williams Fayne has found that today, most of the Black press is owned by corporations and not by Black people, compelling those outlets to treat their communities as markets by focusing more on superficial information and entertainment.[22]

US entertainment media has a complicated history with inviting storytellers across different, intersecting communities. Corporate distributors designed for these historically excluded communities historically treat communities as commodities. This is best exemplified by the acquisition of BET by Viacom at the turn of the twenty-first century, and the emergence of cable channels for women, lesbians and gays, and Latinos, all of which offered culturally specific but sometimes sanitized programming unavailable on broadcast channels.[23] In response to cable's shortcomings, community-minded digital entrepreneurs attempted to recreate the intimacy of early community-based public TV and public access television on platforms like YouTube. Networking technologies enabled communities to talk to each other with greater ease, and short-lived identity-based social media platforms like BlackPlanet, AsianAvenue, and MiGente invited Black, Asian, and Latiné users to gather in digital space.[24]

Reframing our mediated spaces through the lens of the cookout invites us to loosen our standards for who gets an invitation while staying values aligned. I started OTV hungry for a kind of queer church, a diverse and intersectional space embracing difference, with the same ritual of weekly sermons or, to borrow from television, weekly watch parties.

WHO IS COOKING AND WHAT?

Food draws people to gather. Conversations around who's invited to the cookout often start with *what* we expect them to bring. What people bring is based both on skill—using the right amount of salt and spice—and culture—are there raisins in your potato salad? You are free to bring what you want, but if you are not serving the needs of the culture, you may not be invited back or asked to just bring ice. As climate change and capitalism reshape our environments and our bodies, what we eat is increasingly political. The quality of the ingredients and the diversity of what we eat is important for our personal and collective health, raising systemic issues of production (the use of chemicals or monocultural farming), access (food deserts and prices), information (don't serve produce that the government has recalled), and care (make it tasty but if it's healthy too, even better).

Most people are not as thoughtful about who makes their media as they are about what's in their food, even though most of us spend more time consuming media than food. As a scholar of media production, I do. I look at who is writing, directing, producing, and funding everything I watch and engage, from films and TV shows to social media apps. I don't I always eat healthy. I still will taste fried chicken and mac n' cheese at the cookout even though I'm lactose intolerant! But I try to eat a balanced diet so I can show up as my best self.

Just like food, the process of producing culture is as important as the product made. A great example is the Indigenous video game *Never Alone*, developed by Upper One Games and published by E-Line media in collaboration with the Iñupiat tribe in Alaska. "Cooked" in collaboration with a tribal community and distributed independently, the game challenges corporate game aesthetics with an ancestral story narrated by a community elder. The story promotes healing by connecting our relationship to the environment and our ancestors with surviving threats to our community. At the same time, profits from the game go toward the Iñupiat tribe, helping them survive the threats to their ancestral lands because of climate change. Thus, *Never Alone* connects community-led production to community-accountable distribution: "Because the game foregrounds co-productive nature of the design process, it also shifts the relationship between designer and audience. It suggests an invitation to greater understanding of both the designers' intentions and the stories they are trying to tell."[25] Here the global supports the local, independent distribution supports community ownership, and stories become technologies for sharing ancestral intelligence.

This is not to say that products made by people from outside a community cannot offer meaningful pleasures to that community. Before *Reservation Dogs* and *Rutherford Falls*, *Molly of Denali* brought an Indigenous-led TV series to kids; while the creators were not Indigenous, they allowed people from the community to edit the script and used the funding to train more Indigenous writers.[26] In her work on queer gamers, Adrienne Shaw has consistently found that "players/audiences, owing to the complexity of their identities, are able to have strong connections to people unlike them on a regular basis."[27] Therefore, what cooks make matters as much as how they make it. Encouraging queer game creators to tell their stories might create entirely different ways for game fans to engage with the medium, perhaps in ways that are more healing. This is what trans indie game designer Anna Anthropy argues in comparing indie games to "zines," where the author's experience brings value to a text, as opposed to big-budget games largely created by straight white men with large teams.[28] Indeed, in her work creating a vast archive of LGBTQ representation in games, Shaw notes a twenty-year gap from the earliest indie game she could find to Anthropy's *Dsy4ia*, and, in correlation, a lack of games about HIV/AIDS.[29] Today, contemporary artists like Rashaad Newsome and Stephanie Dinkins are questioning the politics of production in interactive media and AI, designing smaller language models with language from specific cultures and communities. Both Newsome and Dinkins have created Black queer and women-centered AI-based avatars trained on ancestral knowledges—Newsome's Being (the Digital Griot) and Dinkin's N'TOO (a composite of her elders). The result is less seamlessly interactive than the large language models of OpenAI, Meta, and Alphabet but more healing and unique.

Most of the media we consume is not made for healing but for profit. How has this shaped our culture, the stories we tell ourselves about ourselves? This does not make it all bad, but it does mean we need to be mindful of what we eat at the corporate cookout and how long we stay. If we seriously commit to trying the indie and community-based cookouts, we might find it more healing over time. We might see our souls expand and soften because we are feeding it something made with more care. I hope this book shows how, though fraught, the community cookout is much more enrichening than the glamorous but shallow corporate alternative.

WHO IS SERVING AND WHY?

Serving is service, an act of care. As hosts, platforms serve communities by distributing culture. Most communities create connections through specific rituals and practices cultivated over time. It matters *why* platforms are serving culture, the intention and legacies behind the gathering. Media is supposed to bring us together, but increasingly our media is private or divisive, motivated by profit over connection. If we want strong social bonds, we need intentionally produced mediated spaces and platforms that promote a loving and pluralistic culture. Our corporate media tries to do this. For some, it is the Macy's Thanksgiving Day Parade or the Super Bowl; for others, it is Verzuz, a celebration of Black music, or *RuPaul's Drag Race*, a celebration of queer culture. So often, however, these events draw crowds for competition, or the events are so watered down as to be for everybody, which is to say nobody specifically.

Reparative platforms serve communities intentionally, using specific forms of care, healing, love, or connection. An example is CyberPowWow, the 1990s "Aboriginally determined online gallery" and "an ongoing community of new media artists addressing Aboriginal issues" that transformed the North American Indigenous celebration of culture and community in the digital age.[30] Before creating the platform, organizers were aware of the colonial legacies of the "blank space" of the internet and made sure that before coming together, the ground was set, via computer code, by members of their community. In the first iteration, the organizers logged on simultaneously to share art and dialogue, but in an open forum, they were interrupted by "nonparticipants." This inspired them to create a website they could control. The next iteration centered Indigenous artists who "customized the chat space with imagery, scripts, and a selection of Indian avatars," guided each other through their virtual art, including dancing. The intimacy of the space and attention to ritual broke down the walls of the digital: "Participants inevitably determined each other's geographical location, discovered who was wearing which avatar, and engaged in some mild flirtation all against a backdrop of brand new Aboriginal art."[31] Intentionally hosted online interaction led to meaningful offline connection.

Today, in film, community-led distributors look like Karin Chien of Distribution Advocates, a collective transforming the crisis in distribution resulting from corporate control. Chien's specific practice entails finding global audiences for uncensored films in China; she was motivated by the terrible deals that corporate distributors offered for films by and about Asian and Asian American people. "We are living in the era of extreme vertical integration, and the business model of today is fueled by predatory pricing. The lower cost to consumers is passed on to the storytellers and the creators. . . . Storytellers are paying for corporations to gain market dominance," she said in her keynote for Color Congress, an emerging collective of diverse documentary producers, distributors, and exhibitors.[32] Noting how most indie filmmakers are not breaking even on their projects, Chien highlights the important work that distributors (hosts) do in supporting story producers (cooks): "Creating more equity in distribution requires cultivating and valuing diverse producers," she said. To resist our centralized distribution ecosystem, Chien works with hundreds and sometimes thousands of exhibitors, many community-run festivals less prestigious than marquee players like Sundance but with deeper connections to audiences.

She found there is wide demand for these complex, diverse, often documentary stories that corporations undervalue. Her work is far from new and follows the lineage of women of color distributors like Loni Ding (National Asian American Telecommunications Association) and Michelle Materre (KJM3, known for supporting *Daughters of the Dust*, among the first features by a Black woman director). "The solution is to create and sustain *many, more, new, different* structures of distribution," Chien says.

Social media has offered new opportunities to organize ourselves through the lens of Indigenous culture and practice. "Ancient cultural values" and Indigenous storytelling traditions are inspiring survival and resistance strategies, mobilizing communities around important political occasions that threaten their sovereignty.[33] These actions take place via "settler computational structures," or what some Indigenous scholars have called digital *terra nullius*—or no man's land. But both Black and Indigenous scholars have shown how communities can enact values and customs in these contested spaces.[34] In interviews I conducted with platform founders of color before starting OTV, I found that leaders intentionally disrupted the extractive logics of corporations. Indie digital distributors like Issa Rae (through her personal YouTube), Numa Perrier and Dennis Dortch (Black&Sexy TV), and Christin Baker (tello films, for queer women) consistently addressed cultural difference by supporting creators in telling stories how they wanted, focusing on material support over notes that try to fit their stories to a platform's "brand." They cultivated fans for these stories by speaking to those communities in culturally specific ways on social media, promoting intersecting cultural discourses. The intention motivating hosts was healing broader systemic exclusions, to heal our culture by uplifting those whose cultures have been harmed, rendered invisible or less valuable.

WHO IS HOSTING AND WHERE?

Hosts curate platforms for community engagement. It is a powerful position: deciding who is invited and where it will be served. At the cookout, hosts manage this power by being as open as possible, defining borders through evolving connections. Reparative platforms are flexible spaces designed to facilitate meaningful engagement and real accountability. At the cookout, I can talk to the people who can help mediate and restore justice, bringing together survivors and tending to their needs and boundaries.

There are people in our communities who are great listeners and communicators, who are respected by most if not all, and who have shown their values through consistent action over time. Proximity of place—*where* platforms are—matters. When hosts are accessible, it is easier for people to seek accountability, which cultivates trust, bravery, and deeper connections that are ultimately healing.

Most corporate social media platforms are headquartered far away from the people they host and are incentivized to sort and segregate our engagement for profit, while adopting policies to limit their liability from the consequences of our interactions. They hire internal human resource and compliance officers, underpay content moderators, or outsource community moderation to algorithmic (AI) models. Julian Posada and Mary Gray have extensively researched the hidden labor moderating tech platforms, the "crowd work" that allows them to host millions of people as data points. These gig workers are far from corporate headquarters, paid less than minimum wage, and depersonalized (their names replaced with numbers).[35] They face incredible mental health stress as they sort through the worst things in the world, not only online but also in their workplaces where harmful language is repeated without sensitivity. "You do feel it in your body, like physically, when someone is using [the 'n'] word, even if someone is repeating it because it's words on a page," one Black moderator told former Twitter trust and safety officer Anika Collier Navaroli.[36] Even then, these jobs are threatened by the AI they helped train, challenging the value of human/community-based moderation. I could not think of worse strategies for cultivating community, tied up with questions of legal liability, job insecurity, or protocols written by engineers who do not represent the communities they serve, who fail to fully comprehend the AI they develop, and who lack training in the humanities or the study of culture.

Platforms are ripe for discrimination because moderation and data curation happen far from hosts and guests. The roots of these discriminatory practices are occasionally made visible. In 2021, Facebook whistleblower Frances Haugen and Google researcher Timnit Gebru exposed the ways tech companies knew platforms were dividing us, obscuring centuries-old racist, sexist, and harmful scripts to predict how we navigate virtual lands. Haugen describes how Facebook avoided accountability for the content they hosted even in how teams and processes were named: "You weren't choosing which social movements to kill or stymie, you were 'disaggregating' them."[37] Social media platforms' users consistently work to combat the proliferation of hate and conspiracy theories, despite the presence of so-called social cohesion teams.[38] Noting connections between natural, urban, and digital environments, Pablo Boczkowski and Eugenia Mitchelstein argue that there are "unique characteristics" to the digital environment "that make it particularly prone to conflict": "winner-take-all markets" and discourse that "tends to intensify preexisting positions."[39]

Less nefariously, many platforms like Instagram, Twitter, and TikTok are spaces that privilege brevity and succinct delivery. Even celebratory narratives are more likely to spread if they engage binaries of Black versus white, straight versus queer, and abled versus disabled as frames. Binary frames simplify narrative complexity for users and analysis for algorithms, promoting conversations that can reinforce harmful norms and avoid meaningful discussion of politics and culture.[40] These frames can amplify extreme narratives, as Safiya Noble found with the presence of pornographic images of Black women on Google, and as Limor Shifman found with "flawed masculinity" as a key factor in spreadability.[41] But in their study of algorithmic invisibility, Brooke Duffy and Colton Meisner conclude that "platforms seemingly favor normative subjectivities and de-politicized content genres," and they question how "regimes of discipline and punishment that structure the social media economy disadvantage marginalized creators and cultural expressions deemed non-normative."[42]

Gathering online vastly differs from how we gather in our lives. Instead of developing platform governance in collaboration with creators and communities, tech companies focus on automating governance, working with legacy corporations, and buying or copying their competitors in service of rapid data expansion. "This process of *data commodification* stands in direct contrast to what makes us human: our sociality," Zhasmina Tacheva and Srividya Ramasubramanian write.[43]

To resist, people curate smaller communities within corporate platforms where they can invite who they want. Whether its Facebook groups, Twitter spaces/hashtags, or Clubhouse rooms, we rent spaces for our cookout on the fields that corporations own. The sacrifice we make is less control over the guest list. We speak knowing anyone can hear. This can have disastrous effects because we struggle to have to the deep, complex conversations that we need to have with our people. This sometimes prevents us from cultivating an intentional culture of care and healing because we cannot fully attend to our wounds, lest strangers emerge to pour salt on them.

To be sure, there are examples of more sustainable community-led hosting on open platforms like Reddit and Wikipedia. Scholars like Casey Fiesler and Zachary McDowell have written extensively about these moderation cultures. Unlike Wikipedia, managed by broad site-wide rules, Reddit has thousands of subreddits, each with contextually specific rules.[44] Both sites face large barriers to representation, as moderators do not reflect the diversity of users, but are nonetheless thriving without automating moderation. It may be better when platforms are designed for a specific purpose by people from that community. Fiesler writes about Archive of Our Own (AO3) as a women-led fan fiction platform that centered identity, inclusivity, and accessibility in its design.[45]

Historically, newspapers are platforms for presenting community-based information and delegating care functions to ombudsman or letters to the editor. But these roles are fraught, often lacking power in/over the space. By contrast, we can think of the late Monica Roberts, founder of the blog *TransGriot*, as an example of a platform owner who hosted her community with care and accountability. Roberts's blog shared information on violence against trans people and celebrated community leaders. As V. Jo Hsu writes, "She chronicled the losses, triumphs, and struggles of Black and trans—and particularly Black trans—people while providing political commentary and advocacy. Throughout her writing, she pointed to the intersectional wisdom and leadership of Black trans women."[46] Building on the writings of Jennifer Nash and Hil Malantino, who respectively theorize Black feminist and t4t (trans-for-trans) love politics,[47] Hsu opens up space for reframing the work of Monica Roberts as a community leader holding space for the difficult tensions between and among Black and trans communities, where harm and love comingle, while also holding accountable "mainstream" journalism for their symbolic annihilation of her communities. At the same time, Roberts uplifted other community leaders in her work, highlighting how good hosts redistribute power to other hosts who have the capacity to care.

Today, we have community leaders hosting on corporate platforms, curating digital space to serve their kin as best they can. I think of the social media work of scholar, artist, and Black Lives Matter Canada organizer Syrus Marcus Ware and writer, organizer, and podcaster adrienne maree brown, who post memes to tens of thousands of Instagram followers, many of them leaders in art and organizing. Memes are tools for identity work, community border management, and cultural politics, often made by those who, as Sulafa Zidani writes of Palestinian memers, hold deep connections to the lands they occupy.[48] Ware and brown don't create most of the memes they share; rather, they are redistributors and exhibitors, curating and serving joyful bits of knowledge and crediting the original creators as often as possible. During the pandemic, these memes offered thoughtful insights on our contemporary cultural environment, and Ware and brown created space online for people to express complex emotions. Many comments express that this is healing to them, especially on a corporate platform known as much for division as for connection.

At some point in our lives, all of us host. We will hold space for someone, online or in person, which means we will learn to bear the responsibility of what we share and how we convene our people. This is a huge responsibility, too much for every person, every day. This is why it is so important to have reparative platforms that have the resources to offer guidance, support, and clear models for hosting in the digital age.

Who holds space for community is so important. If a host has not built trust in the community, with a proven track record of providing nourishment, good vibes, and an appropriately curated invite list, no one will show up, or if they do, conflict or harm can ensue. Any host will tell you that the guest list and menu are the most important tasks, but most corporate media platforms delegate the menu to executives who live far from most communities they serve, to machines that no one fully understands, trained by underpaid workers who users will never meet.

Reparative media require hosts to be accountable to the specific communities they serve—*in the places they serve them*. This means hiring people from those communities that practice artistic, ancestral ways of mediating conflict and paying them well to mediate conflict and moderate content. At OTV, we had a specific team member who lived in our city whose job it was to mediate conflict among artists and develop "Brave Space" agreements for when we gathered our community (explored in-depth in the final two chapters). This is very expensive, but what is the cost to our culture when bad actors keep coming to the cookout and causing so much drama that we can't even talk to each other without yelling or sniping? Can we imagine platforms that not only protect but also help us become our best selves, cultivating deep bonds through media and technology? Every media platform inviting multiple communities to join should have these humans in place.

HOW DO WE CULTIVATE COMMUNITY BETTER NEXT TIME?

The cookout is about how we nurture each other, and we can always do it better. Nobody does it perfectly, just as healing is not linear. Black people who host cookouts know this all too well. Hosts accept the possibility of conflict or complaints about the food, the music, and the general vibe.

Everyday hosts conduct organic forms of research on their programming. Simply, they ask. When people leave, they will let the host know they had a good time. If something detracted from their experience, they inform hosts: sometimes directly, sometimes with a look—or sip of tea—that says, "you better call me later." We debrief about how things went and make changes. Some get disinvited or need to have someone check in on them. Some dishes are adapted or taken off the menu.

Nearly all large media and tech corporations have research departments to formalize the data collection process, but do they *know the tea*? They may get some of it on social media, where their subscribers may organize #hashtag campaigns to revive favorite TV shows, and social media companies will do surveys or ask users to speak back during crises of public relations. But increasingly, corporations rely on "big data" for feedback. They serve too many people to get the tea. Informal feedback comes from the people in the company and their social networks, but we know that employees of these companies are not representative of their user bases, not only by race and gender but also by class and where they live near US coastal cities.

Reparative platforms privilege intimate feedback, even with larger user bases. For example, Chicago-based Black news organization *The TRiiBE* and City Bureau hosted regular gatherings in the city, making the leaders physically accessible to people they cover. The same goes for many of the indie TV channels serving digital entertainment. Social media creators, especially on older platforms like YouTube and Instagram, will say they built their followings by reading and responding to every comment individually; if not, they use other platforms like Patreon and Discord to facilitate an ongoing conversation among the most committed members of their communities.

These creators perform the intimate, community-centered research that the corporations hosting them do not want to fund.

Reparative research is crucial to developing healing stories and platforms. Community-based researchers understand how critical feedback is to improving our work. We often rely on formal mechanisms for feedback like surveys and focus groups, which are helpful, but the process continually adapts to the people and communities served. It is important to be embedded in our communities, where people let their guards down and feel comfortable letting us know how they really feel.

Throughout this book, you will see how OTV enacted these reparative R&D practices organically. Our process was in development during OTV's "beta" stage and continues to evolve as the organization builds capacity. I hope this book serves as a resource to emerging hosts looking to start or grow their own media/tech-based cookouts with intention and sustainability.

2 REPARATIVE RESEARCH: CULTIVATING KNOWLEDGE OUTSIDE THE UNIVERSITY SYSTEM

This work got me fired—conditionally.

"We just don't think you're on track for promotion with tenure *here*," my senior colleague tells me, adding "I think it would be best if you sought employment elsewhere." My heart speeds up and then sinks. The level of research productivity needed for promotion with tenure is one to two books and ten to twelve articles. I'm not *on track*. Tenure-track professors have six years to prove themselves worthy of job security (figure 2.1). I protest, softly, knowing that Black men who want tenure are not allowed to show anger: "Well, I've submitted a complete draft of my book to NYU Press, and I'm awaiting reviews. I arrived at Northwestern University with six single-author peer-reviewed articles, so I didn't have new material to submit to journals but my new project is going well—" I'm cut off. My colleague interjects, "Yes, we are concerned about your new project. You're making a lot of video work but you're not showing it in places we *recognize*, and you haven't published any new articles." I never planned to have my video work to count toward tenure, but the growth of creative work on my CV over traditional research has alarmed the tenured faculty.

At top research universities in the US, community-based creative work is rarely "recognizable," rendering it not only invisible but also a scar, a blemish that must be removed by removing me from the university, lest I besmirch its status in the field.

It's a short conversation. My colleague's voice sounds final. It appears that a decision has been made. "OK, thank you for telling me," is all I can muster to say. They leave, asking if they should close the door, to which I

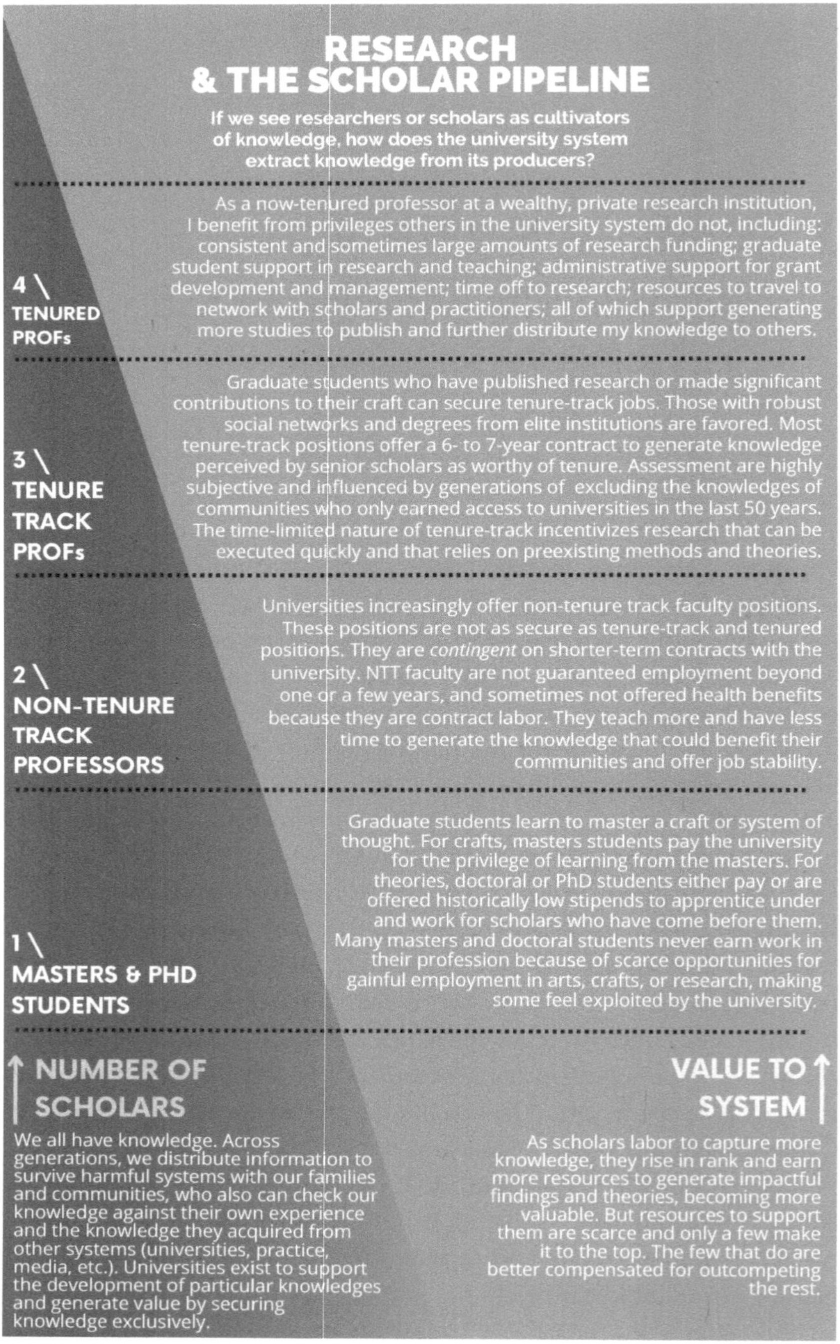

FIGURE 2.1

Research and the scholar pipeline.

FIGURE 2.2
The *You're So Talented* finale party.

say yes. I fear I am going to break down. At thirty-one, I have never been fired from a job.

The day I face the greatest challenge to my career I have to attend a celebration of Sam Bailey and the premiere of the second season finale of *You're So Talented,* her short-form web series about a young Black woman from Chicago "as she navigates her twenties and its inevitable dramas" (figure 2.2). Most indie series only last one season. It is cause for joy. But I show up to the premiere looking so ragged that the series' producer asks me what's wrong immediately upon seeing me. I am at one of the lowest points in my life, and I am disappointed in myself for feeling sad on a celebratory occasion. The event is not only a celebration of Sam, her crew, and my team's incredible achievements. I am also in "the field" as a researcher. As fabulously queer and melanated artists sip cocktails around me, I barely have the capacity to smile, let alone to take field notes. It feels like the end of our cookout just as it was starting to begin.

The event culminates two years of helping storytellers like Sam serve Chicago organically produced stories. She was the seed. *You're So Talented*'s first season launched what was then called "Open TV (beta)," funded entirely from my university research account and my own personal finances. I teach an extra class to donate (not invest) over $4,000 directly to Sam Bailey to ensure *You're So Talented*: *Season 2* is completed by the date I was effectively fired for it.

I spend 2016 drowning in a depression, blaming myself for taking such a big risk with the rarest resource in corporate capitalism: job security via tenure. I feel unable to tell my friends and collaborators that this new project is already running out of money and will have to end the following year, a lack of transparency that would later cause more problems explored later in this chapter. The irony is that I started the project understanding of the power of failure, which Jack Halberstam argues is a queer art that cultivates knowledge and new ways of being in oppressive systems.[1] Following C. Riley Snorton, Cathy Cohen, Roderick Ferguson, and many other scholars who argue for the interdependency between Blackness and queerness, I knew this Black queer-led project was destined to fail in the university, media, and tech systems it was designed to critique.[2]

Every single year after 2016, I make plans to end the Open TV project, unbeknownst to any of my collaborators. The project is precarious by design, but *feeling* failure is different from *knowing* it intellectually. In extractive systems, Black people in America do not have the right to fail, or even make a mistake, without fear of losing respect, connection, our lives, or our livelihoods. I feel that I have disappointed my parents, who like many Black parents told me at five years old that I had to be better than all my white peers because my Blackness would sow doubt in my capabilities. The month after the conversation with my senior colleague, I get the reviews on the *Open TV* book. A senior scholar who had unsuccessfully applied for a job in my department multiple times unleashes a wildly ungenerous review, so petty in its critiques it is impossible to summarize them here. The review is the current that drags me into the sea. I spend 2016 feeling a loser: the lowest performer in the department and eventually the only Black person. For a Black queer overachiever who has defined my identity through education like my immigrant parents taught me, the entire situation feels traumatic, a feeling that would remain even as the tides turn, offering me some air.

The turbulence shifts as cultural systems—academia, media, tech—start to extract (value) our IP and knowledge. Months before that fateful meeting with my colleague, Fatimah Asghar invites Sam Bailey and me to a reading of the script for her first short-form series, *Brown Girls*. Leveraging community support, Fatimah and Sam enter production that summer, but I cannot offer the same cash injection I did *You're So Talented*. I'm pretty much broke by that point. I pay for their insurance out of what personal funds I have left. They apply to the Chicago Filmmakers grant I sent to Sam that she won the year prior, but the two women also organize a GoFundMe that raises $7,000 in weeks. Sam pulls together a local crew who believe in the project and take lower rates than they would on a Hollywood set to make it happen. They release the *Brown Girls* trailer in the fall, and it is clear the show is going to be a hit. Indeed, two weeks after its release in February 2017 at Open TV's premiere event at the MCA Chicago, Sam and Fatimah are in Hollywood pitching the series to eight different TV networks. HBO wins out, and weeks later, the Television Academy honors the team with an Emmy nomination for Outstanding Short Form Comedy or Drama.

It's clear that our little Chicago cookout is incubating stories for a Hollywood system freshly interested in diversity as a strategy for branding new streaming platforms. A month after the *Brown Girls* sale, I fly to New York to give a talk at Vimeo, the alt-YouTube video distribution platform we were using. There, Vimeo's new Black female head of development, Alana Mayo, is in the audience nodding excitedly about my project as the tech company also flirts with investing in media production. Vimeo had a history of investing in indie TV, allowing the creators behind shows like *High Maintenance* and *The Outs* to keep IP in exchange for a cut of on-demand sales. But three weeks after my talk, the company pivots and Alana leaves. Vimeo opts to invest in tech instead of culture. Its parent company IAC buys subscription video platform VHX, rebrands it Vimeo OTT (over-the-top, or video via the internet), focuses on creating video streaming apps for corporations during the pandemic, and then spins off Vimeo for billions of dollars.

At a meeting in February 2017, I whisper to my senior colleague about Vimeo, *Brown Girls'* successful premiere at the MCA Chicago, and its pitch to Hollywood: places my university peers "recognize." My depression wanes as my workload grows: My book is under contract after a new review comes in fall 2016, and I have published my first peer-reviewed article based on the Open TV project in the *International Journal of Communication*. The article makes an argument for my method: why writing, directing, and producing local TV guided by intersectionality allows scholars to understand more deeply the value of representation in digital media. I am lucky that the experiment has so quickly produced "findings" recognizable as evidence of success in the university system. But the article is not my best. The findings are rushed. Cultivating community-based knowledge takes time.

OTV is still running out of money. Thankfully, in the fall of 2016, a faculty member at New York University (NYU) asks if I am interested in applying to a position there. As Sam and Fatimah are pitching *Brown Girls*, I receive an offer from NYU.

The combination of my book, the article, and the success of OTV changes the conversation at Northwestern, and deans are fighting to recruit or retain me. Negotiations result in $100,000 in research funds I can use to continue running OTV and an office downtown for meetings. This is much more than most Black queer scholars receive, though not nearly enough to run the project at its best, I later learned.

I accept Northwestern over NYU because the funds go farther to pay people in Chicago without having to pay for travel to and from NYC. The cost of travel alone would make it difficult to give the team even small raises on the little they were making. Moreover, in the spirit of the cookout, I feel deeply committed to the place whose culture nurtured the project. So I stay at Northwestern not confident my department would tenure me. After all, my department had never promoted a Black person to associate or full professor in its more than one-hundred-year history.

Sometimes beauty and pain coexist, however. Had my department not threatened my job, I would not have pursued the gig at NYU. OTV would have run out of money, and most of the work in this book would not exist. Working with artists in video is resource-intensive and likely not possible outside of a wealthy university that granted me research funding in a city that is not as expensive as New York or Los Angeles. Traditional nonprofit foundations have scant history funding narrative television (outside children's programming), let alone digital media distribution, meaning I needed my university's support to prove that an independent TV distribution platform had value and efficacy in social and cultural transformation. I am grateful for Northwestern's support in making OTV possible with $150,000 in support over the years: $50,000 in start-up in 2012, a majority of which went into OTV, and the additional $100,000 to retain me in 2017. Northwestern's funding is enough to run the project for two more years on a very tight, lean budget, during which I hoped to convince nonprofit foundations that the project is worthy of support. In 2019 the MacArthur and Surdna foundations find me, and I earn tenure at Northwestern—with one book, ten articles, and a TV platform. I feel lucky that my tenure story has a "happy ending" when so many are denied it for taking similar or often lesser risks.

This isn't a hero story. I did not sustain this project on my own. Storytellers and their communities cocreated this project. They taught me that cocreating knowledge in solidarity can repair the inequalities of the university system. It redistributes power and value equitably in our experiments. It challenges methods that extract data from communities to generate theory *for* or *about* them. Instead, reparative research asks communities to theorize *with* us: to cultivate knowledge from the stories they "cook" and their experience of how we serve it. I embarked on the OTV experiment asking myself what information I could share with creators to support them in addressing specific harms, for example, barriers to equity in media. But I also knew that they were already doing this work without me. I could learn from them even if I could not control what they were doing to speed up the process of generating theory for peer-reviewed articles. My role was to support the development of knowledge they were already cultivating and to support them in navigating systems by sharing what I knew about how to survive those systems.

Like any cookout, our process was reciprocal, specific, and evolving. As Patricia Hill Collins writes, "Elites are not the only ones who theorize. Many everyday people offer compelling explanations of their social worlds."[3] Core to our experiment was supporting storytellers in understanding, mitigating, resisting, or transforming systemic oppression. This experiment was inconsistent. It was not replicable or "controlled" as most are. If a single, controllable strategy for repairing systemic harm existed, we would already live in a liberated world. Instead, I had to follow my participants more than they followed me. I learned a lot from them. I shared what I learned with others and hosted spaces for them to share knowledge with each other. Through our cookout, we exponentially expanded our collective knowledge and power.

Reparative research flips power dynamics. It emerges in the borderless space between our questions and the needs or desires of those around us. A good host asks how their community can have a good time. The only way to know is inviting others to share the fruits of their labor and opinions of the gathering. I didn't plan to create a platform. I planned to be of service to those around me and share my knowledge in service of understanding more deeply the question of how to repair harmful systems. The rest, I confess, was up to nature, and as in nature, the elements nearly took me out.

I was pulled into this experiment by future participants. Before OTV began, talented artists and collectives presented me with ideas too good to pass up. My initial idea was to produce and release a series of pilots called

Wide Open. While producing the first one, *Nupita Obama Creates Vogua*, I received an email from Sam, then a first-time screenwriter, asking if I was interested in reviewing *You're So Talented* for my blog. I'd stopped blogging because it didn't "count" for tenure in the university system, but I saw an opportunity to share my research funds to support her. Series as beautiful as Sam's were not common, my past research suggested. The trailer she sent triggered a deep desire to create a platform for its distribution. At the same time, I was becoming familiar with the work of Honey Pot Performance, a Chicago-based Black feminist collective producing an Afrofuturist dance theater work called *Ma(s)king Her*. I was intrigued by their community-driven writing process and thought it would be interesting to document the development of the show, eventually becoming the docuseries *Futurewomen*. Finally, at a dinner I hosted while she was in town producing an all-trans talk show at the MCA Chicago, Zackary Drucker, who I met in grad school filming a documentary on transgressive artists for Penn professor Paul Messaris, expressed a need for funding for an experimental pilot of her own. In each case, I realized I had resources through the university I could redirect to help each artist achieve their goals. I also knew it would also support my intellectual quest to deepen my engagement with intersectionality and its relationship to media production, distribution, and exhibition.[4] Realizing this opportunity for mutual learning and benefit compelled me to expand my vision beyond a series of pilots to a distribution platform called Open TV (beta), now called OTV.

Our experiment began with mutually conceived questions. Elijah launched the platform with a series of questions inspired by my own, distilled for the nonacademic public: "What does artistic/sustainable/expressive TV look like?" Elijah recalls, "It wasn't like we were launching anything. It was, 'this is a thing and we have questions,' which I think created a lot of buy-in from community." We started by asking our community to imagine, to question their understanding of "television," and take action with us. We could answer those questions together, knowing this questioning would never end, but that in our pursuit we would learn more about our collective power and the limits of corporate cultural systems.

I narrate this story because in creative and community-based research, the specificity and nature of our relationships to each other, institutions, and systems are as important as any data we generate. To learn, reparative researchers cultivate knowledge with whomever is available, willing, and aligned with a collective vision. Decentering the researcher's power and control in the experiment allows for the sustainable, ethical cocreation of knowledge, resulting in richer and more accurate data, if less "generalizable" in the traditional framing. Inevitably, scholars bring our own questions, perspectives, and goals to the field, but the answers that emerge will grow organically.

We are not the first or only people to do this work, in the US or abroad, now or throughout history. For over one hundred years, scholars have worked to leverage universities in pursuit of justice and equity. Aldon Morris persuasively argues that W. E. B. Du Bois is the founder of US sociology for the ways he worked in community and with artists to cultivate data on Black American life.[5] Du Bois emerged at a time when statistics was on the rise, but US sociology was theory driven, using questionable data (if any) to argue for Black inferiority. So Du Bois collected specific qualitative and quantitative data on how Black people lived and worked, showing care for life on the margins of America's white power systems: "Du Bois embraced his life's work: the production of careful sociological studies of African Americans steeped in empirical data that could be used to discredit the dominant sociological and popular doctrine that blacks were forever stuck at the bottom of human civilization because nature made them inferior."[6] Morris calls Du Bois's approach the Atlanta School of Sociology: the first uniquely US American sociology, not the Chicago School that emerged decades later and typically gets credit for bringing empiricism to sociology.[7] Du Bois's Atlanta School contrasted sharply with the emerging Chicago School of sociology. While the Chicago School was "still asserting that biological factors played important roles in racial dynamics . . . Du Bois had a vested interest in distancing himself from social Darwinist thought."[8] Here we see how a justice framework inspired scholars to understand how communities generate knowledge to survive oppressive systems. What is organic and natural is not the racial order but the value of all life and our endless capacity to use culture and stories for surviving or thriving. Morris argues that the best of the Chicago School's methods, including the use of personal documents and ethnography to describe diverse ethnic/sexual communities, were practiced by Du Bois decades earlier as reparative acts against the intellectual subjugation of Black people.

Black scholars have never been limited by traditional, extractive methods and have always worked with artists and communities to cultivate knowledge. In the early twentieth century, Zora Neale Hurston transformed the discipline of anthropology with her study of Black American culture, folklore, history, and artistry, even as she also became one of the twenty-first century's greatest fiction writers.[9] Later in the twentieth century, Audre Lorde theorized the complex intersections of race, gender, sexuality, and class in poetry, fiction, and prose: "It is through poetry that we give name to those ideas which are—until the poem—nameless and formless, about to be birthed, but already felt."[10] Hurston and Lorde show how the ways we express ideas invite others to research, to make meaning of their own experiences. In the documentary *Audre Lorde: The Berlin Years*, Dagmar Schultz shows how Lorde inspired Black Germans to write their own histories, previously erased by white German academics.[11] Even Du Bois collaborated with artists to exhibit his data to the public in exhibitions like the 1900 Paris Exposition. He knew that communicating data with beauty and nuance would invite publics into the knowledge production process.[12]

Black, Indigenous, and other intellectuals inside and outside the university have always worked in solidarity with their communities to resist the harm that universities have done to them.[13] In her theory of intersectionality as critical social action, Patricia Hill Collins elevates Ida B. Wells as a theorist, exemplified by her sharing stories about the lynching of Black men under Jim Crow's policing of race and sexual relations.[14] In Canada this form of "research creation" is common and institutionalized, even in the field of media and technology. Canadian artist-scholars like Skawanetti run labs offering Indigenous artists opportunities to develop new work, and Chase Joynt creates films as tools for excavating histories and theories of trans identity.[15]

There is still a lot of work to do to shift how research is done inside and outside the university, but change is happening. Sasha Costanza-Chock's *Design Justice* archives the work of the collectively created Design Justice Network, a network of independent organizations and individuals who commit to a set of principles in organizing and designing justice-based interventions. New groups like Scholars for Social Justice, based at the University of Chicago and the University of Illinois Chicago, or Critical Race and Digital Studies based at NYU, are serving as interdisciplinary hubs to interrogate the systemic exclusion of racialized communities from universities and tech/data institutions. These groups are advancing new ways of being a scholar in the twenty-first century. Today, dozens of scholars are using media and public scholarship in as many ways as their diverse communities will engage. "Communication research should not just stop at critique from the ivory tower but intervene in social justice issues in the cities universities are based," George Villanueva writes.[16]

Today, queer of color critique and Indigenous methodologies inspire reparative research. They offer frameworks for organizing reparative media and tech. Queer practice feels power and oppression in the present to organically cultivate impossible futures.[17] For Muñoz, the "brown commons . . . smolder with a life and persistence."[18] It was important, for instance, for me to feel depressed and queer, a stranger to my university colleagues, as I smoldered and persisted, feeling that the university system was always going to be less life-giving than my community.[19] I felt inspired to queer the university's operating system (OS). Kara Keeling's "queer OS" describes a queer theory of practice that engages technology to dismantle racism, sexism, homophobia, transphobia, ableism, and other harmful systems because these "-isms" are themselves technologies of social control. Queer OS as a method that "unsettles the logics" of disciplinary traditions in service of organic knowledge production: "Queer OS names a way of thinking and acting with, about, through, among, and at times even in spite of new media technologies and other phenomena of mediation. It insists upon forging and facilitating uncommon, irrational, imaginative, and/or unpredictable relationships between and among what currently are perceptible as living beings and the environment in the interest of creating value(s) that facilitate just relations."[20]

Queer OS is foundational to the OTV project. It offers a framework for the messy, deeply relational process of merging of technology and identity in service of knowledge creation. Similarly, an Indigenous perspective focuses our pursuit of knowledge on "facilitating just relations . . . among what are currently perceptible as living beings and the environment" to develop alternatives to toxic power dynamics.[21] To do this highly relational work, scholars must understand ourselves and the systems we study and work in. Only then can we embody the humility it takes to nurture knowledge outside academia's closed fields or disciplines. In *Indigenous Methodologies*, Margaret Kovach describes "the deep self-reflexivity [sic] necessary to do research in a way that resists the colonial, extractive legacy of data collection that plagues academic research."[22] Queer methods pair well with Indigenous methodologies by centering the unending, conflictual, and collective process of asking ourselves questions about ourselves and our environment.

Scholars of media and art are uniquely positioned to experiment with reparative research and have done so for many years. Community-based art and media projects inspire "a different way of doing things—not just in terms of aesthetic qualities and production practices, but in terms of organization."[23] Katherine Cizek and William Uricchio honor the "collective wisdom" of media workers in their book of the same name, "broadening our range of questions about not only *how* to cocreate but also primarily *why* and *why now*."[24] Vicki Mayer has spent much of her career researching grassroots media, applying what she learned in her work in post-Katrina New Orleans to work with citizen journalists. Together, they advanced an "alternative ethics" of media representation, ownership, and distribution, fostering a "messy, unsorted, pluralistic whole."[25] Mayer calls this "small data theorizing," showing how we can use media to generate knowledge for the specific purpose of community sustainability.[26]

Redistributing knowledge changes how we value research. The researcher should not be the only person to benefit from a community-based research project, just as a host should not be the only person to benefit from a cookout. What we often write as benefits to our studies to Institutional Review Boards (IRBs)—for example, one day this knowledge might change the mind of someone in power so this community can live better—is not enough.[27] Contrary to what best practices for extractive research dictate, reparative research is designed to benefit participants. Instead of focusing on making open research more controlled and rigorous for the purpose of generating theory, Jesse Fox and others foreground values that resemble cookout values: respect for persons, ethical transparency, reflexivity, beneficence, and justice: "Individuals, communities, and social groups should have equitable opportunities to be participants, researchers, consumers, and beneficiaries of research."[28]

Reparative researchers, like hosts, are vulnerable and humble. We have a responsibility to our participants and our ecosystems. We respond to our participants as much as they respond to us, constantly changing our interventions based on ever-changing, complex conditions. It is very difficult, rewarding work. It requires that we understand our motivations and open ourselves to critique. The OTV experiment was different every single year, as I worked with the OTV team, storytellers, and community members to optimize it for our own mental/physical health and the health of our local ecosystem. Reparative researching ultimately inspires us to hand power over to our participants. The project may cease to become our own, if it ever was to begin with.

Reparative research values the knowledge that communities held before researchers entered "the field." It honors the ancestral intelligences cultivated for generations among those who have survived systemic oppression. Seeing research through the lens of the cookout shows how knowledge creation benefits from a diversity of collaborators working together organically. Just as the host seeks feedback from their guests and cooks, decentralizing the process of understanding, so too must we cocreate what we know with our participants. What follows are lessons I learned from running OTV | Open Television from 2015 to 2019 before I handed it over to my collaborators to run without my leadership.

HOW DO WE CULTIVATE COMMUNITY KNOWLEDGE BETTER NEXT TIME?

Every host takes time to reflect after the cookout. Following each event, we check in with our community. Asking collaborators what they thought of the cookout helps make it sustainable. Hosts are incentivized to listen and honor our mistakes as much as our successes if we want to keep hosting. We invite others to shape the cookout itself. Decentralizing power and knowledge is core to this ancestral practice. The line between who is a cook, host, or guest is blurry. The process of creating the cookout is collective, so the process of understanding and improving it must also be. This is incredibly complex work, and it is impossible to do it perfectly.

HOSTS SELF-EVALUATE AND SHARE MISTAKES ALONGSIDE INNOVATIONS

Hosts engage their immediate environment, their local community, organically. This method requires deep, consistent introspection, transparency, and an openness to having one's knowledge or authority checked by participants. It resists the legacy of Western colonialist research practices that positions researchers as "objective" outsiders smarter than the communities we study. Instead, it requires that we first be experts on ourselves, knowing that we are ever-changing and consistently impacted by our environment, actions, and communities.

I had to constantly collect data on myself and my impact, engaging in critical autoethnography. Robin Boylorn and Mark Orbe define autoethnography as the use of "critical self-reflexivity and cultural commentary to examine embodied experiences, relational encounters, and intercultural conundrums."[29] Critical autoethnography, combined with other methods, is a tool for excavating how systems of power manifest in specific experiences. It emerges from a feminist, anti-racist, and anti-colonial critique of anthropology's legacy of white men observing "the Other" to define something outside themselves, as if their perspective is neutral. Instead, it asks researchers to consider our position in the field, how we affect others, how they affect us, and how culture shapes our understanding. Today, self-reflexivity is common in anthropology, but there are depths less often explored. John Jackson draws on Ruth Behar's notion of the "vulnerable observer"[30] to counter researchers' impulse to simply list our social identities "as a technique for exposing ideological cards": "Self-reflexivity is not an attempt at greater authenticity, a truer representation of self. It is, more importantly, an instantiation of authenticity's utter impossibility."[31] To say I am Black and queer, without acknowledging how my class and immigrant upbringing challenge normative assumptions of those identities, as well as how my identity is not fixed, limits the questions I owe communities to engage.

Instead of performing authenticity, I focused on my accountability to my people and my environment. This takes time, and it evolves. I wrote my most rigorous field notes when I experienced or noticed conflict with people around me, capturing every detail of my own and others' actions, and then tracking how situations developed over time to uncover how my own identity intersected with broader systems of power and privilege. I felt in every moment I had to show my *sincerity*, which Jackson distinguishes from authenticity as a *relational* form of understanding ourselves and others. Sincerity challenges authenticity's performative scripts: for example, "because I'm Black/queer/etc., I am XYZ." "True reflexivity troubles the categories themselves," Jackson writes.[32] I shared with the artists why I started OTV, my specific history of wanting more Black and queer representation in media, my understanding of solidarity, what I learned from my first book project, and my intellectual reasons for everything from why OTV's contracts were nonexclusive to why we were screening in small, community-based spaces. I also invited artists to critique me, both in formal and informal ways, by letting them know my primary goal was learning, not being right. The longer I was in the field, however, the more I realized that this invitation was not believed, and a few artists refrained from offering critiques until they could not contain their dissatisfaction, to be discussed in the final chapter. I believe my identity as a cisgender man likely contributed to this. Obviously, my being both Black and queer mattered, because I could understand navigating intersecting oppressions, but so much more mattered beyond and including the social categories I inhabit. It mattered how I was acting based on how I identify, how I saw the world, my goals for systemic transformation, as well as how and why I pursued those goals. Ultimately, maintaining consistent integrity in my actions, as best I could, helped me navigate not being seen for who I believe myself to be at any given moment.

Explaining my motivations was key. Still, over the years I came to realize that my position as a researcher was never fully understood, nor could I fully understand my position and impact in the community I was researching. Some people saw me as a community leader or media entrepreneur. They did not realize I had no interest in making money from the project, that my goal was knowledge capital and not economic or social capital in the way they were pursuing it. Hiding my own shame about my struggles navigating my university's tenure process no doubt contributed to this misunderstanding. Challenges to being seen as a researcher became more acute after *Brown Girls* sold to HBO, when individuals in the community started to perceive the project as a pipeline to Hollywood and not a university experiment. The experiment became less sincere when its impact expanded from the local to the corporate and global.

In the early years I had the misguided notion that I could continue to run OTV while also keeping my position as a professor. Yet the more embedded I became in community, the more I realized there was so much I did not and could not know given the amount of time I needed to dedicate to the university. My desire to express sincerity and understand my impact grew more limited the more I advanced—compounded by service to students, the field, and the university. Artists would reveal aspects of their experiences months after their experience shaped their perception of me. In one instance, artists revealed to me that journalists and Hollywood executives were assuming that OTV had produced their series, giving credit to me, a Black cis man, and marginalizing their work as women of color. Not knowing this, I was making mistakes by casually referring to certain series as "OTV's *Show*" as opposed to the names of the creators; this is standard practice in Hollywood, as the press often colloquially refers to series by their distributors (HBO's *Show* or CBS's *Show*) so audiences know where to find it. Here, my identity as a Black cis man and my use of language from an oppressive system impacted my study in ways I did not anticipate. I underestimated how many people confuse distribution and production and how many refuse to give credit to women of color for their work, even though these were obvious to me.

Listening is critical to understanding your position in the field, but time is just as important. A reparative researcher's long-term engagement with community helps us understand ourselves and our impact. Those who have been historically oppressed may need a lot of time to speak our truth due to how we have been misheard or harmed in the past. It took months for those aforementioned artists to reveal to me what they were going through, fearing I would get defensive or combative as many Black men in public do. Indeed, not knowing the full story at first, I posted on Facebook a status update defending myself, because I did give credit to the artists in an interview that caused me to be "called out"—not by name but in a way recognizable to community. I apologized, but it took several more months for the artists to come back to me and apologize in return for the way they acted (an apology I did not request nor need), acknowledging my mistakes were small compared with those of the more powerful people who were misrepresenting their work. We were able to heal the relationship, and both OTV and I still work closely with those storytellers as we learn and grow together. The long-term commitment that reparative research requires is the solution to the panic around "cancel culture."

Reparative research is ideally a long-term effort, with at least a few years in the field, or one that never ends. My knowledge deepened as I spent more time in the field, and many of my collaborators slowly grew to understand me and my motivations. With more time in the field, researchers can build meaningful relationships and *show* who they are. Yet I could have done more to *tell* people who I am and what I was going through. I shared why I was doing this study, my methods, and my capacities and limits, becoming more precise and explicit every year. Over the years, most Chicagoans knew me as queer as I was quite open with my relationship on social media and in public. Deeper truths are harder to share. Family history only came up when asked if I was from Chicago, which did not happen as often as I thought it would, so some people thought I was from the city. It was harder to share my dysphoric relationship to hegemonic Black masculinity, especially since for many years I resisted using they/them pronouns in solidarity with my friends and community members who presented more explicitly as trans and nonbinary in ways that opened them to transphobic violence. Still, I believe my actions spoke louder than words. Apologizing when I made mistakes and taking actions to do better meant more than posting supportive messages on Instagram. Actively supporting Chicago-based and trans/nonbinary artists as much as I could meant more than stating my values. I advised many more artists than anyone knew, compounding my reputation for community care. To this day, I still advise and write recommendations for artists. It takes years to learn and show who you are. This work is thrilling, at best, and, even at our worst, quite fulfilling. And it never ends.

The deepest form of learning is about one's self and our relation to others. Only by taking accountability for our actions and understanding everyone's perspectives can researcher-hosts appropriately assess if the cookout is a productive space for learning and connection. This is an iterative, ongoing process, challenging how universities compel researchers to develop a final product on the constrained timeline of the tenure track. Outside of academic institutions, everyday people understand that learning about oneself, one's community, and our collective impact on the world around us is a lifelong process.

HOSTS MUST BE FLEXIBLE IN HOW WE LEARN

Ecosystems thrive with a diversity of agents evolving strategies for understanding and surviving a constantly changing environment. The cookout thrives when different people come together to share nourishment prepared with different recipes and methods from specific legacies. Similarly, reparative research employs a diversity of methods and ways of knowing: "Indigenous methodologies disrupt methodological homogeneity in research," Kovach writes.[33] I used every method I could, rooted in my training, capacity, and felt need, or what Stephanie Springgay calls "feltness."[34] My learning involved listening to and then acting with the people around me. Community media scholar Tanja Dreher theorizes listening as an essential method for developing systemic solutions: "Listening shifts the focus and responsibility for change from marginalized voices and on to the conventions, institutions and privileges which shape who and what can be heard in media."[35] Listening invites small changes to our process and paves the way for systemic transformation.

I drew on legacies of practice-based research, including participatory action research, arts-based research, community-based or engaged/public scholarship, and research creation.[36] Each method has its own specific history within various cultural contexts, largely outside the US. All frameworks encourage using a diversity of methods for listening. Researchers use surveys, focus groups, interviews, and the act of making creative work, coupled with participant observation, as I did. By publishing artists' films and series on social media, I even had access to quantitative data in views, shares, and comments, the utility of which varied but was less important than qualitative data because most of our work did not spread widely online.

Reparative research disrupts borders in academic fields, or disciplines. We need a range of perspectives to understand the complex lives people lead. The university's disciplinary silos limit knowledge production, but our institutions are still structured to reward scholars who master their fields' methods and canons, be it anthropology, sociology, communication, media studies, and so on. The tenure process tests a scholar's visibility in their discipline. Disciplines have their own language and ways of seeing the world, which makes the process of generating theory and interpreting data more efficient. But they also have internal politics that marginalize the study of specific topics and systems. In my own work I have found it difficult to "place" myself in disciplines. The fields in the humanities that most consistently address intersectionality (literature, arts, history) have been resistant to the study of political economy. Across fields, studying the political economy of media, in addition to intersectionality, is relatively marginal. Studies of the politics of digital cultural production and distribution can find a home in media and communication studies, but they rarely engage television and/or cultural identity. No one discipline could have trained me to execute the OTV experiment. I had to do a lot of reading outside of my field.

Being flexible in our methods and theories are forms of care for the communities we work with. OTV changed every year as the team and I responded to the workload. In the first year, my goal was to release one new video every month, usually at least one episode. It was a small amount of content I thought was manageable. We maximized our limited resources by producing specialized, site-specific premiere events for every project. Yet releasing something new every month meant we were always working, and after a year, my team told me we needed a break. So we decided to pause for more and more months each year. We instituted annual debriefs after each cycle or season. Each year, we condensed the release season to make the work more efficient, especially for Elijah and Chris, who comprised the entire marketing department from 2015 to 2019. They took on a lot of responsibility managing our releases both in Chicago and online. Given the realities of nonprofit start-up life, I was barely able to afford raises in OTV's experimental phase, and since I was not paying much more, the work had to be as manageable as possible. This was difficult because more and more artists and stakeholders were coming to us looking for support even as our funding was not keeping pace.

Constantly refining the project was necessary as it grew organically and as openness posed challenges. Unexpectedly, Chicago's rich cultural soil yielded a bounty of interest in OTV. My method had to evolve to include grassroots field organizing, which yielded a rich data set of local and national stakeholders interested in serving historically oppressed communities. My workload became nearly unmanageable and stayed that way until outside funding came in 2019. I was constantly receiving introductions and unsolicited messages from prospective storytellers, producers, journalists, funders, executives, and other people who wanted help from or who wanted to help the project. I was doing meetings on weekends, in between classes, and after hours, all to keep Open TV truly open—a far too rigorous commitment to my original research question. Soon, I created a scheduler to focus my meetings with artists and developed a rigorous email management strategy, which included a project management system built into it. Through that project management system (Streak), I can see that I connected with at least 428 people from 2016 to 2019, mostly introductory meetings and connections. On top of those, I conducted one to two dozen formal research interviews with creators every year. My introductory calls served as useful data for understanding the ecosystem, and data from my project management system indicates that the majority centered artists and community. Of the over four hundred conversations from 2016 to 2019, roughly 35 percent were creators and producers, and 21 percent were community and exhibition partners, most local to Chicago but including national organizations like the Sundance Institute.

Almost 20 percent were who I called development partners, in that they could partner to help develop OTV artists or the platform as a whole; this included executives at studios, distributors, and management companies in Hollywood, which grew to a database of over fifty by 2020. Then in 2020, as I transitioned out of working in artist development to hand over that work to Sarah Minnie, I met with an additional seventy prospective artists for free one-on-one project and career consultations as a benefit to the first applicants to the OTV Fellowship program, on top of my regular meetings with other stakeholders. Meeting with all these different stakeholders was not part of my original plan, but I was responding to Chicago's flourishing media ecosystem and connecting people who were also actively working to repair media's harm nationally. Still, these contacts and meetings led to the development of internal databases and other forms of information I shared with artists and others to support diversifying the film and TV media ecosystem. It was both energizing and dizzying. As a method, it produced data I hadn't planned on collecting that helped the project and the Chicago film/TV community.

Methods should never remain static, even if making changes threatens data consistency. This runs in opposition to the majority of social science scholars who "demand full control of research design and project execution."[37] Adaptation is particularly important when working with communities facing multiple systems of oppression, as they are more likely to be harmed by traditional methods: "Interdependence, multi-dimensionality and mutually constitutive relationships form the core of intersectionality, attributes that contradict the positivist assumptions inherent in most quantitative approaches."[38] Rooting our methods in *mutually constitutive* relationships means we listen to participants and change the study as needed to *cocreate* knowledge, which makes our data more representative and potentially less harmful.

For example, I soon realized that, because artists' identities are not fixed, my research questions could not be either. Several transitioned their gender identity from cisgender to trans/nonbinary or came out as a variety of sexualities. Others deepened their relationship to national or ethnic identities, religions, (in)visible disabilities, and ancestries. These shifts demonstrate how studies that only engage with participants for short periods of time miss the nuances and ever-changing nature of identity. OTV's community surveys are another useful example of this. We produced live, in-person screenings of every OTV project before publishing them online: fifty-two screenings in four years. After each screening, we surveyed attendees. These surveys served as organic community research, helping us understand who would attend an exhibition of local, intersectional video art and TV and why. I say "organic" because our questions changed over the years.

Demographically, we received feedback from anonymous community members that our gender question was not inclusive. We offered "check all that apply" answers, including "cis-man, cis-woman, trans,* masculine-spectrum, feminine-spectrum, and gender non-conforming." However, these did not leave space for people who wanted to check "transman" or "transwoman," so we added those. We also added South Asian and Middle Eastern after one request, and it made a significant difference in our results. No connection or data point is too small; even just one person asking for a change can have an impact.

Later, with more funding for research assistants, we tried to keep questions open-ended to allow artists to identify themselves in their own words, but open-ended questions were always critical and in flux. Our initial open-ended post-screening questions asked "what stood out to you?" to discover what community members focused on in the narrative, and "what would you like to see in future installments?" to understand their dreams for the future of the narrative based on present inadequacies (a way to model a queer reparative praxis of story development). Noticing an overwhelming tendency for respondents to be positive, I added "what would you like to see *less* of?" to encourage critique, because the post-screening surveys were creators' best opportunity to receive critique from their most immediate community versus executives in Hollywood, who largely do not come from creators' communities. These shifts show how I struggled to balance the need for efficiency in data collection with the need for complex and representative data helpful to artists and the platform.

Moving beyond participant observation to participatory action presented its own challenges. For one, as a researcher whose field was my city of residence, I was "always on." Attending social events to simply enjoy time with my community would often lead to impromptu meetings with new or existing collaborators. Once I become known in Chicago's diverse arts communities, I was often pitched TV shows—despite not having funding to green-light them—at parties, art openings, on the street, even at the gym. I was not always in a place to take field notes or to remember everyone

I met, so I had to focus my field notetaking on moments of tension, revelation, or confusion and resigned that I was not going to get everything. My data set was inevitably incomplete.

Moreover, the more methods we employ, the more we may need financial or institutional support, which many colleges and universities lack. Here, the traditional university research system can benefit community-based research if institutions recognize its value and equitably distribute resources. In the early years I had occasional access to a doctoral student as a research assistant through a negotiated agreement with the university, and I was blessed to be advising the brilliant Chelsea Peterson-Salahuddin, without whose qualitative analysis skills I would have fallen behind. I also had the support of over two dozen undergraduate and graduate students who took field notes, offered creative notes, coded data sets, summarized trade knowledge, and evaluated social media analytics. Still, I found myself constantly needing more support. For one, undergraduate assistants required training on top of a two-month selection process coordinated by the university, and most graduate students were only available to me for one quarter to one year at most. The research process was constantly in a state of flux, but I had the privilege of having some structure via institutional support.

Without institutional support, researchers, like hosts, must lean even more heavily on their community collaborators to produce knowledge. This further shows the importance of having flexible and varied methods for obtaining knowledge that empower the study's participants. An extractive framework for collecting data puts the burden on researchers and their institutions to fully resource data gathering. An open and flexible approach cultivates the relationships and incentives necessary to involve everyone in the process.

HOSTS STRUGGLE TO OFFER MAXIMUM BENEFIT, SHARING WHAT AND HOW THEY ARE LEARNING

Community-engaged researchers carry the burden of minimizing harm and maximizing benefit, which slightly reframes how research is traditionally understood by the university. University protocols, via federally mandated IRBs, focus on minimizing harm because harm is a legal and financial liability. Promises of benefit are supposed to be conservative. Reparative research challenges this system because we must address the harm that participants face to gather data. Working in collaboration with those who have fewer resources requires a clear benefit proposition, however modest. People and communities facing intersectional oppression need support, and there is an ethical conundrum in taking up their precious time to only extract data that benefits us scholars in the short term but *maybe* benefits our participants in the long term.

Designing research for mutual benefit centers abundance and solidarity. It means sharing not only resources but also time and care. The process cultivates interdependency. Throughout the OTV experiment, we all learned from and leaned on each other. No one—not the creators, their crews, the OTV team, nor often community partners—was getting paid "market rates" consistently, because market rates are set by corporations that routinely undervalue or exclude us. In lieu of robust financial payment, we offered skills, ideas, and time to each other's projects in service of liberation.

Recognizing what Linda Tuhiwai Smith identifies as the necessary "humbling" it takes to decolonize methodologies, much of what I did in OTV's early years would not count as research methods in academia and looks more like local/digital community service. I resisted neutrality and extraction to support artists, my community, and the broader local ecosystem. To support distribution and exhibition, I edited our trailers in the early years and sacrificed my personal Vimeo account to give OTV a head start in its online audience. I further supported the development of OTV's online audience by inviting hundreds of people in my own network to follow our Facebook and Instagram pages and nearly every single Facebook event for our Chicago premieres. I posted about the online premiere of every single OTV project on my personal social media, often with a carefully written note offering context about artists' stories, production journeys, or accolades. I also posted updates—especially press and awards—directly to our social media channels in the early years. Anyone connected to me on social media from 2015 to 2020 was probably sick of hearing about OTV.

As my academic peers were gaining larger social media followings posting critiques of harm on the national and global level, mine stayed local and focused on repair, which doesn't spread as widely. To support the development of new stories, I invited dozens of individuals and groups to dinners and brunches in my apartment, from meals with prospective funders to networking gatherings like one I hosted for women and nonbinary filmmakers, or the series of brunches I hosted for the writers' room for my *Hair*

Story pilot. I offered my apartment and offices up for filming, often providing meals I either cooked or paid for knowing I didn't have the research funds for reimbursement. I gave notes on scripts and made countless introductions and referrals.

In terms of production, I donated my labor to artists' productions, working for free as a production assistant, craft services, boom microphone operator, and even lead producer: hiring crews, scheduling filming, and managing the set. If I was not helping physically on set, I was offering advice and introductions, taking calls nearly every day of the week. Sometimes the level of support I was offering reached the point where peers would tell me I should be getting some kind of producer credit on the projects; in a few cases, I gave enough of my own personal money to projects that peers looked at me bewildered that I was not *demanding* executive producer credit and partial ownership. A few times, artists recognized this and gave me credit without me asking; in one case, I found out I was an executive producer on a project when I saw my name listed in the credits upon receiving the final cut for distribution. I never demanded it and never took an ownership stake in any artist's project. Because, of course, for all this work, I was getting the benefit of knowledge and learning, which was my full-time job. And I was not the only one offering more than they were receiving. Most around me were doing similar solidarity work, all for learning and systemic transformation.[39] It made sense I would do the same. Hosts are never too important to cook!

Designing OTV for mutual benefit meant that every moment where I asked for data, I would offer data in return. It was important that I shared insights and strategies into how to navigate the systems holding power over my collaborators and participants. In my first meetings with artists, I would ask them why they embarked on telling their story and what their goals were for their careers. This was both for my own research and a way for me to determine what data I could share that would be most helpful to them. For a creator whose goals included a staff writing position on a corporate TV show, I would share case studies of other writers who had leveraged digital production for career advancement. I would then ask them what stage of the creative process they were in—story development, preproduction, postproduction, distribution, or exhibition—and offer advice on advancing the project, as well as an open invitation for another meeting if they needed help getting to the next phase. Practically, this helped creators complete projects we could distribute, supplementing our small licensing fees of $500 to $2,000, on average. The benefit was mutual. Completed projects offered much more data than incomplete ones. Sharing knowledge requires tremendous care. What works for one filmmaker may not help another. Every creator or project is specific and emerges from different contexts.

In the first year, I fully funded and produced video works, but this grew unsustainable for my budget and capacity. Instead, the team and I would offer advice and free consultation at any stage. The more we helped, the more we were able to help, and the more we learned. Elijah said of these early years, "All of the roles that I have cycled through over the years have been based on need and demand. And I think that's just personally where I thrive in terms of problem solving and creating solutions and developing systems to create sustainability." We shared social networks—people who asked me to connect them with emerging writers who needed support. We shared resources—eventually, local companies and vendors would start offering discounts to OTV artists. Now, OTV offers online film courses to expand and scale the knowledge sharing we were doing on a one-on-one basis.

The cookout, like all ecosystems, redistributes and recycles resources. Sharing and cocreating data benefited both me as a researcher and our storytellers. I shared what I learned from my team and creators with others. For example, Elijah, who both within and outside of OTV consulted closely with the early cohorts of creators, encouraged the *Brown Girls* team to execute a multicity release, which they did, and it worked wonderfully (more in chapter 4). We shared this tip with the teams behind other series, which worked for them as well. To assist with fundraising, my team and I read through grant applications, and successful applications served as meaningful data to help us better inform future applicants. This helped OTV continue to release projects even without much funding for production. Crowdfunding was one of the most common fundraising strategies, and we shared successful strategies gleaned from key creators in the community, like how to structure fundraising events or how to organize requests for donations.

All this support aligned with the goal of learning how to build an alternative platform and ecosystem. I knew OTV needed projects to release so I could have reception or audience data to contextualize what I saw in the story's development and production. After each project was distributed, I interviewed the creators on their experience, asking what challenges they faced, what innovations they created, and how OTV helped or harmed them in the process. In the last year, after revelation of deep harm in our community that I narrate in this book's conclusion, I added a question specifically about how storytellers experienced conflict or harm in the process, what steps they were taking toward repair, and how OTV could support their healing. Yet even these "exit interviews" were mutually beneficial, and in practice, it was often not an "exit" interview because creators would continue to ask me for support long after their project was released. Instead of merely collecting the data I needed, I offered artists a chance to ask me questions as well. They would ask about how the OTV project was developing, trends in the broader media industry, and, most often, the next steps they could take in their career to leverage their project for bigger goals. Those who achieved success in the industry became mentors to emerging storytellers. I tried to make the research process an exchange of ideas, where the researcher and the participants could learn from and hold each other accountable.

Scholars are awakening to the value of opening our data sets and research processes, at least to each other. Our current conversation around open data, led by the sciences and social sciences, focuses on preregistering studies for reproducing and "verifying" results, among other technocratic innovations.[40] The current open data framework does not always accommodate qualitative and exploratory work, which is harder to replicate and for which preregistration holds little utility. Reparative researchers are challenging what they call "hegemonic open science," which "creates and reproduces extractive enclosures that serve colonial–capitalist interests."[41] What does it mean for a study to be replicable? Replicable experiments need rigorous control mechanisms, separating the study from the complex conditions of environments impacted by multiple intersecting systems. Is replicable data representative? Here, the "replication crisis" fails "to engage with decolonizing southern critiques of reductionist knowledge practices in/from the North that have long noted the limits to generalizability in Northern knowledge claims anchored in misplaced confidence in data."[42] Generalizability marginalizes intersectional perspectives that, if centered, would reveal much more about the problems researchers are trying to understand and solve through more controlled studies.

For me, the primary audiences for my data were my participants and collaborators. I wanted them to see how I was interpreting their experiences, being increasingly transparent about my own and my team's mistakes and limitations and what value we saw in the project. This involved publishing on the OTV website for anyone to read or share: annual reports on how the project was developing, reports on surveys of our community at local screenings, and reports summarizing the "exit" interviews I conducted with artists.[43] These reports, written by me and Chelsea Peterson-Salahuddin, explained the frames and codes we saw in the data participants were offering us.

In return for their data, we offered transparency into how we were interpreting it. Of course, I also posted links to the peer-reviewed journal articles I wrote about the project on the OTV website, doing my best to submit to open-access journals while understanding that this wasn't always possible when trying to earn tenure. Still, most of the articles based on OTV data were published in open-access journals: In one case, I fought hard for my article in the *International Journal of Communication* to be published in HTML so the video work from our artists could be embedded and honor their stories as critical sources of data and theory.

My team and I worked hard to open data beyond publishing reports on the process. Over the years, we developed data sets that would directly help storytellers, including databases for hundreds of writing and directing opportunities (labs, fellowships, etc.), funding opportunities (mostly grants), and several internal crew databases to assist us in recommending cinematographers, editors, sound technicians, makeup artists, music artists, and more. My own and our team's personal social media also became sites for sharing knowledge, and many followed my Instagram stories, Twitter, and Facebook posts for new jobs, funding opportunities, mentorship programs, or cultural criticism. Later, the OTV team continued to experiment with new ways to share knowledge, including quarterly Instagram Lives where the team updated followers on how the project is developing, digital "office hours" where I answered artists' questions, and blogs where I shared deeper lessons on what I had learned.[44]

The many ways we shared data using informal channels point to the challenge of scaling open-access data in a community-centered way. At a time of information overload and increasing inequality, we struggled to keep people updated on how the project was developing based on what we were learning. People lead busy lives, and global capitalism takes time out of our days and limits our capacities. People surviving multiple harmful systems face even more precarity. Researchers need to meet people where they are. One-on-one conversations with all our collaborators and participants offered the best opportunities for sharing data and seeking input, but these conversations took time and were incredibly challenging amid my responsibilities to the university. Our universities need to give researchers the space to share data and build truly collaborative projects where power is evenly distributed.

HOSTS CANNOT BE AFRAID TO HAND OVER OR SHARE HOSTING DUTIES

A reparative research process offers more than transparency. It also offers participants and collaborators power over the process. This leads to better data and ensures that the knowledge cultivated serves everyone's needs. Cultural power matters as much as procedural power. As in the cookout, the identity of the host shapes how communities feel about the process, as much as the specifics of where and how projects unfold. Power over process can look like anything from participants codesigning questions to determining how funding is allocated. "*Nothing about us without us!* . . . research about Black people should be in partnership with Black scholars and using frameworks that center Black people and culture," Sheena Erete notes.[45] For example, Erete and her team reversed funding power dynamics by making participants the project's lead recipients, who then sub-grant to researchers, which "completely changed the nature of the research partnership."[46]

Researchers must be mindful of how we structure collective processes, however. We can place an "epistemic burden" on communities to direct research about themselves when we have not developed structures to share power.[47] Without careful attention to how participants can direct the process of learning, we can unintentionally replicate "the pattern of coming into a community; extracting information, experiences, stories, and other data during a participatory design exercise; and then leaving the community without lasting positive impact or appropriate ongoing collaboration or follow-up."[48]

It is more work for researchers to share the responsibility of cultivating shared knowledge. The entire process of organizing OTV involved the cocreation of data. No aspect of the project was possible for me to direct on my own: from organizing in-person screenings (led by Elijah in our early years), to leading the social media channels (Chris Walker), to producing the projects (led by the artists and our first head of production Stephanie

Jeter), and to analyzing the entire process (supported by research assistants). Equally important were the artists as creators of their series, which cultivated knowledge on how to make reparative stories, and the communities that engaged with those stories, which cultivated knowledge on reparative platforms. But it took many years of constant feedback, transparency, critique, and adaptation to develop the structures for ensuring their work came together into an experiment that could run without me.

The project was collective from the beginning. Elijah notes how they conceived of every artist and community member as a founder in those early years: "It's basically having people . . . believe that they are the originators of that thing. And so the whole purpose of the marketing strategy and engagement strategy the first year was around, 'This thing is happening and I'm a part of it. And I'm getting to be one of the founders of this conversation that's happening around artistic open and sustainable television.'" Here Elijah decenters the notion of the single founder of any project or organization. Justice-based projects only survive if communities feel they can actively shape its future. Ceding control over the project to Elijah and the team was an important step in letting it grow into what it needed to be.

Power is collective, but when it comes to a project blossoming into an organization, it is also bureaucratic. Ultimately, reparative research transfers power and full control over the project or ceases the project if power cannot be dispersed equitably. Like Erete and her team, I stepped aside from leadership over the project as soon as funding came in from outside sources. After years of me running the project completely unpaid—in fact, I estimated I went into over $15,000 of debt to keep it going—I received interest in funding OTV from the Surdna Foundation. Robert Smith, a friend and community member who recommended fundraising strategies in its early stages, had recently taken a job at Surdna and introduced OTV to his boss, F. Javier Torres. Javier appreciated the project's ambition and fit within the foundation's "Thriving Cultures" portfolio, so the foundation offered a $175,000 grant in 2019–2020. Upon hearing this news, I asked the entire OTV team if anyone was interested in leading the organization as its first executive director. Thankfully, Elijah raised their hand. The previous year, they had asked about becoming a cofounder, which I agreed made sense because they were doing such essential work. But at the time, I felt we had to wait because the project was still technically an experiment at Northwestern

University over which someone outside of the university would have little control. When outside funding came, it gave us the resources to make OTV an independent 501(c)(3) nonprofit organization.

As I stepped down as the project "founder," Elijah stepped up to become the organization's first executive director and cofounder. A project incubated as a community-based experiment was now led by someone outside of academia whose incredible work supported its development. My ceding of power brought the project closer to its core values of intersectionality, removing the only cis male team member. OTV is now led mostly by Black queer, trans, and woman-identified people. I continued to support the project, writing the organization's grants and annual reports as a board member of the nonprofit.

Transferring power and ownership is hard for researchers. We are trained to "know better." We don't always. Decentering ourselves can lead to innovations and greater opportunities for learning. I was struck by how Elijah offered new ways to care for staff: from tweaks like adding a "check-in" question at the beginning of every meeting so team members could share how they were feeling and their capacity in that moment, to more substantive additions, like including a membership to Haji Healing Salon, a Black feminist space for wellness on Chicago's South Side, as part of OTV's benefits package (something we did not have the budget or organizational capacity for when I was running the project). Elijah is rigorous about protecting staff capacity. Indeed, looking back at my own leadership after watching Elijah lead, I am struck by how often I missed opportunities to check in with the team, which, on rare occasion, led to some tension that inspired some of the changes discussed in this chapter. I inherited from the university and the other institutions that trained me a focus on work as equal to or above overall wellness.

Researchers too often underestimate our participants, to our own detriment. We have a lot to learn from people outside the university working toward the liberation of themselves and their communities. Listening to and working with them opens our own capacities for change. Relieving myself of the responsibility to run OTV allowed me to focus on starting the Media and Data Equity Lab (MADE), supporting other artists and arts/media organizations working to repair systems after a new wave of field and coalition building that resulted from the Black Lives Matter uprisings of 2020.

In all, what we have learned is how reparative practices challenge many of the baseline assumptions in human-centered research. If traditional research empowers principal investigators or research teams, reparative research empowers those who are historically the subjects of these projects. Participants become cocreators in the learning process. They help shape the questions, the methods for answering them, what we learn, and how that learning is presented. If done well, they can take over hosting the entire project. By sharing hosting duties, we free ourselves to support communities in other ways. In our cultural ecology, these cycles of leading and following, founding and retiring, and birthing and letting go are critical to sustainability.

WHAT CHALLENGES SUSTAINABLE KNOWLEDGE CULTIVATION?

Understanding power requires levels of self-reflexivity of which I was not aware and deepened every year. This work is challenging but profound and transformative. Working in solidarity with communities outside of academia clarifies "the significance of being accountable to my political community in scholarship, even if that scholarship is not directly about my political community," Karma Chàvez writes.[49] Accountability to participants is hard for scholars, since we spend most of our time focused on our accountability to our scholarly peers and the institutions that employ us. The challenges are worth the trouble.

Academic institutions, particularly in the US, disincentivize reparative research. The six-year tenure "clock," word limits for journal articles, closed access journals, and more, all impede this work. The limits and norms of scholarship run counter to organic research. It is extremely challenging to summarize the kind of complex findings derived from community-based research in the less than 6,000- to 8,000-word limits that journals often require. Indeed, several of my articles ran closer to 10,000 words, after significant cutting and sometimes at additional cost. Intersectionality is complex. Condensing multidimensional experiences into artificial limits was challenging, especially when many reviewers are not familiar with my communities or the concept of intersectionality itself. Moreover, these journals are rarely accessible to participants, and the condensed nature of journal article writing makes it difficult to simplify complex ideas so our participants can even understand what we're writing and why. More challenging is the prevailing idea from reviewers trained in Western conceptions of research that scholarship must be "generalizable" or generate new theory, whereas organic research informed by intersectionality complicates generalizability and overarching theories. In both their deconstructive and reconstructive modes, this form of research—if done well—offers as much value to the lives of participants and collaborators as to scholarly theory, if not more.

During my tenure track, with so much time devoted to my community, my scholarly productivity slowed, and I had several years of not publishing peer-reviewed journal articles. As noted in the beginning of this chapter, this put my tenure case clearly at risk. While I ended up earning tenure in my department, it was an exhausting feat on top of the work I was doing outside of the university. This is not to mention the service I was giving to the institution, including service on a dozen different search and admissions committees for tenure track, nontenure track, postdoctoral and PhD candidates, and service to the field, including reviewing for journals and university presses. My mental and physical health suffered on the tenure clock. Post-tenure, with time to focus on both regular meditation and yoga, I also discovered I spent my time on the tenure clock with an untreated gut infection that was impairing my cognition and energy levels, partially explaining my inhibited capacity.

The tenure clock is a rigid structure that artificially speeds up the process of knowledge production to the detriment of our collective understanding of what we study and often to our mental and physical health.[50] Maggie Berg and Barbara Seeber advocate for slow research: "Slowing down is about asserting the importance of contemplation, connectedness, fruition, and complexity. It gives meaning to letting research take the time it needs to ripen."[51] I have since cautioned junior scholars about embarking on an experimental community-based project on tenure track because of how my mental and physical health suffered under the pressure. With more institutional support, however, this form of research could thrive. It's important that younger scholars shape it.

It is so important that every professor reading this book understand that *this is not a call for already overworked and undercompensated professors to take on more uncompensated labor*! I acknowledge the privileges I had doing this work, even amid the challenges I faced. I believe more faculty should take on this work but only if people feel they have capacity. Institutions must pledge to offer more support in time and resources, particularly for nontenure track faculty who are bearing the brunt of teaching needs while being starved for resources to conduct research, create art, and engage community. Universities need to invest heavily in this work, giving faculty time to do these projects ethically and money to pay participants whose very existence resists oppression. But universities must also balance existing inequalities between tenured/tenure-track and nontenured/tenure-track faculty, between faculty and graduate students, and between the humanities, social sciences, and "hard" sciences. Redistributing resources equitably will make this kind of work more sustainable and impactful—for example, giving nontenured artist "lecturers" not only good salaries and benefits but also budgets to support their creative practice, as they give research professors budgets for our work.

The benefits to society are immeasurable, but this work also benefits the university based on its own metrics for success. OTV not only led to published research but also public acclaim that attracted student and industry interest to Northwestern; indeed, two years in a row, Hollywood's publication of record *Variety* listed Northwestern as a top film school, citing OTV as a key example. Over the course of running the project, I worked with at least forty of Northwestern's undergraduate, master's, and doctoral students, who earned experience with everything from qualitative/quantitative data analysis, film/video production and postproduction, online marketing, script development, industry analysis, and computer science. These students listed OTV on their resumes and now work for leading local and Hollywood studios, distributors, agencies/management companies, and data analytics firms, among many others. All doctoral students earned academic positions at universities or tech companies.

Reparative research can only grow in a conducive environment, a complex interplay between researchers as agents in the ecosystem and the resources available in the specific location and communities we hope to cultivate knowledge with. I encourage all researchers to look around them in the places they live and work and ask what can be done in collaboration with nonacademics who are already working to solve similar problems. It is incredibly complex and challenging, but the benefits grow exponentially and, in the best-case scenario, sustainably.

Cultivating knowledge is the beginning, middle, and end of the cookout process. We need some understanding of what our community needs before we start a cookout. We need to learn from them throughout the entire process to know if what we are doing is impactful and ethical. When the party is over, we hope they feel empowered to do it again, with or without us. Ultimately, this process supports the development of knowledge but of community itself. If we all engaged in this work, we would learn so much about our individual selves, our communities, and the industries and ecosystems we all must survive.

3 REPARATIVE STORIES: COOKING FILM AND TELEVISION OUTSIDE THE STREAMING STUDIO SYSTEM

To most of the world, the story of Chicago is gangs, cops, and violence: racialized stories of harm. From national news to popular films like *Chiraq* or television shows like *The Chi*, corporate media repeats the myth that Chicago is the most dangerous place to live in the United States. There is a lot of violence in Chicago, but the reasons why and the complex stories of how this happens are rarely ever told. I hear the Chicago story constantly whenever I mention where I live to nonresidents. It always puzzles me. I don't know many Chicago creators who tell this story, and if they do, they don't tell it in the simplistic way I see in corporate news, television, and film.

Inspired by Chicago's legacy of soulful, community-based ways of telling stories, the reparative storytellers I know tell more nuanced stories, culturally specific and trauma-informed but not traumatizing. Instead of reducing Chicago's communities to numbers of nameless victims of police violence, they connect its souls through stories, seeing "stories as a form of compensation or even as reparations, perhaps the only kind we will ever receive," as Saidiya Hartman writes of her own work recuperating the lost stories of the enslaved.[1]

Soul, and its Black roots, has always nourished Chicago's stories. The city played as central a role as New York and Los Angeles in the development of Black radio and music.[2] Throughout the twentieth century, it played a pivotal role in the growth of deeply Black and queer music genres: soul, blues, jazz, and house music.[3] Chicago is the birthplace of *Soul Train*, the longest-running Black and independently produced music TV series in the history of the medium. It was home to the first Black independent film studio and the first Black soap opera on TV. It was home to arguably the most significant publishers in the history of the Black press: *The Chicago Defender*, *Ebony*, and *Jet*. Perhaps its Black history is why Chicago's contributions to artistic innovation have been largely undervalued or understudied. Because of this scholarly gap, I had little sense when I arrived of how important this local culture would be to the development of what I call "social practice television" in Chicago. I had no idea that Chicago's fertile cultural soil had all the nutrients to nurture a reparative media platform.

The community-led ways that OTV creators developed and produced their films and series show how we can make or "cook" stories more nurturing than harmful corporate ones. Rooting our platform in a specific city held us accountable to our community, its complexities, interconnections, and power dynamics. Black and other communities excluded from corporate media tell stories differently out of necessity, just as Chicago has innovated across media forms because it has access to fewer resources than LA or New York. In LA's Hollywood or New York's Broadway, artists and artisans tell stories to advance their careers in a local system designed to extract value nationally and globally (figure 3.1). In Chicago, storytellers come together because we only have each other. This way of making is community based because people form deep relationships and accountability to each other. Storytelling becomes a way to practice solidarity, a means of surviving and thriving, often without much promise of status or capital beyond where we live. In her global study of community media, Clemencia Rodriguez, writes that it "implies much more than simply challenging the mainstream media"; rather, community-based producers "undergo compelling transformations in which established sociological, psychological, and even existential 'givens' are suddenly questioned."[4] What is the value of a story? Chicago stories heal and connect.

We challenged the "given" story of Chicago in how we platformed collectives of artists and bridged the city's divides. For example, OTV cofounder Elijah McKinnon's work as a storyteller served as a platform for Chicago artists to showcase their work. They started with *Two Queens in a Kitchen*, a talk show where two artists from different identities and perspectives have an organic conversation and make a meal together (figure 3.2). Elijah designed the series to elevate the writers, directors, and community organizers critical to Chicago and OTV but not always given space to share their knowledge. Both my own pilot, *Hair Story*, and Elijah's series, *Good*

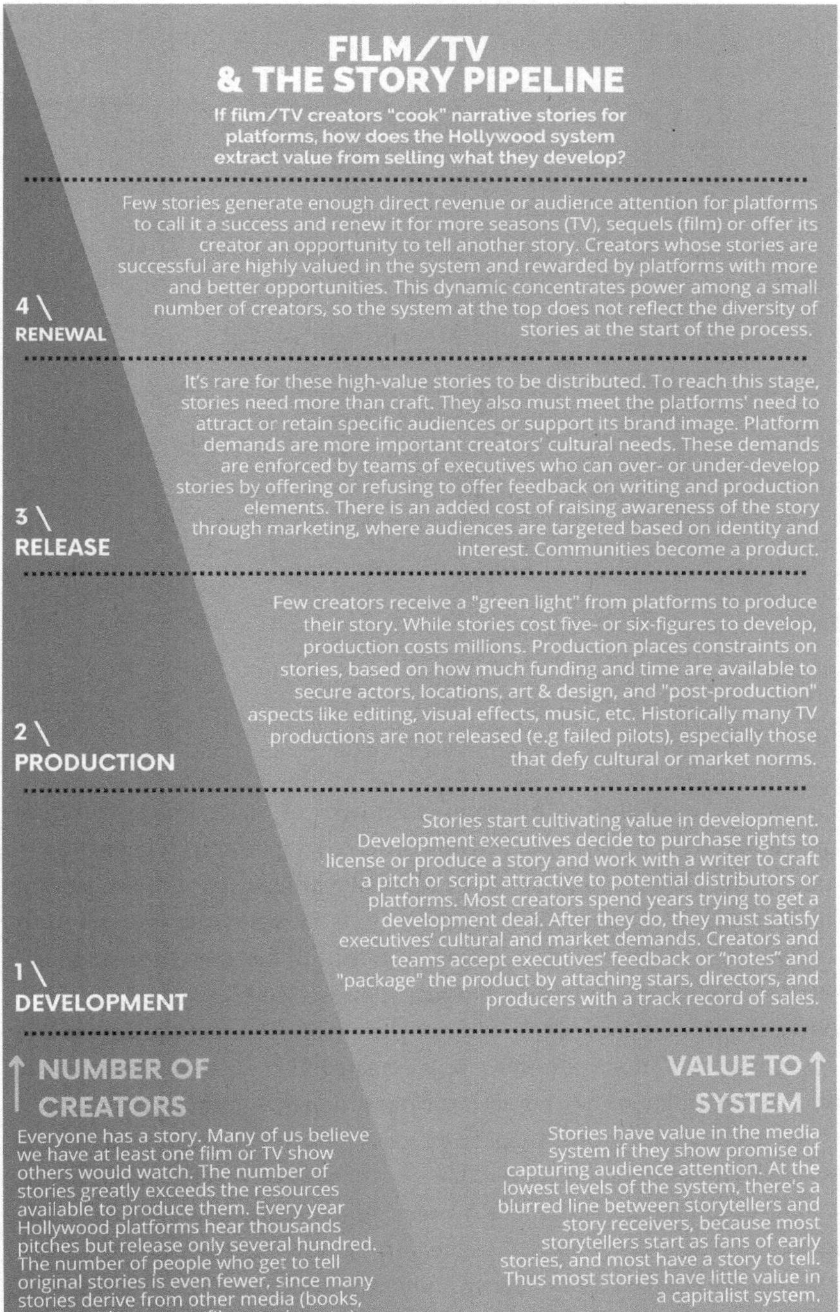

FIGURE 3.1
Film/TV and the story pipeline.

FIGURE 3.2
E. Patrick Johnson, Britt Julious, and Ashley Ray share soul food recipes during *Two Queens in a Kitchen*, season 3. Credit: Dorlan Curtis.

Enough, featured diverse, interconnected casts of Black and Brown queer people navigating chosen family on Chicago's reportedly "violent" South Side, set at the Breathing Room by #LetUsBreathe, a space of art, healing, and organizing that emerged out of the #BlackLivesMatter protests of the early 2010s (figure 3.3). In addition to directing her own film, Stephanie Jeter advised artists on how to produce their work ethically and effectively, doing the work of a producer without the credit. Her next project on OTV, *HIVE*, is an ambitious pilot for a series created by a team of three creatives and showcasing multiple characters from different communities.

We expanded Chicago's legacy of social practice to the digital era, cultivating stories about the everyday experiences of diverse communities. Unlike corporate media's focus on sensational crime and criminal justice as key to Chicago's story, OTV's creators centered the mundane, complicated issues people face including and beyond trauma. OTV also deepened the city's tradition of creating platforms for independent and community-based artists to tell their stories unapologetically to create value for each other even amid scarce resources and investment. I estimate the entire

FIGURE 3.3
The *Hair Story* and *Good Enough* casts and crews. Credit: Jaclyn Rivas.

budget for OTV's operations and budgets for dozens of individual productions at around $1 million, maybe less, over just five years (2015–2020), less than the cost of *one episode* of traditional broadcast series like NBC's *One Chicago* that focus on crime and death. Yet we arguably did as much, if not more, to support the development of stories by and about Chicago communities, both locally and even in Hollywood given the training we offered storytellers to enter that system. OTV shows the disproportionate value that under-resourced communities contribute to the media market and overall economy.

Our growth did not emerge in a bubble; we benefited indirectly from the rise of big productions in Chicago. In the next section I discuss how Chicago became both an attractive site for Hollywood to produce more "plastic" stories and how OTV recycled Hollywood's resources to incubate reparative stories. Productions like NBC's *One Chicago* kept crew members in the city working so they could discount services in the indie economy we were cultivating. However, while large corporations like NBC indirectly helped make our work possible through individual job opportunities, they could not sustain our platform. OTV also benefited from Chicago's vibrant, collaborative communities in theater, literature, poetry, dance, performance, and music, all of which embody the city's legacy of collaboratively making art by and for artists and communities. Film and TV are inherently interdisciplinary and draw from diverse artistic inputs.

After a discussion of Chicago's role cultivating social practice—essential to reparative practice—I then delve into how OTV and our artists organically developed grassroots processes for developing and producing film and television. Collectively, we worked to repair our systemic exclusion from film and television—the mediums that draw from all other art forms.

We planted seeds for a sustainable media ecosystem more representative of its peoples. My hope was that OTV could help repair Hollywood's cycles of exclusion and inclusion, underrepresentation and misrepresentation, through *independent distribution*, an indie channel *serving* intersectionality. Distributors like OTV are critical nodes in cultural systems, buying stories (inviting) from creators/producers (cooks) to serve to communities. At the corporate level, distribution is a tool for value extraction. Hollywood's power has always been rooted in distribution even though scholars and critics tend to focus more on producers, stories, or audiences. Without broadcast, cable, or streaming distribution channels, and the exclusive contracts they require, TV distributors like NBC or Disney+ would have no way to amass large audiences and earn revenue on series (IP) they also own. Without exclusive relationships with cinemas, film studios would have nowhere to place their blockbusters (also IP they own). A critical problem in US culture is the scarcity of independent, community-driven distributors that can broaden our cultural perspective with more sincere stories: organically cultivated IP.

At OTV, we asked what it would mean to have a TV channel for intersectionality, distributing stories by and for people surviving multiple systems of oppression. We learned that at the grassroots level, intersectional distribution provides a way to structure solidarity in stories and labor. OTV's distribution model challenged Hollywood's extractive practices. Creators retained ownership of their stories, and distribution agreements were nonexclusive, meaning they could release projects outside of OTV too (e.g., if Netflix released whole shows on YouTube for free). Following intersectionality's lessons of liberation and honoring the power of one's specific story, we invited creators to trust us and join our collective struggle by protecting their agency and power over their own work, their recipes for liberation. In turn, we offered what little financing we could and all the knowledge, resources, and social networks we could share.

We cultivated systems to share the responsibility for repairing Hollywood's exclusions and distortions. People in the US have leaned too heavily on storytellers and audiences to bear the weight repairing our culture, subjecting them to capitalism's boom and bust cycles. This is unfair. The weight is too heavy. Those who have never produced a film have little idea of the intensity of this labor. We need grassroots distributors—cultural cookouts—to nourish the storytellers and communities that our culture marginalizes.[5]

In reparative media, artists and storytellers have a lot to teach us about how to "cook" connective, healing stories for us to consume. They inspire us to ask of the film and TV platforms that serve us stories to binge, Who is invited to create, what dishes, and with what ingredients? What's on the menu? How are you serving the most nourishing, sustainably produced stories?

WHAT ARE YOU SERVING?

The cookout is organic and local: What and where cooks make matters. Reparative stories are produced in a specific place by specific people, with recipes and values emerging from specific histories in the community. To understand OTV, we must root ourselves where the platform emerged and how harmful narratives about Chicago took shape. Large-scale, fast story production from people outside of the city conflicted with its legacy of intimate, community-based, and restorative storytelling.

Big studios perpetuated the story about Chicago and violence. *Law & Order* creator Dick Wolf, pioneer of assembly-line television and among the most powerful showrunners in television, created four different interconnected procedural dramas about the city: *Chicago Fire* (NBC, 2012–present), *Chicago PD* (NBC, 2014–present), *Chicago Med* (NBC, 2015–present), and *Chicago Justice* (NBC, 2017). Much like he did with *Law & Order*, Wolf designed *One Chicago* to be an episodic mega franchise. Each series' simple plot structure sustains hundreds of episodes, making Wolf even richer. *Chicago Justice* only lasted one season, but ten years in, the other three were still releasing new episodes: a total of twenty-six seasons, over five hundred episodes. With drama episodes averaging over $3 million each, we can estimate that producing the *One Chicago* franchise cost well over $1 billion and counting.

Before *One Chicago*, the city was best known as a pass-through state for big movies to film specific scenes on the cheap. In 2004, Illinois launched a tax credit for production, tripling the amount of productions from the year prior.[6] *One Chicago* and Cinespace benefited from a years-long public-private effort to woo Hollywood to Chicago. Wolf's style of production was just what the city needed to build itself into a production hub.[7] To the state, TV was more valuable than film: "TV work has a bigger impact economically than most movies. . . . TV . . . even if it's less sexy in some ways, really creates the jobs," Illinois Film Office managing director Betsey Steinberg said the year the first *Chicago* series premiered.[8] The state tax credit gave *One Chicago*'s studios a 30 percent rebate on more than $1 billion in production costs, a generous incentive to support the corporate industry. By 2021, Illinois reported over $600 million in revenue from film/TV production and over 13,000 jobs, down slightly from pre-pandemic 2019. In 2019 I was invited to stand behind Governor JB Pritzker as he signed the tax credit's renewal until 2026. There by his side was Dick Wolf, congratulating the state of Illinois for taking appropriate action so NBC would not move production to one of the other states offering robust savings on big productions: "I have to tell you, if the tax credit goes, we go," Wolf said.[9]

The culture of Chicago was valuable too, perhaps as much as its tax benefit.[10] The city's heartland authenticity distinguished it from Hollywood's plasticity: "If you set this show in Los Angeles, people would say, 'Oh come on.' But this is about the heart of the country. It's real," Wolf said.[11] Chicago's "brand" of soulful realness brought freshness to the stale broadcast procedural.

The real Chicago is a rich, complex place, but *One Chicago* is not known for its complexity. It is not "real" representation of Chicago culture from the perspective of many Black or Brown residents. The story of violence in the city is far more complex than Hollywood has generally represented. *Chicago PD* shows an effective albeit occasionally corrupt police force, but Black community organizers describe a police force too uninterested in whether they live or die. During my time here, numerous Black people have been shot and killed by Chicago police, guilty until proven innocent, with police rarely facing justice. Corporate media focuses on Chicago's crime rates, sensational cases, or celebrity cases like that of Chicago-produced *Empire*'s lead Jussie Smollett. But so-called mainstream journalism routinely fails to mention that the Chicago Police Department (CPD) is one of the most corrupt and inefficient city police departments in the country, solving proportionately fewer homicides than their counterparts in New York or Los Angeles despite having more cops per capita.

So corrupt is the CPD that the US Department of Justice investigated it for detaining people without charges and holding them in undisclosed, untraceable black sites.[12] This is the tip of the iceberg of corruption. So corrupt is the CPD that Chicago became the first city to pay out reparations after Chicago Torture Justice activists spent decades seeking reparations for the survivors of John Burge, who tortured hundreds of mostly Black prisoners for decades.[13] In 2012 organizers coined the hashtag #SayHerName in response to the CPD's killing of Rekia Boyd, a twenty-two-year-old Black woman.[14] Two years later, a group of activists revived the report "We Charge Genocide" and brought it back to the United Nations. They accused the CPD of the mass killing of Black and Brown youth, placing Chicago "center stage in national and international stories about policing," wrote scholar and BYP100 founding national director Charlene Carruthers.[15] In 2015, OTV's first year, the city released a previously suppressed video of a CPD officer shooting and killing nineteen-year-old Laquan McDonald, whose crime was refusing to put down a knife.[16] The night we premiered Rashida Webb-Miller's healing-centered *Let Go and Let God*, thousands of protestors swarmed the city streets to protest the city's disregard for Black life.

I move around this city as a young Black man amid persistent police-enabled violence and systemic disinvestment in Black and Brown people. While I have lived in Chicago, there has been a never-ending epidemic of missing Black girls and women, which residents suspect is the result of serial killers going unpunished by the criminal justice system. Stephanie Jeter directed a beautiful short film, *Searching for Isabelle*, that uses artful surrealism to represent the city's neglect of its Black women and girls. Her film renders the horrors and effects of missing Black women in ways that facts and data cannot (figure 3.4). Perhaps it is because Black women feel the multiple, intersecting effects of over- and under-policing that Chicago's style of Black activism in the twenty-first century has been led by Black women, queer, and trans people, supported by elders like scholars Barbara Ransby and Cathy Cohen.

Hollywood rarely gives us these narratives of justice and repair. For decades, NBC and the other broadcast platforms spent billions of dollars on shows that misrepresented the culture of policing in America. Color of Change's comprehensive study of representations of police found that TV narratives perpetuate myths that police violence stops crime, police only follow the law, and when police ignore the law, they do so in service of justice and not power or hate.[17] In an analysis of 1,678 episodes of 234 series in the 2016–2017 season, Darnell Hunt and his research team found

FIGURE 3.4
A still from *Searching for Isabelle* (dir. Stephanie Jeter, 2018).

that "none of the episodes acknowledged that Black people are routinely racially profiled in America or noted that police disproportionately brutalize unarmed Black suspects. The episodes also did not acknowledge that Black people are more likely than others to be pressured into plea bargaining for crimes they didn't commit, routinely face harsher penalties for committing the same crimes as White people, or make up a disproportionate share of those incarcerated."[18]

TV's warped perspective on policing reflects the politics of production—none of the police procedurals in the sample, like *Chicago PD*, had a Black showrunner. Who tells the story matters: series with Black showrunners were more likely to "acknowledge that racial inequality still exists; attribute racial inequality to structural racism; and place Black characters on par with others in terms of whose stories were being told."[19]

(Who tells our stories matters, but who corporate media listen to also matters.[20] Four years into running OTV, my cousin, Botham Jean, was infamously killed by a Houston police officer simply for opening the door to his own apartment. If America had only listened to officer Amber Guyger's side of the story, we would have placed blame on my cousin as her defense was her own fear of Black people. Police lie all the time because they are so rarely held accountable for it. Nowhere are Black people safe from police, not even our own homes.)

I arrived in Chicago in 2012 amid this tension between the coming wave of big-budget TV productions and Chicago's history of small-scale, Black-led artistry and activism. I eventually uncovered the roots of these practices for producing reparative stories in Chicago's many community-based or social practice art traditions, its legacies of serving *soul* through art as Black people serve soul food at the cookout. Born of the pressure of segregation after Black people fled Southern white terrorism in the late nineteenth and early twentieth century, Chicago's artist communities have always produced art by and for each other as a survival strategy, inspiring and holding themselves together with soul. Starting in theater and performance,[21] Chicago's "social practice" tradition extends to visual art, radio, film, and television from the midcentury Chicago Renaissance and into the social media era. Intersectionality—Black women and queer people in particular—has been critical to this history. Even writers, largely considered solo practitioners, worked collectively in Chicago through groups like Young Chicago Authors (1990s) and the International Black Writers Conference (1970s and 1980s), dating back to the Southside Writers Group (1930s), led by Margaret Walker and including Richard Wright. Social practice, guided by intersectionality, has a lot to teach us about how to develop reparative stories.

Chicago's legacy of producing stories with and for community contrasts with Hollywood's history of highly professionalized, often managerial teams writing for profit. Most TV shows are written by collectives—writers' rooms—under the leadership of the creator or showrunner, who is part creative, part executive or manager in charge of balancing the story's needs with that of the distributor providing most of the funding. In her exhaustive history of the Writers Guild of America (WGA), Miranda Banks notes that writers' "white-collar labor . . . is inarguably part of an assembly-line production," even though "many writers try to seek a balance, making the most of their talent and passion while complying with the needs and expectations of the executives who pay them."[22]

Even when they sit down to write, however, writers historically face norms of how to do so. Jess King notes that screenwriting manuals adopted by professionals, universities, and even the WGA standardized normative perspectives to help writers "straddle the line between the goals of the artist, with their concerns about craft, and the goals of the business, with their concerns for efficiency and profit," particularly as films grew longer and more expensive throughout the twentieth century.[23] Of course, writing and producing for corporations is complicated. Both John Caldwell and Derek Johnson find that industrial authorship is a collaborative endeavor, with everyone from crew members to executives claiming creative power.[24] However, for Black and other racialized writers, creativity in industrial production, while collaborative, is historically limited. Television producer and scholar Felicia Henderson experienced consistent struggles in sincerely representing the Black experience in writers' rooms, where Black voices were routinely questioned and discounted.[25]

By contrast, Chicago has resisted the bureaucratization of story development and production as an innovator of social practice. "Social practice" is a term most often used in the art world but can manifest in film, music, radio, music, performance, theater, and, yes, television too. I'm not here to make a case for television as art, as that case has been made by many scholars in recent years, such as Maeve Connolly, Jason Mittell, and Lynn Spigel.[26] What is most important for social practice is less about the story than how it is made, how "people constitute the central artistic medium and material."[27] Focusing on *people as the medium* reorients our understanding of media away from the message or product to the *process and politics* of making: "Socially engaged art practice prioritizes relationships, process and action," Stephanie Smith writes.[28] Because TV is not only a collaborative, normative medium but also one increasingly supported by large corporations whose processes focus on fast extraction over slow cultivation, we can see why TV's social practice history remains relegated to the margins of our understanding.[29]

Chicago was a hub for early innovation in television, music, radio, and film, with both Black and working-class storytelling at the forefront: social practice art as a cookout that served American culture. In music, Chicago was critical to the emergence of communally created forms like blues, jazz, rhythm and blues (R&B), and soul—"genres which defined popular music in America."[30] White-owned corporations extracted and stole from independent Black artists and distributors: "It was almost as if their work—some of the most innovative, original and imaginative artistic work ever produced in America—was . . . freely usable by anyone."[31] In film, Chicago was an early innovator of the medium. Jacqueline Stewart writes that in 1913, William Foster founded the first Black-owned film production company in the country, producing at least a dozen films that screened in the city.[32] Foster started in vaudeville, known for its racist/blackface portrayals, so he used film reparatively, to show the fullness of Black life. Allyson Field identifies Foster as an innovator in "uplift cinema," writing that he "sought to create a cinema that would be interracial in its origins" and centered around "multiple and intersecting kinds of practices, including comedy, drama, actuality, local film, and official public record."[33] Both Field and Stewart argue that these early Black cinemas spaces were critical sites for the Black community to come together in the context of the Great Migration, where Black Southerners migrated to Northern and Midwestern cities like Chicago to flee the Jim Crow South and rebuild their communities. Decades later, in the context of white flight, Black Chicago made its mark on Blaxploitation with the classic film *The Spook Who Sat by the Door*, one of the few Black films at the time that imagined collective resistance to power.[34]

The emergence of radio and television brought new opportunities for representing Black people's collective struggle and innovation. Richard Durham has been under-recognized for his decades-spanning innovations in these serial mediums. In radio, he created *Destination Freedom* (1948), a show for NBC affiliate WMAQ that dramatized the lives of Black historical figures, from national and global figures like Crispus Attucks and Toussaint L'Ouverture to local Chicago figures like choreographer Katherine Dunham and writer Gwendolyn Brooks. Durham went on to create the first Black soap opera in US TV history, filmed and set in Chicago, called *Bird of an Iron Feather* (1969), for public TV station WTTW. Funded by the Ford Foundation, which also funded other Black public affairs programs nationally (few scripted), *Bird of an Iron Feather* unflinchingly dramatized the lives of working-class Black Americans in ways that would read as radical even by the standards of contemporary television. Many episodes tackled issues of racial discrimination in bold ways: one unaired episode even dramatized a story based on the murder of Chicago activist Fred Hampton, the basis of an Oscar-nominated film fifty years later.[35] Durham drew from family and community stories for the series, because at the same time he was editing a weekly TV newspaper, *Muhammad Speaks*, for the Chicago-based Nation of Islam. Leveraging community activism, the show fought and won to have a mostly Black crew,[36] which included people like a young Pemon Rami, who would go on to produce independent Black films and theater for decades with legends like Robert Townsend.

In television, Chicago was critical to the development of both sitcoms and soap operas.[37] Chad Raphael and Joel Sternberg write persuasively that before television's mass adoption throughout the 1950s, Chicago developed its own "school" of television, "a searching for television forms where no forms had existed."[38] The Chicago School of Television was defined by values key to social practice, including "liveness, spontaneity, informality, intimacy, and experimentation," and "distinguished itself through its collaborative and improvisational mode of production [and] its embeddedness in the local culture of Chicago."[39] We can see its program innovations most prominently in live variety shows that embraced the real-life stories of its cast members—actors as writers. This collapsing of hierarchies is critical to social practice, where "the division of labor and hierarchy of creative roles was less pronounced than in New York or Los Angeles," stemming from "relative scarcity of resources."[40] In Raphael's analysis of acclaimed writer Studs Terkel's *Stud's Place*, he argues that the variety show relied on local knowledge to represent "a semi-utopian vision of Chicago culture as a unique space in which popular and elite culture, working class and intellectual, could meet in mutual respect."[41] But even before its artistic innovations, Sternberg writes that Chicago television experimented in management, sales, engineering, and production.[42]

In the late 1960s to 1970s, before BET, Black-produced television emerged in full force after urban rebellions following the death of Dr. Martin Luther King Jr. Chicago had several programs produced by and for the Black community, including *Our People* (WTTW, 1968–1972), *A Black's View on the News* (WCIU, 1968– 982), *For Blacks Only* (WLS, 1968–1979), and *Common Ground* (WBBM, 1972–unknown). As evidenced by the titles, Chicago's programs explicitly focused on Black community uplift in branding and focus. Indeed, the host of *A Black's View on the News*, Don Cornelius, would go on to create *Soul Train*, which started in Chicago on WVON before moving to Hollywood.

Soul Train shows how Chicago's social practice tradition cultivated innovations for the broader industry. It is best known for representing community in the program itself, and it was famously sponsored by Chicago-based Black-owned media company Johnson Publishing of *Ebony* and *Jet* magazine: Black TV production funded by Black media distributors.[43] The program reinvented the live music TV show by bringing in young dancers from its surrounding community and highlighting community-created dance moves. Because it was on a local network, it was able to represent what young people were authentically wearing, unlike corporate programs like

American Bandstand.[44] *Soul Train* thus leveraged a hyperlocal production process to set a new standard fusing music with television. This focus on unapologetically representing the lives of young Black people continued well into 1990s local TV with church-produced shows like *The Awakening* that used television as a medium to discuss intra-community issues in Chicago in ways that national platforms could not accommodate.

We have undersold the role of Chicago, and particularly Black Chicago, in producing and distributing new forms of subjectivity that we associate with twentieth-century modernism and innovation: the idea that the advancement of a community is an experimental political project that combines individual innovations with collective ambitions, working organically together outside of institutions to organize culture. I experienced its continued relevance in my own practice as I worked with communities in the city to develop independent television in the twenty-first century.

WHO IS INVITED AND HOW?

We care if our kin, the people closest to us, will be at the cookout. In Hollywood, we are lured to support what we can never access. Because it's always been this way, it can be difficult to see how our absence in the story development process shapes our experience of films and series. Reparative media, by contrast, helps us see what it looks like when platforms intentionally invite historically excluded storytellers to cook what they want for the people they know.

Hollywood is exclusive, and that is the source of its power. From the Oscars to the Emmys, to the cottage industry of celebrity tours where we gaze at LA's gated mansions, film and television thrives on shutting the gates to those outside the system. To get a studio to develop your story, you must pass through gatekeepers: agents, managers, celebrities, executive producers, and others in the system to value your idea. There are scores of talented writers and directors who have great ideas but no access. Streaming technology has not changed anything about this legacy of exclusion. The early entrants to the streaming market like Netflix, Amazon, and Hulu took a page from the broadcast/cable playbook, hiring most of their executives and buying shows from the same agencies as the "old media." People who come from communities that have been excluded by Hollywood face even higher gates to climb. In my first book I theorize how the web created the idea of "open TV" through open-access platforms like YouTube: No longer did you need exclusive access to get your story seen. Everyone was invited to the cookout. Black, queer, and other marginalized groups embraced the web with zeal.

I designed OTV to be a streaming platform that supported diverse writers in owning, producing, and releasing their shows independently so they could cultivate community through their stories and enter Hollywood more resilient if they wanted to crash the gates. Our goal was to be an open distribution platform but not open to everyone like YouTube. Instead, like at the cookout, we tried to balance the power of local connection and a curated invite list over scaling up to generate big data. Our goal was to help creators accomplish what previous generations of indie web producers did—cultivating community and IP—but more sustainably. I shared the knowledge I learned from interviewing creators for my first book and from producing my own indie work in grad school so creators could leverage indie work to gain employment or deepen their relationships with their communities. Instead of taking IP, we made sure creators retained ownership of their own stories. In turn, they shared ownership with each other and occasionally sold IP to Hollywood studios. Instead of forcing creators to exclusively release with OTV, we shared ownership over distribution, cultivating specific online and local experiences that built connections and bonds. We invited and invested in Chicago's artists to heal past and current harms in media and to mitigate future ones.

How does an open invitation, structured by place and identity, affect who and what we see? We found that our process yielded storytellers who were majority Black and people of color, women or trans/nonbinary-identified, and overwhelmingly queer.[45] Most of all sixty-four original works were made by Black creators (66 percent), and overall, 83 percent were created by racialized people (e.g., Black or Brown, Latinx, or South Asian). That our body of work is largely Black is indicative of a possible revival of the Chicago Renaissance. Yet to test the boundaries of intersectionality, I also allowed white creators to contribute to the platform if their stories met the requirement of centering characters who lived at the margins of multiply marginalized identities. This was designed to acknowledge that white creators can work with people of color and occasionally steward stories that other communities enjoy, for example, Norman Lear (*Good Times*) or Stephen Spielberg (*The Color Purple*).[46] Surprisingly, this decision was uncontroversial and did not spark any discussion or debate in our community; though, as I discuss at the end of this chapter, many white creators struggled in cultivating solidarity with their collaborators of color, revealing a key finding that power dynamics are critical to intersectionality in the development process.[47] Our creators were also largely college-educated, evidence that some class privilege mediated by race, gender, and so forth assisted in the development of indie productions. Creators who could tap social networks for crew referrals and funding benefited disproportionately (see the appendix in the online version).

Disrupting Hollywood's development process cultivated more complex, connective, and collective stories. What emerged from this open, grassroots process is a true representation of what stories creators wanted to tell in this period, unfiltered by platform demands or strategies. We could not "greenlight" or buy shows. All we could do was support storytellers in making what they wanted to. This was organic representation, a stark contrast to what Kristen Warner identifies as the "plastic representations" produced in Hollywood. Reparative stories value the storyteller's unique perspective, unencumbered by executive notes that try to fit the story to a distributor's brand or their perception of the audience. By not giving notes, I was experimenting with what might happen if storytellers viewed their first audience not as executives for brands like HBO or FX but as their community, because they knew we would screen it in person before it went online. This is what a media cookout looks like.

OTV was designed to resist how corporations leverage intersectional creators or communities for future gain. In Hollywood, diversity is for "buzz." In US history, few distributors or platforms have consistently invited creators across intersectionalities.

Hollywood executives develop stories to exploit IP for the enrichment of global corporations removed from the communities they serve. Yes, executives use the word *exploit*. The development process is structured around the pitch to executives. Development executives assess the value of stories using various metrics based on anticipated economic, cultural, and social capital in the existing system: the brand of the channel, the popularity or critical acclaim of producers' past work, or the audience size if the series is based on preexisting IP (ratings, book sales, etc.).[48] This top-down development process obviously does not center the reparative power of stories to address deep cultural wounds. When that happens, it's a bonus. There is an "all-or-nothing" approach to development. Executives reject almost all story pitches and bet big on a select few that have the right metrics, the pitches that meet distributors' demands, or the ones that their competitors want. Stories are bought, sold, and exploited, not nurtured so creators and audiences/communities can be in conversation with each other and collaboratively shape their development. This capitalist process does not lead to stories crafted by people who represent our country or global diversity. It turns culture into trends.

OTV never purchased projects for development. I said "yes" far more often than "no." We nurtured as many as stories as we could where we were located. We did not have enough resources to buy stories, and it would have challenged our efforts: Artists would not have trusted us. We also never heard pitches. In fact, over the years, I sensed artists pitching me, leading me to explicitly state that we lacked the resources to green-light and produce their projects. Instead, within our capacity, we would work *with* them to support story development, connecting them to the material and community resources needed to complete and own their stories.

The stories on OTV are by creators who could best leverage the offerings of our team and their community. OTV is a truly organic platform developed by and for community, not by the platform as a distributor deciding what the community wants. What you see on OTV is what stories emerged naturally in Chicago in that period. We were able to take risks and be honest. We had no other choice.

This diverse, digital media ecosystem is not new. It follows decades of cycles of inclusion and exclusion. New technologies and market trends historically force film and TV corporations to invite or disinvite storytellers. Black, Indigenous, and racialized people have always produced and exhibited stories to repair our systemic exclusion and exploitation. From Blaxploitation to Black Power TV, from public access TV to New Queer Cinema, artists have produced and shared stories amid widespread political neglect and aggression. We have made and released our own stories out of necessity because capitalism has treated intersectionality as a product ingredient, adding a little flavor when the market grows stale.

Throughout film and television history, inclusion has risen and fallen in response to changes in technology, regulation, and the organization of the industry. When companies need profits or innovation, we show up. Critical periods in film, radio, and television history all featured representations of Blackness and queerness, warped through a white supremacist lens. Throughout the history of representation, race and gender have led innovations in the forms and technologies of storytelling. Kara Keeling persuasively argues that race, gender, sexuality, and class are central to how we interpret cinematic reality, shaped by these dynamics throughout film and television history. Corporations use the periodic under- and overrepresentation of racialized, sexualized, and gendered representations to regulate flows of capital by exploiting our desire to see what was previously excluded.[49] Alfred Martin calls this "surplus blackness," the idea that "Black audiences are rarely explicitly courted as anything other than a value-added audience."[50]

A key disruption in TV's limited view of US culture happened on public television and the national movement that Devorah Heitner calls "Black Power TV" of the 1960s and 1970s.[51] It expanded the reach of government-supported television[52] through locally produced community media.[53] Nonprofit foundations and city governments funded this Black media-making to create outlets for Black rage and political thought in the aftermath of the collective trauma of Dr. King's death.[54] Nowhere was this more evident than New York's *Soul!* (WNET, 1968–1973), created by Black queer producer Ellis Haizlip in collaboration with a team of Black women, including Nikki Giovanni. I first became aware of *Soul!* in 2014 when Heitner was presenting her book at the Jane Addams Hull House in Chicago. I was blown away by *Soul!*'s raw expression of Black political power and cultural discourse using conversations, poetry, dance, theater, and music in ways I rarely see on television today, especially outside of plastically packaged talk shows and competitive reality series (the series' best scenes are well-documented in the stunning Peabody Award–winning documentary *Mr. Soul*, produced by Ellis's niece, Melissa Haizlip).[55] Seeing *Soul!* was one of the strongest inspirations for starting OTV and inspired me to collaborate with performance artists and dancers in its earliest years.

The national Black Power TV movement coincided with other US community-led film movements, enabled by cheaper technologies for filming and by emergent queer, feminist, and Chicano/a activism. Black, Chicano/a, and feminist cinemas grew in the 1970s following the collapse of Hollywood's distribution and exhibition model, after the 1948 *Paramount* case outlawed the vertical integration of the original Studio System. Freed from the glut of corporate productions, cinemas became diverse sites for erotic intercommunal exchange during a period of white flight and growing movements for Black, Latinx, feminist, and queer liberation. Writers describe screenings of Blaxploitation films as full-bodied experiences.[56]

As we approached the twenty-first century, media corporations increasingly co-opted cultural marginalization for niche marketing and buzz. They purchased independent film distributors and cinemas while hiring emerging indie directors and producers to work on their own productions, drying up the indie film market. Television largely took over the work of representing America from film. New TV distribution channels emerged following the deregulation of broadcast television in the 1970s and the proliferation of cable in the 1980s. Media conglomerates bought cable distribution channels that segregated communities by race, age, and gender. BET became a channel for Black Americans, MTV for young people, Lifetime for women, and Logo for queers by the 2000s. Yet cable channels largely treated communities as markets,[57] following broader trends in niche marketing.[58]

To support the expansion of the television market, the government forced telecommunications companies to pay cable channels for transmitting their feeds, but it also called for cable companies to carry channels owned by the public. Truly revolutionary and community-based television emerged in the art world, universities, and on cable's public access.[59] Most of the "guerilla television" on public access did not reflect our country's diverse cultural ecology, with rare exceptions like the short-lived Black Power TV movement. Yet there were exceptions, most notably PBS airing the work of Marlon Riggs, whose explicitly Black queer films stoked fear among PBS affiliates that persists to this day.[60] Still, public access cultivated generations of talent who would go on to global fame, such as RuPaul Charles, creator of the first global queer franchise in *RuPaul's Drag Race* decades later.[61] Amid public television's retreat from politics following the Riggs's scandal, public access served immediate community needs, albeit inconsistently. Alex Juhasz covers how queer community leaders used television to share healing information during the AIDS crises, and Frances Negrón Muntaner notes how Latino queer videomakers did the same.[62]

By the 2000s, film and television gentrified. In the 1990s, broadcast television distributors released dozens of Black stories to compete with newly ascendant cablers.[63] Yet by 2000, conglomerates that owned broadcast networks started to buy cable channels too, killing the competition and the need to appeal to historically underserved communities. The result was the near-total decline of Black TV by the time UPN merged with the WB to create the CW in 2006.[64] Meanwhile, cable earned its prestige by greenlighting buzzy, "edgy" Black and Brown stories—*Oz* for HBO, *Soul Food* and *Resurrection Boulevard* for Showtime, *Any Day Now* for Lifetime, *Noah's Arc* for Logo, and so on—only to jettison those communities once their channels reached critical mass. They used the "risk" of diversity to differentiate themselves from the more culturally conservative fare on broadcast TV.[65] But cable's flirtation with "authentic" and diverse stories was short-lived. Instead, by 2010, before Netflix started ordering original programming, cable was largely the domain of who Amanda Lotz calls "the cable guys," white male anti-hero leads who resolve moral ambiguity with violence, sometimes—as in one of the best written shows of this time, *Breaking Bad*—at the expense of the lives of Black and Brown people.[66]

I graduated with my PhD from the University of Pennsylvania around this time. Stuck in my apartment writing my dissertation and unable to build community in the city where I lived, I binged cable dramas to escape Microsoft Word. I started to notice how corporate television differed from the diverse programming of my childhood and from what I was seeing on YouTube. The first years of the 2010s saw waning diversity on broadcast and cable before the rise of corporate streaming.

As Hollywood shut its doors, open-access digital platforms like YouTube invited new creators to tell diverse stories. Indie creators and producers fled to the internet in the 2000s, cultivating new media ecosystems that would face incredible pressure from corporate power by the late 2010s. I started interviewing people like Issa Rae and Ruth Livier, who said in interviews that Hollywood executives were not taking pitches about Black women and Latinas seriously. "It was a learning experience, but the process just felt really, really outdated to me, really inefficient for writers," Rae told me of Hollywood's development process in 2014, the year she and Deniese Davis launched their Color Creative independent pilot initiative that also inspired OTV.[67] "They're really relying on the same formula and not taking into account how much we've grown as a society," Rae added. In 2011 Issa Rae told *New York* magazine that she wanted to be the first Black woman to have a show on HBO; forty years after HBO launched and became the premiere cabler, they still had never done it.

Amid the intensifying debate over net neutrality—an open internet—both Rae and Livier testified to the Federal Communications Commission

(FCC) and US House of Representatives that the open internet was a critical distribution channel for their communities. The first person to join the WGA based on a web series, Livier told the US House Committee on Energy and Commerce that "net neutrality changed my life as a Hollywood entertainment professional. I shared that the open internet put worldwide distribution of media content at the fingertips of independent artists, like me. . . . Latinx communities are largely misrepresented, symbolically annihilated, and/or positioned as peripheral characters in someone else's story. With net neutrality rules in place to ensure that internet access service would remain open, with low-barriers to entry, artists could actively participate in balancing Hollywood's irresponsible exclusions."[68]

Livier describes what it is like to be a woman and ethnically marginalized in the corporate media ecosystem and how the internet's openness offered her hope. Yet despite the testimony of these visionary women of color, the FCC's net neutrality rules left big loopholes for corporations and made scant mention of open-access platforms like YouTube and Vimeo, focusing instead on protecting big-budget players like Netflix. Under the Trump administration, policies designed to support local and educational broadcasting based on the sale of spectrum for 5G were rendered toothless, reflecting the FCC's consistent dismissal of "localism."[69] Nowhere was the government imagining what it would be like to expand public access TV to networked open access.

I was deeply inspired by emerging storytellers building curated, community-focused distribution platforms on top of corporate platforms like YouTube. Indie entrepreneurs knew before Netflix the power of diversity in the "networked era."[70] Unbeknownst to most, Rae was a distributor before she was an HBO series creator. She cultivated a community of Black storytellers in Los Angeles by distributing web series and short films via her YouTube channel, a practice she continued even after her HBO deal. Numa Perrier, Dennis Dortch, and Jeanine Daniels grew a subscriber base of thousands of people for the indie platform Black&Sexy TV, based on the indie feature *A Good Day to Be Black and Sexy* (2009). Several indie queer and Black platforms built passionate followings off indie TV series hits, including SLAY TV (*No Shade*), GLO TV (*Ski Trip*), Between Women (*Between Women*), tello (*N&N Files*), and BRB TV (Ballroom Throwbacks).[71] Still dozens more doggedly worked to cultivate internet channels for historically marginalized creators, including several still in operation like Kweli TV (Black stories),

Revry and One More Lesbian (queer TV), Zeus (started by diverse YouTubers), and WOW Presents (taking us back to the legacy of public access as it was built off global franchises for *RuPaul's Drag Race*).[72]

Community-based indie distributors drastically differ from corporations in how they invite storytellers into the story creation process.[73] As I argued in my first book, *Open TV*, Hollywood's current development process disincentivizes risk and empowers top executives, not the actual storytellers or the communities watching them. The process requires massive multimillion-dollar investments in buying scripts, producing pilots, and/or ordering shows straight to series production. A showrunner like Dick Wolf might get paid upwards of $250,000 just for an idea, let alone a script. Most development money is wasted, as not all scripts or pilots produced make it to series. When shows get the green light, producing full seasons of shows for at least $1 million per episode is a massive gamble that only occasionally pays off in series viewers who want to watch a second season. To alleviate this risk, Hollywood often relies on preexisting IP—popular books, comic book franchises, reboots, remakes, and adaptations—that replicate existing inequalities from cultural history or other industries (e.g., discrimination in the book publishing business).[74]

How can we bring the cookout ethos to Hollywood and transform the politics of representation? Instead of overpaying for ideas or gambling on pilots no one ever sees, studio and distribution executives could release organically developed short-form series to solicit community feedback before larger investments. Lowering the cost of development would incentivize more risk-taking and more deals for younger or less experienced storytellers, which would increase and sustain the diversity of stories and creators. Short-form series with episodes under fifteen minutes are less expensive to make but still offer enough story to introduce characters and worlds. For over twenty years, audiences have shown interest in this form, but the industry has never fully invested in it because it is not as marketable or profitable as IP. Short-form stories let studios and distributors pilot stories *with* community and for communities to offer feedback before they spend more money on longer narratives. Grassroots, social practice development strategies require short-form or smaller-scale storytelling.

In Hollywood, writers create stories to sell and hit the jackpot, alongside cultural, social, and personal motivations. Most US media is still fast food, manufactured with prescribed ingredients and distributed by algorithms and other forms of AI without enough care for those represented. Kristen Warner's theory of "plastic representation," extending her argument that color-blind casting erases histories of harm,[75] connects the art of storytelling to the systems that support its creation. Alongside scholars like Racquel Gates, Cael Keegan, and Jack Halberstam,[76] Warner argues for a shift in focus away from visible diversity, from "positive" or "negative" representation, where "the degree of diversity [becomes] synonymous with the quantity of difference rather than with the dimensionality of those performances."[77] *Meaningful* representation emerges in writing, supported by directing and producing: "Actual progress would involve crafting a more weighted diversity, one generated by adding dimension and specificity to roles."[78] Warner refocuses cultural politics beyond what we see to the systems that determine what can be represented and the creative freedom of the people who craft its narratives. These systems privilege simplicity and marketability over cultural complexity, machine deep learning over deep communal connection.[79] A systemic view resolves representation's many contradictions.[80]

Outside of Hollywood, creators express greater motivation to tell stories to meet and heal personal and community- and system-wide needs and harms. Early in OTV's development, I started to ask artists why they created their series both in our first and last meetings. Not once in over one hundred meetings did creators ever mention the opportunity to sell their project. My research assistant coded their responses and found the top reasons were improving representation or stories about their communities missing in the mainstream, exploring their own history or identity, the need for more complex representations of their communities, specifically representing intersectionality, focusing on the gender and sexual diversity within their communities; representing their unique point of view on culture, representing multiple points of view of culture, and exploring historical counternarratives in intimate stories.

Adrian and Andrew Nuño, creators of the family drama series *Border'd*, were motivated by personal experiences as queer Latinos growing up in a predominantly white neighborhood. Andrew Nuño told me, "I felt many times growing up that I had to be sort of the spokesperson for communities that just weren't terribly prevalent where I grew up. Whether it was having to speak up for the Latinx population because I was in classes where there really weren't a whole lot of Latinx people and people would have opinions about illegal immigration. And I had to chime in and be like, 'Hey, my mom wasn't a legal immigrant. I'm not sure if you knew that.'" Here the personal is political, especially for people who hold specific intersections—for the Nuño twins, who are Latino and queer. A focus on intersectionality reveals specific forms of harm that artists write stories to process and heal. Adrian noted how *Border'd* draws from personal experience to portray Latiné people differently from corporate fare, which disproportionately focuses on crime and on people who speak Spanish, often ignoring the many different nationalities and experiences in "Latinidad."[81] *Border'd* draws its title from the borders that the Nuños felt divided them both from the white people around them and from their Spanish-speaking family.

Creators attend to cultural complexities through personal stories, counteracting tropes and stereotypes that corporations view as marketable. For instance, Deja Harrell, creator of the sitcom *Seeds* about four young Black women, told me, "I wanted to write about Black women that I knew . . . [versus] the idea of the strong Black woman. And I know, especially, the women who raised me are strong Black women, but . . . are they strong? Or are they just hoping in a way? I think it's a myth. Because it puts us in a box. Like, we can't be vulnerable and we can only be this one thing. I wanted to challenge that, and I wanted to show Black women are nowhere near perfect." Harrell's series *Seeds* uses an organic metaphor (the seed) to show the complicated ways young Black women grow into adulthood, inspired by her friends and family, whose strength stems from the messy process of surviving a white supremacist world (figure 3.5).

At our cookout, all dishes that honor the culture are welcome. By inviting producers to create smaller, short-form stories, we cultivated a space for experimentation, new recipes using different kinds of art to expand the form of TV. Episode and season lengths could vary because indie TV doesn't have the legacy of half-hour comedies and hour-long dramas corporations developed to manufacture stories on a large scale. On a smaller scale, OTV welcomed video artists trained in traditional "art world" disciplines from performance to textiles, in addition to music, theatre, dance, and literary arts. These artists created everything from nonnarrative works that could be shown in galleries to more traditional scripted comedies and dramas that became some of our most award-winning projects.

It was important to engage artists who were not traditional screenwriters and TV creators. In the first year, I made one exception and produced

FIGURE 3.5
Seeds (2018).

a short film in Los Angeles, as opposed to Chicago, for my friend Zackary Drucker. Zackary would go on to be a producer for Amazon's *Transparent* and award-winning documentaries for HBO and Hulu, but I knew her as a video/performance artist and photographer who exhibited in galleries and museums. Her experimental short *Southern for Pussy* subverts TV family tropes, the mother-daughter dynamic, to queer our expectations of gender in subtle, boundary-pushing ways. Meanwhile, drag artist Shea Couleé's *Lipstick City* uses drag to queer the women's revenge fantasy, whereas the music films of opera and performance artist Alexa Grae upend our understanding of classical virtuosity through their Blackness, gender nonconformity, and the mixing of pop/R&B with French poetry, sung through Grae's incredible vocal range. Interdisciplinary artist Derrick Woods-Morrow's brilliant *The Roach Is Coming* weaves his personal story growing up Black and queer in the South and his experiences in Chicago with the police, with images of two twin white boys playing as a meditative exploration of masculinity, vulnerability, and power. Dancer Rashida Webb-Miller, whose sensual pedagogy would later be featured in Lizzo's Amazon reality series *Watch Out for the Big Grrrls*, artfully represented her recovery from an abortion by blending Black church "praise dance" with the erotic style she uses as a healing tool for Black women.

Inviting these diverse producers expanded TV's limited representations of art. For example, NIC Kay described themselves as a "mover" in interviews. Their performances press the limits of race, gender, and sexuality. In their docuseries *Bronx Cunt Tour*, NIC takes their Chicago-born show globally to New York and Europe. NIC asked for support, and I offered a $2,000 nonexclusive licensing fee in advance of production, for which they sent five episodes beautifully filmed on their phone. The series lacks a traditional narrative structure and includes long sequences of performances produced for the camera and for live audiences, in addition to extended conversations and travelogues with friends. The "cunt" in the series' title refers to the style of hyperfeminine performance from the ballroom community, a Black queer community practice dating back to the nineteenth century but expanding in the 1980s. The series reconfigures "cunt" performance through NIC's gender nonconformity:

> My ultimate gender performance is that cotton silk robe on the porch with my iced tea in my underwear. . . . When I started to grow a chest, it was a really surprising moment for me, and in some way has always been a point of contention. I just think it's ridiculous that male dancers or male bodied or male-presenting people with no chest, with like, not a fleshy chest even, are able to like, walk in the world, dance onstage, in little to nothing and it be not a problem. . . . I was exploring taking my shirt off in clubs with my cis-gay male friends. And going through that sort of struggle internally. And that's something that I wanted to share. And sort of the freedom that comes with realizing that you can do that. And that there will be repercussions in terms of the way people view you.

Here we see how complex race, gender, and sexuality can manifest in specific experiences and how performance becomes a critical technology for disrupting norms and creating space for other ways of being.[82] As brilliant and nuanced as they are in the history of film and television, series like *Pose* and even *Paris Is Burning* miss or skirt the internal tensions within the ballroom scene, how the codes of gender and sexuality can become rigid even in Black queer community spaces. Someone like NIC would have a difficult time selling Hollywood a series about Black queer performance that isn't based on glamour, fantasy, or competition. Aside from their Blackness and gender nonconformity, their lack of credits would discredit them from even getting the opportunity to pitch; indeed, it is telling that white cisgender queer executive producers are behind both *Pose* and *Paris Is Burning*. Simply put, NIC was not "ready" for Hollywood by its exclusionary standards, but at OTV's cookout, we invited genre- and identity-defying artists, believing their cultural offerings could heal deep divisions.

"Readiness" is a slippery qualifier in Hollywood's development process, highly subjective yet somehow never-changing. In Hollywood, a project's cultural merit is only one of many factors determining your invitation to produce. Often, projects need powerful producers or studios attached, a built-in audience (franchises, preexisting IP), the "right" audience (a desirable demographic), and a story that is acceptable to LA executives, advertisers, and/or the press, all of which are brokered by agents, managers, lawyers, and unions. Streaming has done little to change this. William and Deniese Bielby's systematic analysis of how 1990s TV executives evaluated potential hits still holds true today.[83]

Capital is so concentrated in Hollywood that corporations hear many more pitches than they can fund for development deals. Meanwhile, during OTV's second cycle, before *Brown Girls* drastically increased the number of artists interested in us, sixty projects were "pitched," meaning an idea or treatment existed but there were no resources to start preproduction. Of those, thirty-three projects were eventually produced and released. By contrast, broadcast TV networks alone can receive two thousand pitches each season for only several dozen opportunities for full series licensing.[84] Thus, executives are tasked with valuing a tiny number of pitches over others, relying on status, norms, and various forms of capital.[85] LA-based executives rarely represent US diversity along lines of race, gender, class, and sexuality, thus inhibiting representations before projects can enter production.

By contrast, I met with nearly every artist who reached out wanting to develop with us. We were truly "open television," which is how we were able to expand the art of television itself to include brilliant minds like NIC. Creators were invited into development after they met with me and we agreed to work toward collaborating on a project. Yet many projects came to OTV already produced or in preproduction. When creators were merely looking for a distributor for a completed project, they moved through development faster. A project that was already ready—a creator arriving with a dish ready to serve—was an asset to OTV, unlike in Hollywood where fully produced projects are often cast aside because the studio or distributor cannot shape it to conform to its brand.[86] Most OTV projects were not produced by me or our team and did not need direct production support. Otherwise, projects in development need funding and a production team before we can enter preproduction.

At OTV, a project in development never left development. We rarely rescinded an invitation. In other words, once we started development with a creator, we knew that we may always be supporting their work, even after it was served. For example, we would assist with the development of a second season or advised an artist's overall career.[87] Initially, I tried to help every artist and pitch I received, even if it was not exactly right for the platform, to support a community of producers who I may need for their assistance or work on future projects. Our support typically involved referrals to individuals who could assist in production, distribution, or exhibition and suggestions on how to achieve funding. Yet most pitches aligned with OTV's goals, with the big exception of pitches from outside Chicago. We kept it local with very rare exception.

An open, organic development process is a necessity when access to financial capital is low. For the platform to function, we needed more projects in development than were ready to release so we could pursue different forms of financing at different levels of production—budgets ranged from virtually nothing to as high as $70,000, still inconceivably low by corporate standards. Funding sources at this level came from various sources: nonprofit grants, crowdfunding, sponsors, and investors. Thus, it helped to have a variety of programs to develop to increase our chances of releasing a full slate.

Our flexibility shows how we responded to what was already growing in our local ecosystem, what stories were nourishing artists, crews, and community. Opening who was invited to our cookout showed us the many reasons why people tell stories and how to think specifically about their value. Next, I will show how storytellers specifically produced—or cooked—these stories, similarly leveraging community relations to create the most edifying story to serve.

WHO'S COOKING?

Cooking is at the heart of the cookout, just as stories are at the heart of our cultures. We are what we make and consume. For Black folks, food at the cookout is known for being *soulful*—soul food. Sadly, "soul food has become a toxic cultural asset inside the Black community and a cuisine stigmatized from the outside," Adrian Miller writes.[88] In reality, cultural systems theorist Tony Whitehead argues that "what we are calling a core African American dietary content can rarely be seen today in its purest form"[89] because of the complex influences over Southern Black cuisine. Soul food blends

African traditions maintained throughout slavery, with influences from European and Indigenous practices conditioned by a variety of local environments. In recent years there have been many efforts to "save soul food,"[90] from popular healthy cookbooks to documentaries like Netflix's *High on the Hog*, which focuses on the healthy elements of soul food. Indeed, Chicago has a unique place in the history of "saving" soul food as the purported birthplace of "soul veg," vegetarian soul food distributed by Hebrew Israelites whose arguably anti-Black American rhetoric was rooted in a critique of soul food.[91]

Debates about soul food reveal how what we consume is so important to our culture and how politically charged and important these questions are. It exposes the essential work of tracing food to its cultural roots and uses, the way food grounds people's identities, the stories they tell themselves, its power to gather communities to share information and cultivate bonds. Community-minded culinary artists know healthy and organic ways to make soul food that retain ancestral traditions and meanings. At the same time, as soul food is appropriated and castigated, Black people are continuing to reinvent traditions, organically, at the local level. These practices resist the extraction and stereotyping of local, ancestral ways of making.

It matters how we cook what we consume, and production ethics inform the quality of the product. The antidote to extractive production is cultivating local ingredients sustainably from diverse ecosystems. This is as true for media as it is for food. Communities developing and producing their own food or stories can repair cultural harms. Hollywood stories are produced in high-stress, high-stakes environments, a context akin to fast-food chains or, at best, world-class restaurants, with regimented hierarchies for production, rampant exploitation, and lack of diversity.

Hollywood is vertically integrated. A small number of conglomerates produce most of the stories consumed by the US and a significant portion of the world. The result of these power inequalities is increasing stress among the people who both create and produce our stories. Creators who write our stories are facing pressures on job stability. Increasingly, they have no right to own their IP (seeds or recipes) nor profit from its distribution as global streamers absorb the syndication or residual markets. This inequity in story ownership is particularly troubling when you consider that most women and people of color have historically had less access to owning IP, Black people have *been* property, and Indigenous people have had land stolen. Lack of ownership changes *all* creators' relationships to the stories they tell, since they neither have the power to keep their shows on platforms nor are they paid if it stays on platform (the 2023 WGA strike changed this last point—slightly).

Throughout the 2010s and early 2020s, we saw TV series developed by and for historically excluded audiences, from Black and Brown people to adult animation fans, canceled by distributors too early or even mid-production, while others were pulled from platforms without notice. We're starting to see threats to diversity and labor equality that coincide with industry downturns. Research from Stacy Smith at USC and Darnell Hunt at UCLA has shown that much progress has been made in ensuring Hollywood writers, directors, and executives represent the country, as well as how much more work needs to be done and how fragile progress has been. The most recent WGA data, for example, shows that while the number of women and minority writers reached population-size representation, they remain underrepresented at the executive producer level, who have the most power over the story and most IP ownership.[92]

The Streaming Studio System has not improved inequalities in production. Crew members, like camera operators or sound technicians who execute writers' visions, are in demand but disempowered. In the months leading up to a 2021 vote to strike and shut down production in Hollywood, an Instagram page for the largest crew union, the International Alliance of Theatrical Stage Employees (IATSE, @ia_stories), spread like wildfire, acquiring over one hundred thousand followers in a few short months with an endless stream of anonymous stories about working conditions in Hollywood. The first story was short: a production assistant who worked for twenty-four hours straight and nearly fell asleep driving home. It opened the floodgates. During the COVID-19 pandemic, television and film streaming rapidly expanded as the world sheltered in place. By 2021, streaming platforms had a backlog of stories in development but increasing demand for them. When production resumed, Hollywood raced to produce stories as quickly and as cheaply as possible, leading workers to notice the increasing demand for their labor without the increase in its value. Early in the campaign, workers identified streaming as a critical context for their concerns, releasing spreadable images. The use of bright red with white and black text strikes contemporary viewers as a sly reference to Netflix, with the arrow referring to Amazon and the "play" sign referring to other streamers.

Increasing demand for stories to binge combined with centralized control over the process worsened already problematic working conditions. In the first two months of the Instagram campaign, my lab analyzed a sampling of 115 anonymous submitted posts from crew members. We found thirteen themes, almost all about harm: financial instability, issues with labor and financial distribution, poor leadership, physical health compromise, mental health compromise, long work days, fear-inducing circumstances, unfair compensation, threat of replacement, harmful effects on personal lives, positive experiences, pressure from management, and support for the Instagram account or union action. The three most prominent themes discussed in these posts were instances that posed a threat or compromise to physical health, long working days of either ten or more hours in a day or fifty or more hours in a week, and poor leadership in the form of out-of-touch, apathetic, or abusive supervisors.[93]

We wanted to assess whether the anonymous accounts on @ia_stories reflected conditions in Chicago, so we conducted a survey of almost two hundred of the city's film and TV workers in partnership with the Independent Film Alliance. Of those, 41 percent said they had experienced harm in the industry, and 35 percent openly described the type of harm they experienced. In their answers, respondents focused on four key types of harm they experienced: being overworked, experiencing race- and gender-based discrimination, experiencing sexual harassment, and being used or manipulated. To a much lesser extent, some participants mentioned experiencing toxic work environments, lack of safety protocols, being blacklisted, having funding dropped, lack of communication or leadership, and verbal abuse or bullying.[94]

Harm is embedded in how Hollywood cooks its stories. OTV's storytellers organically took a reparative approach to story creation across the entire process: fundraising, preproduction, and production.

HOW ARE WE COOKING?

In Hollywood, executives green-light stories, and shareholders, mass audiences, and corporate advertisers fund story production. In reparative media, communities green-light and fund stories. Storytellers are accountable to the people they represent before they start filming. Practically, to supplement the $500 to $2,000 that OTV paid to nonexclusively license their series, most creators needed to crowdfund for their work, as seen here with

FIGURE 3.6
OTV's page on Seed&Spark showing creators green-lighting shows from community funding.

our partnership with Seed&Spark, the leading platform for indie TV fundraising (figure 3.6). Some teams also secured state and nonprofit grants that we helped them find and prepare for.

Even short narratives cost a lot of money, especially for communities that historically lack capital investment. The average minimum cost of producing an industry project in the state of Illinois at the time was at least $50,000 for thirty minutes of story. Primarily through crowdfunding from their communities, artists raised well over $500,000 to green-light productions from 2015 to 2020 ($450,000 between 2015 and 2018). This greatly exceeds the nearly $100,000 that OTV gave to artists over the same period (though that sum represented 60 percent of OTV's total operating budget, showing how proportionally we as a platform valued storytellers as much as we possibly could).

Having some funding via OTV alleviated stress for some creators. In 2016 Sam Bailey recounted that the financial support made a big difference in the production process behind her first series, saying it "changed everything: having a significantly larger amount of money going in. Also just like dealing with insurance. It honestly felt like we stepped our game up and I don't think that would have happened without you." Similarly, NIC Kay noted that financial support from OTV was one of the key drivers in helping them to complete the work, stating "Open TV was most beneficial in providing me with the platform and finances to make a project that I could have produced on my own, possibly, but would have never been able to produce with the same confidence because I had the financial support." Jess King, the cocreator of *Full Out*, also noted how OTV's funding alleviated the tension that artists often feel between making their work available to the public sooner and restricting distribution to recoup financial losses: "It helped us to not have to worry about trying to monetize in any way. It was really valuable to us to put it out in the world on Open TV for free. If we had been in the hole and not gotten that funding from Open TV, we might have talked about it a little bit more, 'Should we try to monetize it and then go on Open TV?'" In this way, the financial support provided by OTV alleviated the pressure they may have felt to put their work behind a paywall, limiting public access to their project.

OTV's funding was marginal compared to what creators did outside of the platform, showcasing the power of their communities and innovations. Victoria Lee and the late Shervin Bain, cocreators of *Low Strung*, completely self-financed their project. As Shervin recalled, "I think we were putting away $20 each a week. . . . And then having that add up. We just started doing that as we started writing." Similarly, others mentioned saving money and using personal funds to pick up the cost associated with production. For instance, Ashley Lackinger, creator of the show *For Better*, noted that since she could not afford to pay her actors, she used her personal finances to purchase food for the crew and compensation in the form of gift cards. In this way artists used their own funds, derived from other sources of income, to make up for the limited or lack of budget, caring for their crew as best they could.

The OTV team supported creators by offering connection and consultation, but creators controlled story development and production. Upon request, we would offer suggestions on grants they could apply to or strategies for crowdfunding. After watching creators get certain grants or, in my case, serving on juries myself, my research assistants and I offered to read drafts of grants before they submitted them to increase their chances. Funds from organizations such as the Chicago Digital Media Production Fund provided large boosts in production budgets; indeed, from 2015 to 2020, Voqal Fund's Chicago Digital Media Production Fund granted well over $100,000 to OTV projects. Because we did not own or produce these stories, we often did not know how creators were structuring their budgets, schedules, crews, and so forth—their recipes for production. What they brought to the cookout was not prepped in our kitchen. We could only point them to places to find ingredients and resources.

Grants posed unique challenges. Creators' success in securing them relied heavily on making their work legible to jurors who may not identify with their community. Creators who could succinctly communicate an authentic or uplifting narrative about marginalized communities—trans people or disabled people—were more successful. As one creator noted, "We were just the thing to hit their little diversity checklist. . . . Instead of focusing on how long we've been working in the arts and wearing all sorts of different hats, although that stuff is true, we always knew that that was going to be the biggest selling point." We see here how institutional sources of funding curtail artists' ability to fully express their talents and who they are, unlike crowdfunding from community that relies heavily on showing both one's connection to the culture represented and one's ability to get the story done at a high level of quality. Artists here felt compelled to flatten the complexity of their identities—"diversity checklist"—to attain institutional funding even if their actual stories exposed the nuances of identity.

Crowdfunding, on the other hand, requires flexibility and attentiveness to the diversity and nuanced relationships within communities and social networks. As one creator put it, "I started to rely on just connections that we had built separately in our artistic careers up to that point. . . . The finesse of it all is that I can't just go to someone and be like, 'Hey, money please.'" As the creator highlights, this approach to tapping into community networks is not purely transactional and can often be trickier than just asking for help with services. In addressing this, they had to "code-switch" between communities to underscore the ways in which donating to their project would be beneficial beyond the individual, from the value of the story to its value to the people making it: "For this demographic, for people in our shared communities, the queer folk and activist folk, our statement about representation and how much we care about that and how much we want our set to reflect our beliefs in terms of representation, that kind of verbiage I feel like incites a sense of purpose . . . so you feel like you're a part of a movement." Appeals to community values worked for creators differently. Robert Cunningham's comedy *How to L0ve,* about a mostly Black, Asian, and queer group of tennis "ball" people, reached out to Black tennis organizations and even famous queer players like Billie Jean King to fund their series. Eventually, through personal connections, they received a large grant from pop star Halsey, who is Black and has history with tennis.

Watching artists fundraise was very instructive. We learned from them. We noted successful strategies and platforms and shared that knowledge. Most successful campaigns were run on the film-focused platform Seed&Spark, which offered consultation to creators and eventually developed a partnership with OTV. Julie Keck, cocreator of the series *Full Out* on OTV, also worked for Seed&Spark and conducted a series of workshops to help people develop strategies for crowdfunding. The biggest lesson in crowdfunding is leveraging community. Many creators—such drag star Shea Couleé and writer Kyra Jones, who would go on to write for ABC's *Queens* and Hulu's *Woke*—produced local events to raise money for their campaigns and build buzz. Each event harnessed the artists' connection to community. Shea Couleé's was hosted at long-running Lakeview bar Berlin and featured performances from local drag queens and homemade desserts from the film's costumer designer, Tiger Lilly. Kyra Jones and *The Right Swipe* team held two separate fundraisers for their romantic comedy series, leaning heavily into the show's queer and Black feminist politics with a fundraiser at Early to Bed, a feminist sex shop, and #MeetCute: A Hoetation Lituation with performances from Chicago-based queer performance mainstays like JuJu Minxxx and Cruel Valentine.

All of this was a lot of work. Robert noted that crowdfunding "truly becomes a full-time job." Robert had every person in the cast and crew list ten to fifteen family and friends they could ask for money, making templates for text, email, and social media to support them. Inspired by Kyra Jones and the crowdfunding class from OTV, Robert offered unique perks specific to the series, including customized tennis "player cards" and even offering to read scripts for a select number of donors. Donations came in from family, friends, and the Chicago creative community, and Robert beat his $20,000 fundraising goal, reaching $35,000.

OTV's grassroots, community-based strategy for fundraising also revealed deeper inequalities. Over the years, I noticed that the most successful projects came from artists with more social, cultural, and sometimes economic capital: people who had large social media followings developed from tight social networks in college or university, and artists who tended to live on Chicago's wealthier North Side over the South and West Sides.

Once they have secured funding, creators enter preproduction and recruit a team to start filming. This is the planning stage before projects enter production and start capturing the footage they need to complete the story. Producers hire the crew, find locations, schedule filming days, and troubleshoot the whole process.

It matters when creators have control over hiring, so who is behind the camera represents who is in front of it. Many creators find it very challenging to do this in Hollywood because of how unions, talent representatives, and historically exclusive social networks structure hiring. These systems historically exclude women, queer people, and racialized people of color, though there has been some marginal improvement depending on the type of role.

In Hollywood a matrix of gatekeepers structure hiring: executive producers, studios, distributors, unions, and guilds. Distributors have more power in production. After selecting stories to license from studios, they oversee production and supply most of the funding for writing or developing the story. They also approve key crew members to ensure "quality" via experience, which benefits the historically empowered. Scripted comedy and drama series generally hire union workers, both "above the line" (creative leads like writers, producers, and directors) and "below the line" (the crew who execute creators' visions, like camera operators). In both cases, this privileges workers who are already in the system and perpetuates legacies of discrimination.

Conversely, at the cookout, community and social networks structure hiring. Often, friends of the creator or the crew perform roles at no cost or at below-market rates in exchange for skill building or assistance on their own projects down the line. Rates are often negotiable. Production companies and local vendors offer "family" or "community" rates to projects that align with their politics, promote their talent or wares artistically, or have the possibility of getting developed by a larger institution that could later pay higher rates. At times, filmmakers use traditional methods for preparing for production, including storyboards, call sheets, tax credit and insurance applications, and work-for-hire agreements or union contracts (several guilds have offered "new media" contracts that allow producers to pay below minimums). Yet in the case of very small-scale productions, such as the three-person crew for Rashida Webb-Miller's story of surviving abortion, *Let Go and Let God,* or Andre Perez's docuseries about trans people of color in love, *Been T/Here,* these norms are less necessary. Most indie series are the result of a single or very small team of writers and producers, so the process of staffing series with several writers and larger crews is far less common. Casting is expensive and time-consuming, and thus most creators work with actors they already know and often write scripts with those performers in mind. In all, the flexible and community-centered nature of production at the cookout can avoid the persistent problems of discrimination in corporate contexts.

Community ties are critical resources. Like with fundraising, artists relied heavily on their closest connections to support different aspects of production. For instance, in casting her show *F*ck Stan,* Marrissa Coccaro said that she found people through her networks who she "felt convey[ed] the characters well." Similarly, Jake Noll, the creator of the romantic comedy *Just Call Me Ripley,* highlighted several times throughout production that they used existing relationships, tapping into their network of improv and acting colleagues and soliciting friends for recommendations for production roles. Jake also mentioned that they worked on other people's projects without pay in exchange for them returning the favor and offering their free services on the project. In this way, Jake leveraged their participation in community to fill several production roles at little to no cost. For some, OTV was a key part of this community network. Jake recalled turning to me and OTV for production advice throughout filming. Likewise, Nine Blackmon, creator of the darkly erotic Black queer thriller *Night Night,* recalled how I helped fill one of his biggest gaps by recommending a cinematographer that understood his vision for the series (Christian Meijia).

The intimate scale and low budgets of community-based production put pressure on workers, often causing stress. Yet lower resources engender innovation out of need to wring as much value out of every participant's time, thus showcasing their talent and potentially serving as evidence for greater investment from larger institutions, communities, or crowdfunding. OTV productions lasted anywhere from a single day to two weeks to several months. Producers took on multiple roles, amplifying their "hand" in the project. As I have noted elsewhere, small-scale productions have crews that take on multiple roles, often crossing the above-/below-the-line divide, or what I called "off-the-line" labor.[95] For example, I wrote and directed *Nupita Obama* but also provided craft services, served as an extra, and hired some crew; in *Brujos*, writer Ricardo Gamboa also starred, codirected, and helped cast the series; *Lipstick City* creator-writer-star Shea Couleé also cast the film, whereas art director Dan Polyak also edited it. In all cases, the above- and below-the-line crew also helped promote the project in Chicago and online.

When cooking for family and friends, anyone can help, no professional experience required. Similarly, it was common for creators to perform several roles in the process of making their film or series, whether or not they had training or accreditation in that role. While stressful and occasionally risky, it also created critical space for learning and growing. "We did it all by ourselves," *Yogma* creator and *Renee* producer Karla Huffman said of her and her partner. M. Shelly Conner, creator of *Quare Life*, said, "One of the things I have to do is be the producer, executive producer myself and then do the extra work to find out what that entails." Rachel Relman, creator of the show *Kings and Queens*, said that production was "a big learning experience." They noted, "I got all of the locations, I got all of the food. Paige [Hochstatter], my DP, helped me secure the equipment, but that was something that we worked on together." Similarly, Victoria referred to their crew for *Low Strung* as "scrappy," but cocreator Shervin said it worked because he, Victoria, and writer Ruth Perret-Goluboff had "good synergy": "A lot of it was us just kind of learning on set. You know, a lot of times while we were acting, we were also helping carry equipment around, and move cameras around, and move lights around, and make sure that the cords were plugged in. . . . It was really just kind of us doing everything that we could behind the scenes, as well as in front of the scenes." Artists learned on the job, switching back and forth between different roles and responsibilities. This precarious labor reveals inequalities but also avoids the hierarchies and problematic power dynamics of the legacy system.

Reparative productions challenge hierarchies, making it easier for creators to empower those involved and prioritize the cultural value that workers contribute to the final product. Creators see their crews' cultural experiences as equally valuable as their technical skills. As Sam Bailey told *Okayplayer* about *Brown Girls*, "To the best of my ability, I try to make sure the people in my production crew mirror the story they're helping to tell in front of the camera. . . . I wanted the actors to feel like they were entering a safe space to tell this story without being exoticised or judged. . . . So much of the talk surrounding diversity in media begins and ends with the characters but I think we do ourselves a disservice if we don't extend that to the people crafting the stories behind the scenes."[96] Here Bailey calls attention to the space of the set as a site for creation of cultural value through specific performances. Cocreator Fatimah Asghar agreed that the set's culture shapes the final product: "Everyone was so open, and I'm a huge believer that process is as important as product."[97]

"Production value" dominates film and TV executives and critics assess quality, yet no clear definition exists. Generally, production value describes the quality of all aspects needed to complete a creative work—performances, design, sound, photography, or visual effects. More is almost always better in the corporate system. In general, more expensive or labor-intensive productions have higher production value. As corporate TV studios and distributors have sought "legitimation," production value has been increasingly associated with below-the-line technical aspects, including "cinematic features . . . in real locations and soundstages . . . where manic stylistic virtuosity is materially produced by groups of production workers who labor in dedicated hierarchical teams."[98] Legitimating media in this way can "reproduce unequal structures of social position more generally—certainly those of class and gender—[and is] inherently troubling."[99]

Production value is calculated by time and space: the more time, space, and crew available to film each page of the script, the higher the production value. Scripts correlate to the time of the overall narrative—for example, one minute per page—and producers want each second of the film to have the highest-quality production elements. Managing space—where producers film and with whom—is integral to managing time and value. The more time directors have to try out different "takes" of an acting performance, the more options for the editor in postproduction, and thus the more likely a performance can be read as quality. The more spaces available for production, the more captivating the world of the narrative. The more people on staff to manage production, the more expertise available to fix problems and devise ingenious solutions. Traditionally, money buys you time and more skilled or experienced labor, which is presumably scarce.

Increasingly, in Hollywood, story is less valuable than technique, which is easier to quantify. Stories are cultural in nature. They are necessarily more subjective and contextual than technical aspects. Story and character are the most difficult to define in terms of value since viewers have different cultural perspectives.[100] It makes sense then that film, historically the more valuable form of IP compared to TV, invests more money per minute than television. Standard studio film budgets start at upwards of $20 million for 70–120 minutes of story; conversely, standard budgets average $1–$2 million per 22- to 30-minute episode for comedies or $2–$5 million per 40- to 60-minute episode for dramas.[101] Compared to film, television historically invests less in technical and design elements and more in characters by hiring teams of unionized writers to shape them. Films rarely have more than three writers, but TV writers' rooms historically range from half a dozen to over a dozen. Television sees more value in narrative than film because its business model requires aggregating audiences over time; the more narrative, the more time and opportunities to reach new people, engage current viewers, and monetize their attention. Yet as competition for viewer attention increases, so have television's investments in technical and design execution, while writers' rooms have been getting smaller on average, as cable and streaming shows order fewer episodes, suggesting less investment in story and character.[102]

Like comparing the spread at the cookout to the menu at a restaurant chain, community-based productions rarely meet corporations' technical consistency or levels of capitalization. Yet, these more intimate productions render visible the relationality of production value as cultural as opposed to quantifiable. Reparative productions show us how corporations undervalue the social, cultural, and symbolic capital of their stories. They balance time, space, and capital through intimate collaboration, relying on cultural knowledge instead of big investments in technical capacity. We can see this in Sam Bailey's directing for *Brown Girls*, for example. She recounted the importance of having a queer cinematographer (Hannah Welever) and other crew when directing the coming out scene because she's not queer identified. The emotional reactions of the crew clarified which was the right take to use. Having seen *Brown Girls* screened in front a range of diverse audiences, from the Chicago Art Department to the Frameline Film Festival, I can attest that this worked.

Hiring people you trust but who may not be the most experienced saves potentially thousands of dollars. However, this approach also presents drawbacks in securing sustainable commitment. For instance, Shelly said that when asking for help from friends, "people, they're like, 'Wow, we want to help you. Please call on me for insight and advice,' but no one wants to commit to it." She continued, "the few people that I know who are in film . . . were like, 'Hey, love the project but can't commit. Can give you advice, but can't commit,' you know?" This statement highlights both the advantages and limitations of drawing on community and social networks in the service of DIY production. On the one hand, community networks share knowledge and support. However, because this is voluntary, friends and associates may not be a steady source of support due to their own obligations and limited financial, time, and emotional resources.

First-time creators inevitably face learning curves, and even with community support, it is impossible to foresee all potential challenges. For instance, Arnetta Randall, who created the show *Hook Ups*, said she faced issues when estimating the cost of caring for the crew: "I went over budget because I was like, 'Okay, I didn't really need certain things.' And craft [services] was like one of my biggest ones too, like feeding people. . . . You know you have to, but I think sometimes you can kind of underestimate how much that would cost." Similarly, Derrick Woods-Morrow noted it would be helpful if artists understood upfront what was feasible and required based on a given budget. This lack of experience with what may be needed on set was cited by several artists as a key roadblock in trying to successfully produce their stories.

Ideally, hosts fill gaps in resources and knowledge for those offering to cook food to serve at the cookout, but OTV's hosting did not always meet this ideal. Many noted how OTV could potentially play a larger role in supporting and shepherding their grassroots approach to production. Derrick added, "If left to the devices that I have myself and doing all the work myself, I would hope that OTV would do more because I don't have the time to do all of it. . . . Less getting the materials together but just telling me would be super helpful." As Derrick highlights, while creators often choose a DIY approach for financial reasons, many of the independent artists producing with OTV have little prior experience with production and thus require more guidance from entities like OTV. We lacked the capacity to do this at the time, and it seemed like artists who benefited most from us were those who had experience in production and knew what to ask for.

Several other creators suggested that OTV offer primers on the key roles in production so they can get a sense of what they might need. As one person noted, this "checklist" of sorts could also help prepare filmmakers in how much it would potentially cost to hire paid labor for one of these jobs, giving them a sense of when and where they could afford paid labor and what parts of production they could do themselves or do without. This would also prevent them from cutting potentially critical resources. For instance, in the case of *Seeds*, creator Deja Harell's team cut hair and makeup to save on production costs, which they later realized was problematic on a show with four Black women leads. After 2020, with more resources, OTV created a suite of film courses, including one where Stephanie Jeter taught key roles, budgets, and scheduling.

It is important to note that despite these critiques, many artists cited the important role OTV played in helping to connect them to potential production resources. Many also said that OTV was a potential resource for accessing members of the community who may be able to aid them in their production. For instance, Puja Mohindra, creator of *Geeta's Guide to Moving On*, compared OTV to a "broker" bringing together artists and production professionals such as sound technicians, musicians, and directors of photography. This highlights the importance of distribution platforms as hosts supporting independent creators as chefs for stories.

WHAT ARE WE COOKING?

Chicago's fertile soil for producing community-owned and created stories nurtured OTV. What stories emerged from the city's ancestral practice of socially engaged ways of making? Of sixty-four original pilots, series, short films, and video art works we released from 2015 to 2019, nearly two-thirds indicated a social practice orientation to story development and production. To identify the range of storytelling in OTV, I open-coded these stories released in the first five years in terms of representational strategy. The following themes emerged:

(1) *intersectional friendship*, featuring two culturally different leads who share equal weight in the narrative;
(2) *ensemble stories* featuring stories about
    (a) *love across difference*,
    (b) *difference within sameness*, and
    (c) *true anthology/decentered stories*;
(3) *community as a character*, featuring community/community-based organizations prominently in the narrative; and

(4) *collaboration as a character*, showcasing cross-disciplinary collaboration as central to the narrative.

The other one-third I categorized as solo works: focusing on one person's story or created by one person who held multiple credits (creator, writer, director, etc.). Yet of the few solo works, most were experimental films and series resisting norms of representation to explore the multiplicities within the self. For example, Aquarius Ester's *ambivert* shows her across Chicago in a variety of contexts to uncover how her mental health changes in relation to space. Like *ambivert*, Chloe Fourte's meditation on loss, *Ghosts and Where They Lay*, leans heavily on abstraction to convey complex emotions. Marshall Green's poetic *Triggers* is a letter to his younger pre-transition self that features original dance and music. Similarly, Alexa Grae's *Sur La Nuit* and *I LOVE ME* showcase the various dimensions of their queerness by exhibiting multiple styles of music and abstraction. Rebba Amaris's *Conspiracy Theorist*, Rachel Greenhoe's *Symbiotic*, and Nine Blackmon's *Night Night* explore characters navigating shifting impulses related to neurodivergence. Of course, not all solo-created works fit this description and include a few zany comedies, like Arnetta Randall's *Freaky Phyllis* about a horny grandmother and widow, and Tracie Roberson's *Uneverything*, a hilarious sitcom about a directionless single woman.

In all, however, OTV's cookout served stories with a collective orientation, emphasizing how we survive and heal together. Perhaps because most OTV creators did not have degrees in screenwriting, their stories rejected characters' linear agency and resolvable conflicts that Jess King notes are characteristic of the corporate narrative form. Instead, they embraced what King calls "the interplay of character and setting" that "captures a more equitable, inclusive, and holistic view of the world" emblematic of intersectionality.[103]

I was struck by how few stories focused on community trauma and pain and instead focused on joy, resilience, and solidarity. OTV productions were trauma-informed but not traumatizing. Only around 11 percent or seven productions centered their narratives on trauma or violence, and half of those that did were dramas where all but one left room for joy. The majority were stories of solidarity that decentered individual heroes and victims in favor of collective narratives that focused on the value, complexity, and diversity of marginalized communities. At a time when Hollywood released "Black Lives Matter" collections overrepresenting sensationalized oppression, OTV's stories represented our everyday realities in their intimacy and complexity.

Creators produced the stories they thought would value and nourish their communities. While some of OTV's programs might stylistically bear some similarity to corporate fare, the platform's programming slate skewed more closely to community-based storytelling developed through a social practice orientation.

Collaborative and community-based writing were key attributes of OTV projects. Nearly one-third of our stories had multiple creators, and several had three or more. We encouraged community in the writing process through specific programs, like our OTV Writers Group hosted during our residency at the Chicago Cultural Center; the one-week, twenty-four-hour collaborative, interdisciplinary livestream *OTV Marathon* on ACRE TV; and through specific productions like the *Hair Story* pilot. But Chicago has cultural infrastructure for community-based making. Many writers participated in long-running collectives outside of OTV, including Free Street Theatre, Young Chicago Authors, the weekly curated open mic Salonathon, the Dark Noise poetry collective, the queer hip hop platform Futurehood, Pilsen-based co-op The Dojo, and more.

Overall, nineteen projects had *multiple creators*, writers, or directors—sixty-five people total—meaning the average project had three core collaborators. A few projects had large teams of creators, including *Velvet*, a three-episode series about Black female friendship, which had seven creators, and *Hair Story*, which had two directors and thirteen writers, each of whom contributed characters from their own series. Much more common were projects that had two creators sharing writing, directing, and producing duties, amounting to nearly half of the projects with multiple creators. These creative teams worked collaboratively not only to share the labor and hold each other accountable but also to reflect the complexity and interdependency of identity.

Cocreated works challenged the myth of the solo author. Each of the first OTV projects were collectively imagined by a team of creators. One of those projects featured the work of performance collective Honey Pot Performance (HPP), who Coya Paz identifies as a key practitioner of "ensemble made" or social practice art, now for over twenty years. In 2014, HPP was devising their show *Ma(s)king Her*, an Afrofuturist dance theater work inviting community to cocreate the characters and story of Black journeywomen across time and space. Paz writes that "finding ways of welcoming in the community is key to Honey Pot's practice," where HPP member Felicia Holman says "every HPP show, every HPP public humanities program, every HPP project or event starts from the consideration of improving quality of life for our communities."[104] I started filming the development of *Ma(s)king Her* in 2014 and throughout 2015 to peel back the curtain on their process. In workshops hosted on Chicago's South Side, HPP asked questions of their collaborators and community, mostly Black women, and integrated their experiences, dreams, fantasies, and fears to develop four diverse characters, all played by the collective. Each character spanned Black histories—from the Haitian Revolution to the 1919 Chicago riots—and space—from Earth to unknown worlds. What we see in *Futurewomen*, the docu-series about *Ma(s)king Her*'s development, is an expansion of Black womanhood that goes far beyond corporate TV representations to show how Black women collectively create whole worlds as containers for healing and discovery.

I was most struck by what appeared to be the emergence of a new genre of storytelling in Chicago: *the intersectional friendship series*, where two people of different cultural backgrounds come together to support each other, sharing the narrative, challenging cultural homogeneity, and representing cross-community solidarity. Overall, thirteen series explicitly split the narrative between two or more central characters who hail from different cultural backgrounds, excluding projects with ensemble casts with more than two central characters. Several of these series represent Black and Brown (South Asian) solidarity and connections, something virtually unexplored in Hollywood, including Sam Bailey and Fatimah Asghar's *Brown Girls*, Priya Mohanty's *FOBia*, Nikkita Duke and Aalisha Sheth's *United States of Aliens (US Aliens)*, Karan Sunil's *Code-Switched*, and Vincent Martell's *Damaged Goods*. Other series showed Black-white friendships, including Wanjiku Kairu's *Models* and Kyra Jones and Juli Del Prete's *The Right Swipe*, and Black-Latiné friendships, in Michelle Zacarias's *THOTless*. Still, other shows focused on friendships of characters who have the same race but claim different genders, sexualities, or body types, including Zak Payne's *Kissing Walls*, Shervin Bain and Victoria Lee's *Low Strung*, and Rachel Relman's *Kings and Queens*.

Intersectional friendship series highlight each individual character's journey while also showing where their struggles intersect. They resist the ways corporate platforms segregate lead characters by identity. They are also substantially different from Hollywood's "buddy comedies," where two characters of different identities are put on an explicit mission that drives the narrative, often focusing on policing crime (e.g., *Rush Hour* or *Naked Gun*). Instead, these series illustrate how systemic oppression impacts people differently. In *US Aliens*, Duke and Sheth's characters, Rishita and Uduak, are Chicago-based immigrants from India and Nigeria, respectively. They face issues common to many immigrants, like accessing healthcare or fearing deportation, as well as specific challenges. In an opening scene on video calling family back home, Uduak's long-distance sexual play with her partner is interrupted by their country's poor internet infrastructure, while Rishita ends her call with her dad early when he starts talking marriage after she mentions meeting one guy, once. Sheth said they explicitly collaborated to bring out these themes of the similarities and differences in cross-cultural immigrant experiences: "We don't see multicultural friendships onscreen. It's always like two brown girls or two white girls. Why? Because we live in a world where people of all backgrounds, of all races, of all ethnicities are trying to survive things together. . . . It's almost like the support system that they're creating while surviving individual experiences." We can see the importance and value of intersectionality as a framework for guiding collaboration and dispersing ownership over the narrative.

Ensemble works challenged singular, "representative" narratives. Works that focus on two or more characters offer even more possibilities for representing communities onscreen. Creators highlight diverse groups of people largely excluded from the ensemble genres on corporate television. Adding more characters increases production budgets: You have to pay more actors and spend more time in production capturing sound and choreographing scenes. Yet, despite small budgets, a strong plurality—twenty-one projects—featured ensemble casts. I categorize these projects by three broad approaches: (1) love across difference, (2) difference within sameness, (3) and true anthology/decentered stories.

Stories about *love across difference* show people of different identities supporting each other. Amid the lack of Latinx and queer community representation, Ricardo Gamboa's *Brujos* accomplishes this by representing three Latinx leads who have different orientations to class, family, and different superpowers. They rally queer people of color against the descendants of colonizers, showing "the importance of fighting back in coalitions against systems that grind us down," as William Orchard writes of the series.[105] In the show, we see characters who deal with family members who do not understand what it's like to be in academia (played by writer Isaac Gomez) and characters with complicated relationships to other Latinos (played by Ricardo). Sam Bailey's *You're So Talented* focuses on three friends—two Black women and one white man—and their broader diverse creative community who are all struggling for recognition. Abby Pierce and Cassidy Slaughter-Mason's *Exquisite Corpse* features the rare story about co-op living; cultural differences are collapsed here to show how living together raises more intimate issues, like when and how it's appropriate to have sex. Similarly, Marrissa Coccaro's *F*ck Stan* follows three women of different races who come together to seek revenge on a mutual "fuckboi," slang for a man who uses women for sex without seeking a meaningful relationship. In Julie Keck and Jess King's *FCK YES*, characters of different identities face the complexities of consent—in a sexy way; we see a gay male couple navigating consent in a "hookup" situation and a couple of queer women in a more consistent partnership.

Stories exploring *difference within sameness* focus on characters who share one identity and show differences within the community. Responding to the lack of series about Black queer women's community, Ahya Simone's brilliant pilot *Femme Queen Chronicles* does similar work with a diverse cast of Black trans women in Detroit. In Fawzia Mirza's public service announcement series *You Should Know This by Now*, Asian American actors and comedians from across the diaspora educate viewers on common mistakes and misconceptions of their diverse communities. In Mia McCullough's beautiful drama about a women's shelter, *The Haven*, women of different identities struggle to support each other amid their own triggers, traumas, and histories.

Karan Sunil's *Code-Switched* explores a friend group comprising South Asian, Korean, and Black people. The comedy focuses on how different South Asian people—Hindu, Muslim, Indian, Pakistani—navigate the romantic and professional growing pains emblematic of the quarter-life crisis. Sunil created the show to disrupt the largely solo South Asian narratives in Hollywood (*Master of None, The Mindy Show*).[106] Knowing his own South Asian experience is specific, he spoke to dozens of people and spent countless hours participating in Chicago's art scene before filming: "The process was long, fun, and interesting. . . . I spoke to focus groups of South Asian millennials between 18–25 in Chicago and Seattle about their experiences.

I handpicked the cast, who are mostly comedians, stand-ups, and improvisers. I scouted comedy shows in Chicago for months, everything from paid tickets to open mics at Mexican restaurants and sports bars. I wanted to find five people that embody the character's roles in some way."[107] Here we see how much work it took for Sunil to include multiple voices and artists even as he was representing a community with which he identified, embodying Chicago's social practice values.

Some OTV projects were *true anthology/decentered stories*. These include some of the aforementioned anthology series, such as Christian Mejia's *Born and Raised*, a drama that showcases his historically Latiné home neighborhood of Logan Square through the lens of three different stories that show a range of perspectives on gentrification. In Arnetta Randall's *Hook Ups*, Black people across gender and sexuality experience awkward and life-changing sexual situations; each character is connected to a character in the previous episode, painting a beautiful and hilarious portrait of how the Black community is connected by our different sexual desires, healing homophobia and misogyny in the process. Kate Royal's *In Real Life* performs similar work representing Chicago's queer community, featuring queer and trans characters in various stages of sexual self-acceptance and exploration.

In other series, the *community is the character*, the sole focal point of the narrative. For example, *The North Pole*, created by Josh Healy and Yvan Iturriaga, focuses on the gentrification of Oakland and its impact on Black and Latiné people, whereas Jenna Anast's *Craft Service* takes us from Pilsen to Johannesburg to showcase community organizers and everyday people reflecting on how where they live influences their craft. But we see this theme clearest in Sohib Boundaoui's *Arabica*, which is in part inspired by his sister Assia Boundaoui's award-winning documentary *The Feeling of Being Watched* that explores the real-life story of the FBI's surveillance of their Muslim and Palestinian community outside Chicago in the 1990s. Sohib's approach feels like a documentary. Using handheld cameras, real locations in Bridgeview, and largely untrained actors, he plays a filmmaker trying to uncover the mystery of unmarked vans appearing throughout the neighborhood. The community expresses a wide range of reactions to his interest, from complete dismissal to burgeoning curiosity. Yet the story spends as much time on more mundane narratives of life in Bridgeview, from the customers at the local store who are skeptical of white patrons, to the kids who take the wrong routes home from school. When asked why he made the story, Sohib started immediately by describing the neighborhood and the circumstances of his upbringing as a Muslim millennial: "I started off in film exploring my friends' perspective, what they thought being in the community. . . . [I'd] write scenarios that could easily have happened in that community. I feel like it was a space that wasn't explored, and by having so many connections in the community and being able to rally so much support . . . it was inevitable that these stories were going to be told and it would be a shame if someone outside the community came in and told our stories."

Sohib mentions community several times, signaling the neighborhood as the lynchpin for all his storytelling, not just *Arabica*. Still, it is in *Arabica* that we see his love for the richness and fullness of Bridgeview. The series reframes the community away from their misrepresentation by the government as criminals to a complex array of people who all share Muslim identity but also embody varying perspectives on what it means to live in the context of surveillance. By contrast, a USC study found that slightly more than one-third (39 percent) of Muslim primary and secondary characters in Hollywood films and series were shown as perpetrators of violence.[108] However, *Arabica* marginalizes police presence to show the actual community, which is both specifically Muslim and Palestinian as well as very ordinary in other ways (thus revealing why they didn't need to be surveilled).

Several other OTV projects *feature community organizations* or issues prominently in the narrative. We filmed *Hair Story* at the Breathing Room, a Black-run venue for healing and activism in Chicago's Back of the Yards, and our narrative reflects the pleasures and challenges of organizing as Black queer and woman-identified people. Kayla Ginsburg and Ruby Western's *Afternoon Snatch*, which explores the genre of the break-up comedy through a queer and gender-expansive lens, centers multiple episodes on Chicago-based organizations well-known as critical nodes in the community at that time, including Salonathon, a weekly "performance-based open mic" that ran for six years in Ukrainian Village, and About Face Theatre, the city's LGBTQ+ theater. We see in OTV's programs how community emerges as a character through very specific local neighborhoods, organizations, and contexts.

Finally, we see in a few works the idea of *collaboration as a character*. These stories feature artist collectives working collaboratively to make new works or worlds, challenging the dominance of competitive artistic production in corporate reality TV. The core driver of the plot and the emotional arc of the story revolves around the shifting dynamics of different people making something together. Certainly, *Futurewomen* fits into this rubric but so do other dance-focused series, like Diana Rivera's *Darling Shear* and Jess King's *The Furies*. *Darling Shear* is centered on one character, Chicago-based Black trans choreographer and dancer Darling Shear, who was widely known and celebrated in both queer performance and dance spaces throughout the city. Still, the actual narrative of the show focuses on their developing their biggest show to date for Links Hall, a space well-known for collectively generated and experimental performance, in collaboration with dancers they hired. A critical part of the narrative involves Darling working with dancers to reinterpret dance sequences from classical Hollywood films. As a Black trans woman, Darling's embodiment of that work, even when scenes were implicitly racist, reconfigures its meaning, but the dancers do not share all Darling's identifications. We see how different identities grapple with the politics of identifications in nuanced, embodied, and divergent ways, in ways we rarely see in dance documentary.

It would be overly simplistic to say that these story development and production practices are completely absent in more corporate, national, or mainstream media contexts. It is not that Hollywood lacks ensemble TV shows or stories that focus on communities. But I would argue that few, if any, corporate TV platforms' original programming slates, in total, represent the diversity and complexity of community in the ways we see on OTV or have seen in Chicago historically. What's more, the hierarchies of production necessary to produce at the level and speed of Hollywood means that even when the stories themselves resonate with some social practice values, the context of creation and production rarely does.

These stories were lovingly crafted, nutritious offerings that OTV proudly served at our cookout. What is remarkable about Chicago's artistic production is the consistency with which creators privilege the social and communal, the improvisational and decentralized ways of making often more difficult to achieve in global media hubs. Indeed, if we look across and outside the US, we will likely find a lot of similarities in how stories are produced and told outside of power centers. Amid scarce resources and absent institutional norms, artists and organizers find fertile ground for social practice. With OTV, I was surprised how most programs we developed cultivated this orientation to storytelling. Through Chicago, we see how vibrant, if a little less technically polished, our nation's stories could be if we distributed resources more equitably across all our localities.

WHAT CHALLENGES DO WE FACE SERVING SUSTAINABLY?

Creator- and community-driven practices cultivate a different kind of media system. We see how short-form and collective writing reshape creators' relationship to their stories as IP and the types of stories made. We see the power of community development in financing production. We see how our understanding of production value expands beyond the technical, which big budgets can secure, to the cultural, which is harder to buy and sell.

Reparative TV platforms succeed when they center what storytellers and their communities need and provide the capital to meet those needs. But many hosts like OTV struggle to meet those needs. As mentioned earlier, most OTV creators brought their own social and cultural capital through college-educated networks. Combined with evidence that these stories emerged organically, meaning creators largely fundraised for and staffed productions without much assistance from OTV, this suggests that reparative platforms have a lot of work to do correcting for deep economic inequalities throughout all of society. I met with several creators who were trying to fundraise for and staff projects but struggled to do so because their networks were not as rich. My main strategy for counteracting this was through a queer form of syndication.[109] In the early years of OTV, I "picked up" existing projects and rereleased them on the platform. This was my way of supporting people whose communities were underrepresented on OTV. We rereleased Coquie Hughes's *If I Was Your Girl*, a Chicago-based drama about Black queer women from different class positions navigating relationship and friendship drama amid state and domestic violence; Kalup Linzy's *Melody Set Me Free*, a very Black Southern melodrama produced through drag and lip sync; and the transmasc-led diary vlog series *Outtakes* from Sylvan Oswald, among others. Most of these works did not have the same level of technical production value as other OTV works, but they served important roles in diversifying our slate.

Cookout hosts' core role is serving culture by inviting cooks to serve community. Studios focus on telling storytellers what to serve to match corporate expectations of what people want. With scant resources, OTV generated value for the entire US media ecosystem by focusing on supporting storytellers instead of telling them what they should serve and how they should make it. This is a time- and resource-intensive practice from which corporations shirk but benefit. Over five years, several projects sold to major studios, and over two dozen writers and directors earned work at major media companies. These artists viewed OTV as helpful to their careers. The depth of our support, limited by resources and broader inequalities, inspired them to continue to support the platform and other artists working to gain employment. In the later years of my tenure at OTV, I started hosting brunches during my trips to Los Angeles. From 2019 to 2020, the size doubled, showing a steady crew of writers, directors, and actors working in the industry but eager to maintain a connection to the "OTV community." OTV was not just the viewers of the programs; creators were also our audience. OTV cannot take full credit for its growth. Storytellers were organizing themselves, and we just cultivated a space for them to meet.

Centering storytellers as our core community inspired us to focus on how we care for them throughout the project, even as we also had to care for ourselves. As the platform grew, we had to negotiate between the desire for organic, grassroots development open to as many artists as possible and streamlined processes to ease the stress and workload for the team as more artists sought our help. We started by offering writers' workshops, including a several-month residency at the Chicago Cultural Center that became the testing ground for the *Hair Story* writers' room I created later that year. Sarah Minnie, our head of artist development, formalized the pitching process, including a website for projects seeking distribution.[110] Elijah, Stephanie, and I created the OTV Fellowship program, now in its fifth year, to provide four writers production funding and mentorship: both by staff and by more experienced professionals through a two-day intensive in partnership with the Sundance Institute. We also started a suite of online film courses called OTV Study Hall that ran for four years, providing guidance on how to write, fundraise, produce, and market projects from experts. These broadly distributed the knowledge we were sharing one-on-one. The scale of development greatly impacts how artist- and community-centered platforms can be. The more people and projects in development, the less artisanal the process.

In our first program with Sundance, we were confronted with the tensions of being community oriented and helping as many artists as possible leverage our platform to launch their careers in the industry. Hosted at Lana and Lilly Wachowski's North Side studio, festooned with their Oscars and other awards, our "Emerging Storytellers of Chicago" multiday workshop was designed to connect executives who'd reached out wanting to meet storytellers. Here, I faced the tension of scarcity: There wasn't enough time or time and money to give every storyteller a meeting with two Sundance filmmakers and three executives at Netflix, WarnerMedia, and Issa Rae's Color Creative. I had to select them, as neither I nor the team had the budget or capacity for a jury process at the time. I focused on a dozen storytellers with completed or near-complete series who had expressed interest in being staffed as a writer or director, since that was their most likely entrée into Hollywood. It was my experience that those with multi-episode series with consistent technical production value were more likely to be staffed.

This decision, however, left some writers who had only produced pilots, or produced series with more technical "flaws," feeling marginalized. One even stormed the meeting session uninvited, leading to an awkward encounter. Another shared years later that they felt excluded because of their identity, not their work, a misconception resulting from my lack of transparency over the inclusion criteria. My attempt at inclusivity—inviting thirty artists, nearly half of all OTV creators—backfired. After the event, the team decided we could not do that again. All OTV programs now have jury processes, and all those invited have access to every part of the program. But because of this streamlined process, fewer storytellers benefit.

There is more we can do for storytellers beyond career development. In the conclusion I will discuss how OTV started to deepen our understanding of care in production. Production is incredibly high stress and prone to conflict, at whatever scale. OTV fellow Marlo Abril-Viriña told me, "On every film set there's going to be high tensions and some amount of stress, even some of the most relaxed sets have some amount of stress to them. People are going to get frustrated at some point." They noted a situation where a crew member struggling with their own mental health spit on another person, during the pandemic, necessitating letting that person go and a pause in production. In indie contexts, low budgets often require workers to perform multiple roles or lack the resources to solve problems. In OTV projects, creators are often also producing their projects, which can be deeply personal and often tools for healing. One creator said, "My project was very specific because I came into it with very personal needs and it was a part of my healing process that I managed independently." Because of this, we started to notice that some storytellers were leaving production triggered. That same creator said, "I do think I approached that in a very different emotional space. . . . I was very unfiltered, raw." That artist finished a beautiful production but needed mediation afterward, which we were able to offer at no cost.

Conflicts often continued long after production ended. Indeed, I started to notice that some storytellers who cocreated works, or worked closely with a producer or crew member, left production not wanting to work with each other again. The biggest problems I saw in collaboration fell along cultural lines. It was heartbreaking to see, but most collaborations I saw between people of color and white people—usually between cocreators, between creators and directors/directors of photography, or between creators and producers—did not last. I wish this was not true, but there was too much evidence to avoid it. I noticed it at least a dozen times over my four years running OTV. Conflicts can fall along other lines as well: cisgender versus transgender, queer versus straight, and differences in class, nationality, disability, and even religion can amplify conflicts. Here it is important that we understand what Patricia Hill Collins calls the "matrix of domination." Everyone experiences oppression differently depending on how they identify, a matrix of oppressions and privileges. But people who are privileged—and most of us have some privilege—must acknowledge that our identity may be amplifying conflict. We need to "sit down" or "step back" to listen and allow the other person who may not have those privileges some time to process their feelings.

The specific reasons why racialized people and white people struggle to collaborate is different every time. Often, the question is about power and control, though sometimes the issues are complex and interpersonal. Sometimes personalities just don't match! Different levels of experience among people of color and white people can bring out triggers. Often, white and/or class-privileged people are more experienced in film, a result of broader inequalities that give white people more opportunities in the corporate sphere. This can make people of color feel "talked down to." These feelings of inadequacy can intensify during the high-pressure environment of production, where time is money and every second wasted brings changes and compromises to the story. The feeling of marginalization can be particularly acute when it is the person of color's own story they have written to heal. If production is running behind, as is common, the story becomes compromised—scenes cut, acting compromised, design flaws accepted. This can feel harmful even if unintentionally.

Later in the book, I will discuss how OTV is creating systems to mitigate these harms, but it is also clear that people of color need to own their power in production as a necessary precondition for healing the harm that can emerge in the process. I have seen creators of color get sidelined by white creators. I have seen Black and Brown people have white people write their stories, only to be dissatisfied with the authenticity of the project. I have seen people of color sign contracts that give executive producers complete control over the project, when writers of color who originated the story should be able to decide who the show sells to and who gets to profit. I have seen people of color partner with production companies that offer no support services, leaving all the fundraising and preproduction work to creators of color while the company takes credit for doing much less work. Storytelling reclaims one's authority and history from a world that may devalue one's power, value, and ancestral intelligence. It can be incredibly healing if this power and value is asserted and respected throughout the process.

Despite the challenges, I see tremendous reparative power in producing stories for the cookout. I have seen how community heals even when we also hurt each other. Developing reparative stories makes us aware of our cultural wounds, the stories never told or the lies in the stories we tell ourselves that storytellers are desperately working to repair. Reparative production reveals how the way we make stories draws on organizational practices and technologies that were not designed for healing—basic safeguards like intimacy coordinators or on-set therapists or healers are relatively new in the over one hundred years of cinematic history.

Healing can be painful at any scale. The corporate film and television industry is also struggling with these problems on a much larger scale. At the smaller scale, we have more opportunities to center survivors of harm and pursue restorative justice. I view challenges in indie, local contexts as a reminder that the broader process of healing always involves engaging pain, as well as the importance and intimacy of community in starting the healing process.

Healing how we tell and make stories will take generations, but we will never heal if we do not start now.

4 REPARATIVE PLATFORMS: HOSTING COMMUNITY OUTSIDE ALGORITHMIC SYSTEMS

The power of social media creators surged in the early 2020s, but it took over a decade to manifest. Many creators are independent—writers, visual artists, journalists, dancers, and so forth—and people who work outside of corporations can struggle for legitimacy. When YouTube, Facebook, and Twitter emerged in the 2000s, advertisers were skeptical of creators, the platforms they used, and the massive amounts of data generated from their fan communities. Advertisers stayed loyal to the legacy TV business, the broadcast and cable corporations with whom they had decades-long relationships. They worried that new platforms were cooking the books, inflating views and other data. But in the next decade, creator power became undeniable. Traditional TV viewership declined, platforms strengthened metrics for counting users, and creators engaged millions of young people who saw film and television as old media. By the early 2020s, YouTube generated more ad revenue than legacy TV channels, fueled by thousands of creators.

Creators are also hosts, just like the platforms extracting the fruits of their labor. They create community, not just "content" or stories, and that is the source of their power. Their best asset is not only their talent but also who follows them because of what they share or serve. They engage communities, generating data. This data helps tech companies develop sophisticated algorithmic recommendation systems that sort and discriminate our interactions, generating ad revenue and AI. To maximize revenue, platforms focus on accumulating large amounts of data, compensating most creators proportionately little for the engagement creators attract.

Working as a creator is becoming more sustainable but unequally so, with automated, artificial content moderation partly to blame. Many creators, particularly nano- and micro-creators who identify with communities historically marginalized in legacy media, are undervalued in these systems (figure 4.1). In their study of the "influencer pay gap," Angèle Christin and Yingdan Lu find that social media metrics are racialized. People of color are paid less than white creators, if at all; when they complain, they face online harassment from brands.[1] We often think of these platforms as expanding access for racialized people, but Tressie McMillan Cottom argues that expansion without equity and transparency is extraction: "To both expand and exclude, the platform-mediated era of capitalism that grew from Internet technologies specializes in predatory inclusion. Predatory inclusion is the logic, organization, and technique of including marginalized consumer-citizens into ostensibly democratizing mobility schemes on extractive terms."[2]

Platforms are inclusive so they can extract value unequally. Only a small percentage of mega- and macro-influencers can make money exclusively from writing/producing either independently online or with corporate studios. In their retelling of YouTube's "adpocalypse," Thomas Poell, David Nieborg, and Brooke Duffy describe how network effects meant that smaller creators experienced mass demonetization and marginalization as platform power increased: "An increase in viewers, advertisers, and creators makes the platform more valuable to each of the other groups, which in turn further inflates the number of viewers, advertisers, and creators."[3] Like the broadcast media they overthrew, social media platforms love mass audiences but control creators' ability to cultivate and profit from them.

As social media platforms dabbled in the television business, they ironically copied the Hollywood system's "mass media" logics. Creators and communities with intersecting identities became too small for development or too complicated to target. As the platform with the most video creators, YouTube has never prioritized original programming initiatives, reviewed in my first book's discussion of "big data TV."[4] YouTube's efforts to develop creators and their stories have been scattered, underfunded, and inconsistently representative of its vast global user base. Facebook's Watch program never took off, with perhaps the exception of *Red Table Talk*, Jada Pinkett Smith's talk show showcasing three generations of Black women, another example of how intersectionality offered brand marketing buzz to

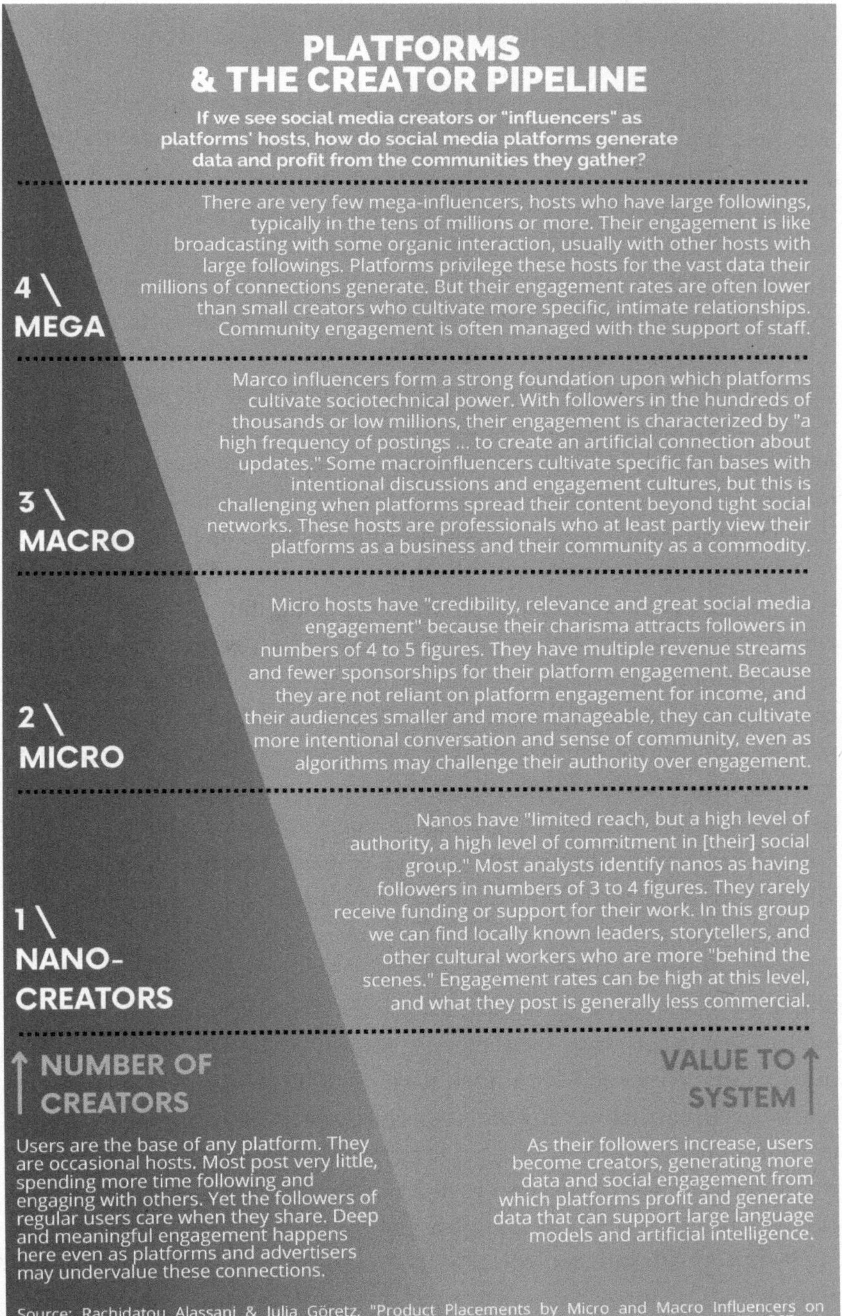

FIGURE 4.1

Platforms and the creator pipeline.

new channels. When I met with Facebook executives in the fall of 2018, they told me that, while they had started licensing diverse shows from other companies like Nicole Byers's *Loosely Exactly Nicole* from MTV, recent Facebook Watch originals were all Facebook owned, just like the rest of Hollywood. Facebook-owned programs needed to be "globally appealing" and "broad," they told me. They were focusing on genre (fantasy, horror, etc.) and drama, with themes that appealed across borders. Comedy was too "culturally specific." When I met with a YouTube Red executive around this same time and sent them a range of OTV programs, the executive liked the acting and writing but said they needed more of a "hook," suggesting platforms' sensitivity to attention-grabbing names and concepts to simplify marketing efforts. These strategies did not work: Facebook and YouTube shuttered their original programming initiatives soon after we met.

To most corporate platforms, OTV is a micro-creator, or host. We were never designed to be broad or globally appealing but culturally specific. Our followers did not exceed 20,000 across Vimeo, Facebook, Instagram, Twitter, and Tumblr during the period of this study. Despite serving our communities rich stories that took years and around $1 million to make, we were not valued as hosts on corporate platforms. The data we generated was not large enough to matter. Many creators we supported went on to develop larger followings and graduate to bigger platforms, but our hosting and serving, which supported the broader cultural ecosystem, had no value. This pushed us to create our own app in 2020 so our community could support our hosting directly.

Hosts anchor gatherings as platforms for community engagement, online or in person. This chapter compares OTV's hosting in Chicago to our hosting on corporate social media platforms. Our work shows what corporate hosts cannot achieve at their scale. At OTV, we valued our creators as hosts, decentralizing hosting duties to support the communities we wanted to engage. Instead of automating or exploiting curation and moderation, we listened to our creators and their communities. This was healing, individually and collectively. Reparative platforms reveal how complex hosting is, how much care and community accountability it requires, and how automating the intelligence needed to do it is in tension with the deeply relational work of bringing people together.

That creators cultivate platforms for community is not new to the digital age. Storytellers, artists, and entertainers have always brought people together. This work has always been valuable, especially at the micro level. Historically, in queer communities, trans and gender nonconformists, from drag queens to performance artists, have been essential hosts and community leaders. In her classic study on drag queens and transfeminine performers in the 1960s, Esther Newton describes how queer community catapulted them to the stage.[5] They helped ignite the US LGBTQ rights movements, and scholars like Jenn Jackson remind us how Black and trans artists were central to everything from the Stonewall uprising to HIV/AIDS activism.[6] Today, drag queens and trans people remain targets of hate in local communities across the US. Queer artists' work has often been undervalued, or when it is valued today, it is more often in competitive contexts on corporate television. Precious few make a living from the stories they tell and communities they gather, on social media or in person.

In the age of global social networking, however, local hosts can become global superstars, showcasing the value of their art and community-building skills, or how small data informs big data. Perhaps best known as a contestant on *RuPaul's Drag Race*, The Vixen spent years as a host for Black Girl Magic, a platform for Black drag queens who are often marginalized and underpaid in Chicago's mostly white gayborhood. Hailing from Chicago's historically Black South Side, The Vixen has spoken eloquently about the importance of Black queer spaces to her artistic development, particularly Jeffery Pub, one of the oldest Black gay bars in the country dating back to 1965, where she started her career in 2013: "A drag queen happened to stumble upon my show and invited me to the Jeffery Pub to perform—and it changed my life."[7] Queens like The Vixen and Shea Couleé crossed Chicago's segregated landscape to create brave spaces for Black queer people wherever they are in the city. Knowing the importance of Black community, The Vixen started Black Girl Magic as a platform to promote Black drag queens in Chicago's North Side. The show started at Berlin nightclub, but after *Drag Race* and an increase in her online community, The Vixen moved it to Roscoe's and started touring the show, promoting local drag artists around the country.

After the onset of the COVID-19 pandemic, we lost our ability to gather in physical space, but Chicago's Black drag queens persisted in cultivating community online. The Vixen knew Black drag queens would be hit even harder by bars and clubs closing, so she took Black Girl Magic online to Twitch, a livestreaming platform that had been purchased by Amazon.

Leveraging The Vixen's hundreds of thousands of social media followers, *Black Girl Magic* was a hit on Twitch, attracting thousands. Digital drag helped the show go global quickly but organically: Queens from Portugal to South Africa submitted videos and performed alongside Chicago queens (always) as well as rising and established drag artists from across the country. As a form of what T. L. Taylor calls "networked broadcasting," Twitch offered gamers a powerful tool to "transform private play into public entertainment," whereas it allowed drag queens to *transform local performance into global entertainment*, bringing the local gay bar to an international community.[8]

However, Twitch was not the most hospitable environment for digital drag. The platform did not pay its creators much for the work they streamed and uploaded. Creators largely supported themselves with tips, just like in gay bars. A former Twitch employee explained the platform's strategy before its longtime CEO stepped down: "It was a bet against creators. . . . We didn't need to be paying millions of dollars. It wasn't necessarily that we didn't fully need [big streamers]. It was that they don't have anywhere else to go. And we need to be profitable."[9] Moreover, Twitch streamers found themselves in a poorly moderated, under-regulated space. Community discussions on Twitch were often interrupted by bots, or creators were targeted with harassment or DDoS attacks.[10] As a host, The Vixen took great care in reminding *Black Girl Magic* fans to keep comments positive, and the vast majority followed the host's rules. But her platform faced another problem: Because of Twitch's collaboration with the record labels that owned IP rights to the music to which drag queens lip-synced, *Black Girl Magic* streams were always immediately removed from the platform.

Seeing an opportunity to attract higher-paying fans and prevent takedowns of the show, The Vixen approached OTV about potentially streaming *Black Girl Magic* on our platform. Executive director Elijah McKinnon negotiated a licensing deal with OTV, seeing an opportunity to attract The Vixen's fans to become OTV subscribers the year we launched our app. OTV streamed *Black Girl Magic* live on our app until the end of 2020, when digital drag in general fell out of fashion as our community became "Zoomed out."

That a small local nonprofit platform like OTV was able to woo an innovative, globally relevant show like *Black Girl Magic* away from a massive platform like Twitch shows how little support social media companies offer their most groundbreaking and community-building creators, especially those embracing intersectionality.

Creators need more support from social media platforms—but not just financially. Platforms are spaces for discussion and discourse, which can be joyful or harmful. We know from many studies that Black, Brown, queer, trans, and women-identified creators are disproportionately facing harm, harassment, surveillance, and censorship, even as their work is most important for showcasing the beauty and diversity of our country and world.[11] Corporate platforms undervalue creators' social and cultural capital as they exploit them economically. Indeed, the Black drag queens on *RuPaul's Drag Race* have for years decried racism proliferating on platforms. They also struggle to attract followers due to censorship and our culture's toxic beauty standards, even as these queens bring so much artistry (and occasionally some much-needed drama) to the franchise.[12] Platforms' automated and exploitative moderation processes have failed to protect them. The Social Media Safety Index of the Gay and Lesbian Alliance Against Defamation (GLAAD) has given "low and failing" scores to the five major social platforms (Facebook, Instagram, TikTok, YouTube, and Twitter) in both 2022 and 2023. "Dehumanizing anti-LGBTQ content on social media such as misinformation and hate have an outsized impact on real-world violence and harmful anti-LGBTQ legislation, but social media platforms too often fail at enforcing their own policies regarding such content," GLAAD president Sarah Kate Ellis said.[13]

Cultural toxicity cultivates solidarity among drag queens, online and offline. In 2020, amid a reckoning on racism and inequality across all sectors globally, Chicago's Black drag queens banded together to form the Chicago Black Drag Council (CBDC). The CBDC "called in" the owners of North Side gay bars to account for their systemic exclusion, mistreatment, and devaluing of Black drag queens. In late June 2020, livestreamed on Twitch, popular Chicago queen Lucy Stoole hosted an accountability session with an expert in restorative justice and several other local queens. As local hosts, bar owners committed to specific acts of repair such as pay equity. Trannika "T" Rex, white queen and staple host at Berlin and Roscoe's, was also called in and committed to stepping down as a host after revelations of racist acts. Shea Couleé appeared in the livestream to tell her story of when T Rex suggested Shea perform Britney Spears's "I'm a Slave 4 U" for Black History Month and then enacted retribution when Shea demanded an apology: "You directly attacked my livelihood, which is an act of violence. . . . You blacklisted me in the community until I got on *Drag Race*. . . . But even after that, you came for my [drag] daughters. . . . My daughters are still experiencing these microaggressions." In a full circle moment, Shea's brilliant daughters—Bambi Banks-Couleé, Kenzie and Khloe Couleé—took over hosting a weekly night at Hydrate, where Shea once hosted, soon after the accountability session.

The success of the CBDC shows the power of queer artists/creators as local hosts and community leaders. Organizing where we are, we can leverage community for accountability and healing, which is much more challenging on global platforms where AI-driven moderation replaces human hosts. This is not to say that accountability is impossible online. As Raven Maragh-Lloyd writes in her study of cancel culture, "The shattering of barriers of communication that social network sites accomplish cannot be overstated; it gives those on the margins opportunities to hold those in power seriously accountable for their actions."[14] Meredith Clark identifies canceling as a "socially mediated phenomena with origins in queer communities of color," one that has always been mediated, whose power has been amplified through digital distribution.[15] Both Clark and Maragh-Lloyd find legacies of canceling in ancestral Black practices for accountability, like boycotting and blacklisting. History tells us that these practices are more successful when supported by community-owned institutions and platforms like the Black press and similar organizations.

Queer people are excluded or marginalized from many institutions, so historically, we look to highly visible artists to take on some responsibility for caring for the collective. Unsurprisingly, in 2020, with the official corporate- and state-sponsored Pride parade canceled, it was Black drag queens and trans activists who led Chicago's Pride March as a protest for Black Lives Matter. That year was also the fiftieth anniversary of Chicago's first Pride "gay-in" protest. Both The Vixen and Shea, rising leaders in the drag community, gave passionate speeches channeling collective rage and resilience. At the same time, Elijah created #4theQulture, a three-day primetime livestream and platform for fifty Black artists to celebrate Pride with skits (including those from the Banks and Couleé families), music performances, and panel discussions among members of the local community (figure 4.2). It was the first program that launched OTV's app, a platform

FIGURE 4.2
Elijah McKinnon and Jenna Anast channel Black trans icon Marsha P. Johnson's Stonewall resistance in the promo for #4theQulture.

doing as much, if not more, to host queer artists as corporations that simply change their logo to a rainbow for one month every year.

Seeing creator culture through artists as hosts reveals the power of ancestral, social, and cultural intelligence over AI as platform protocols. Using intersectionality as a hosting framework, community leaders show platforms how to cultivate global engagement without overly relying on machine learning trained on proprietary, biased, and big data sets. Locally, drag queens hone their crafts and create platforms for others to do the same. In front of audiences of friends and chosen family, they perfect art forms popular on platforms, including comedy, acting, makeup, fashion, high-concept photography, lip-syncing, dance, music, design, film/video storytelling, and even the art of conversation. Building on these ancestral skills, passed down from generations of queens, they also learn how to produce and curate spaces for community engagement, how to talk to other creators, fans, sponsors, distributors, and exhibitors of culture. As we know from scholars like Brooke Duffy, creators like drag queens perform a feminized form of labor that balances authenticity with aspirational aesthetics that are very valuable in global corporate capitalism.[16] As André Brock argues, Black performance also brings libidinal pleasures to platforms, making them cool spaces to digitally congregate, thus enriching the corporations that fail to recognize the power of this labor.[17] Popular drag stars master balancing craft and sincerity, joy, and irony. They attract fan communities that appreciate their mastery and celebrate their specific cultural intersections informed by their gender, race, ethnicity, sexuality, and so on.

The communities that queer creators cultivate are incredibly valuable to the platforms that host them, even as these platforms consistently fail to fully recognize this solidarity work. Instead, platforms can encourage the formation of "neighborhoods" that activate otherwise "inert" users by binding them to those who are similar and repelling them away from those who are different.[18] Like the twentieth-century real-world segregation that created the Black and white neighborhoods in Chicago that The Vixen transgressed, algorithms use this form of "homophily" to "reveal and create boundaries within theoretically flat and diffuse social networks."[19] The term homophily implies love of the same, but Wendy Chun argues it is like the segregation that inspired the network science that gave rise to algorithms, "a call to hate your neighbor as you hate yourself . . . a tool for discovering bias and inequality and perpetuating them in the name of 'comfort,' predictability, and common sense."[20]

Some might see the work of drag queens of color as perpetuating networked segregation and data extraction by congregating similar people—lovers of queer art—making them easier for platforms to target and harder to "convert" homophobes and transphobes. But this fear of "echo chambers" or "preaching to the choir" underestimates the diversity of the choir and the value of historically oppressed people having our own spaces that can meet our complex needs. So much of the discourse on platform "polarization" fetishizes integration and assimilation as ultimate goals, taking a politically neutral position on the harm that happens when different people come together in spaces without hosts who care. Similarly, much of the discourse on "misinformation"—divisive, propagandistic speech—fails to acknowledge that not all information is equally harmful, and some communities cultivate knowledge that necessarily resists official narratives because of how institutions have lied or harmed. Black people know that some neighborhoods and narratives are more inclusive than others. Chicago recently celebrated the one-hundred-year anniversary of the 1919 riots, where a Black boy was killed simply for crossing a neighborhood boundary *in a lake* because of cultural norms: the racist misinformation of segregation. These lynchings continue today and partially inspired the 2020 summer of protest led by Black women and queer people.

OTV's cultivation of "brave space"—because "safe space" eludes our communities—reveals how hosting the choir is much more complex than platforms acknowledge. Because we hosted in-person premieres at the same time as digital premieres, we saw how Black, queer, and trans leaders like The Vixen attracted everyone from white, gay, and straight people to trans people of color to their engagements. As interdisciplinary artists, drag queens also attract diverse fans of fashion, music, makeup, dance, acting, and performance from around their cities and the world. The history of drag and trans performance is one of diverse fandoms, including consistent interest from straight people.[21] The history of Black performance—from literature, jazz, hip hop, and TV—consistently shows interest from white audiences.[22] While we cannot assume that these communities are "inherently progressive," my data suggests that a reparative media framework informed by intersectionality largely resists what scholars like Rebecca Lewis have found: how platforms advanced the kind of white-supremacist-fueled polarization that emerged in full force throughout the OTV experiment.[23]

Hosts guided by intersectionality challenge the extractive and segregationist logics of AI-driven platforms. These automated processes cannot yet fully capture or make sense of the rich, interdisciplinary work of queer and differently marginalized creators. Creators like Shea and The Vixen and platforms like OTV offer tools for combating division and extraction while promoting solidarity and reparation. Even online, we see in our work the enactment of what Catherine Knight Steele identifies as core tenets of digital Black feminism: "the prioritization of agency, the reclamation of the right to self-identify, the centralization of gender nonbinary spaces of discourse, the creation of complicated allegiances, and the insertion of a dialectic of self and community interests."[24] It's not about integration for the sake of scaling healing. It's about creating intentional spaces for people to be their fullest selves, which inspires them to change the culture wherever they are in discreet, impactful, and deeply relational ways.

In reparative media, artists and storytellers are leaders who have a lot to teach us about ethical, sustainable hosting. In the spirit of the cookout, they compel us to ask of all platforms, online or local, Who is hosting and where? What's the occasion? What rituals do we need to celebrate it? Who oversees the vibe, safety, and protection?

WHO IS HOSTING?

At the cookout, the two most important questions are who's cooking and who's hosting. The cookout does not happen without a trusted host, who has cultivated that trust over many years. The host signals to guests who's invited, the vibe of the space where we gather, and the values we expect to be upheld. Hosts maintain meaningful relationships with the guests and cooks. They know who is going to bring what dish (offerings to the collective), what struggles they are going through, what significant life changes they are navigating, who they conflict with, how they will shift the vibe, and how to handle conflict if it disrupts. Good hosts know that inviting people who have done harm and have not taken accountability for it can ruin the party. They may mediate conflict before the party and seek restorative justice if a guest wants to continue to be in community. Hosts know if that person has earned reinvitation, and perpetrators of harm are incentivized to take accountability and stop doing harm to have access to community, knowing the host is not here for nonsense. Hosts collect data from survivors and other people in community to determine if justice has been achieved, by talking to people and listening. Because the host's main task is bringing people together, they know which rituals, ingredients, and information will cultivate a sense of community and solidarity: a sense that we're all in this together.

Hosting is a lot of work, and increasingly the US does not support this labor. Inequality makes hosting difficult. Rising prices for housing drive hosts and their communities away from each other, and rising food prices increase the costs of hosting. People are working harder, and more often, to pay off medical and student loan debts, leaving less time for the intimate work of hosting. All these inequalities are amplified online: Who has time to cultivate community sustainably online when doing so in real life is increasingly challenging? When corporations prioritize short-term growth and profit for shareholders, what incentivizes them to take this much time and care for us, their community of users, even though they have the resources to do it? The toxic inequality in systems affects how communities seek accountability, giving rise to the least sustainable aspects of "cancel culture."[25] We need well-funded, locally accountable, cooperatively owned platforms to support sustainable community building.

I've used the word community so many times in this book, but what is it? For me, community is *the group of people to whom we are accountable.*

This definition expands the notion of community beyond its place-based assumptions, classically defined by nineteenth-century sociologist Ferdinand Tonnies: "one's family, one lives from birth on, bound to it in weal and woe."[26] Indeed, twentieth- and twenty-first century scholars writing in the age of the internet have convincingly argued that community need not be rooted in a physical place.[27] Some argue community is "post-place": "networks of people tied together by solidarity, a shared identity and set of norms, that does not necessarily reside in a place."[28] Too often, research on communities as social networks focuses on individual users and their connections—the nodes and edges in network analysis—and not the work necessary to maintain them, nor threats to the sustainability of the whole.

In a global and digital era, community borders are porous. We can participate in many overlapping communities unbound by place or shared norms, simultaneously. As a Black queer scholar living in Chicago and present on several social media platforms, my communities include my friends, my neighbors on Chicago's South Side, the people I know throughout the city, and my Northwestern University peers as well as, through social media, a global community of scholars, community organizers, artists, and, of course, Black and queer people, generally, across multiple platforms. That is millions of people. I am not accountable to all of them every day, but my allegiances are revealed through digital media's porous networks. Many people have realized this, often negatively without their consent. Every day, somebody tweets or posts something that offends networked communities and suddenly finds themselves besieged by "Black Twitter" or some other online community. We realize that we are part of global networks unbounded by physical space. Online, we are accountable to people we have never met, so we treat each other harshly or competitively, without care. This produces a lot of anxiety on platforms that are designed for increasing the quantity—over quality—of engagement.

Intersectionality is a critical framework for understanding how to organize community, but solidarity struggles to thrive under the automated rules and codes of platforms' algorithms. Instead, it thrives when hosts show awareness of the complex, contextual, and culturally specific rules of power and privilege on interpersonal, intra- and intercommunal, and structural levels. Reparative legacies of community building show how this is incredibly intricate, intimate work, as we see historically in Audre Lorde's call for white feminists to center Black women and women of color in their gatherings or in Yuri Kochiyama's call for both separatist and integrationist frameworks for social justice.[29] This work requires a tremendous amount of self- and community care that most of us are not acculturated to or trained to do. Because of this, it is best done intimately at the local level or in small groups online, where hosts can respond to the complexity of their environments and the people in them.[30] For example, the social media platform Front Porch Forum, moderated and hosted by the people of Vermont, promotes much healthier civic engagement and higher satisfaction rates than any large social media platform.[31]

Corporate hosts like Twitter, Facebook, or TikTok struggle to cultivate containers for sustainable, healing engagement. They delegate accountability to crowds, bots, or algorithms globally. To be sure, there are many types of platforms, and the broader effects of so-called platformization are varied. As Poell, Nieborg, and Duffy note, platformization is not only "top-down" and different outside the US. Here, platforms are somewhat accountable to creators but not for what they create: "If platforms are considered *hosts*, its owners have limited responsibility for the content that circulates."[32] But they are not completely "bottom-up" either. Corporate platforms are not open to everyone and everything even though they want to be seen as that: "There is not one platform that does not impose rules, to some degree," Tarleton Gillespie writes.[33] These rules, however, are outsourced to underpaid workers and the algorithms that drive monetization. Because of this, "platform companies . . . rarely have the interests of cultural producers at the top of their priority list. . . . Instead they are primarily focused on growing audiences and revenue, protecting their brands, and avoiding risks," Gillespie continues.[34]

A key problem with corporate social media is that creators are doing the hard work of hosting but cannot dictate platform rules nor are they given ample support. As platforms incentivize and reward creators who grow their communities, the challenges of hosting increase: "Users within that community will have competing values; the challenge only grows as the community does," Gillespie writes.[35] Platforms do not offer much support for this labor, preferring to instead automate and outsource. They also refuse any politics, let alone a perspective that accounts for generations of oppression and harm to the cultural and physical environment, nor do they claim responsibility for the billions of data points they generate. Contrasting the effective local and digital activism against violent white supremacists in

Charlottesville, Siva Vaidhyanathan notes how it was Facebook that enabled this anti-racist action as well as the disproportionate spread of racism. "Holding Facebook responsible for filtering too strongly or not strongly enough misses the point. The problem is the very idea of Facebook multiplied by more than two billion users,"[36] Vaidhyanathan says.

How do you moderate a conversation with two billion people? Computational algorithms built on machine learning have helped platforms host the largest cookout ever created, processing vast amounts of information to understand our cultures, knowledges, and patterns of congregation. A core focus of algorithmically driven platforms is content moderation, which can be read as a form of categorization and simplification antithetical to the idea of individuals hailing from intersecting, inextricably linked communities. Algorithms and other forms of AI must learn to identify specific inputs and constantly develop new rules to determine outputs, often relying on legions of underpaid workers to develop these protocols.[37] Categorization based on prior data—unequal historical contexts—may limit the extent to which complex, intersectional experiences can be incorporated into machine learning processes. The promise of machine learning is not to capture all the world's complexities but rather to capture *enough* similarities and patterns to provide profitable insights. Therein lies a tension, however, between efforts to highlight stories depicting complex, neglected identities or experiences and the processes of categorization that necessarily reduce and limit their complexity in favor of broad interpretability or generalizability. Algorithms control the visibility of content and, in doing so, also control and threaten content's invisibility.[38] This reality bestows enormous power upon platform owners, who are wholly unrepresentative of the world population.

Despite apparent openness, platforms' algorithmically based processes operate like legacy media institutions in their regulative, normative, and cultural-cognitive functions: "Algorithms . . . have the capacity to directly structure user behaviors, impact preference formation, and impact content production decisions," Phillip Napoli writes.[39] It echoes legacy media's twentieth-century processes for categorizing audiences and selling them to advertisers. Skeptical of the value of demographic information, companies like Netflix are targeting individual users based on their actions within its walled garden, and marketing agencies bring this efficiency to the broader ad-based marketplace that supports the big social media companies.[40]

For generations, institutions have adopted technologies to sort and segregate communities unencumbered by cultural identity, in service of capitalism's focus on the individual consumer.[41] Yet these efforts obscure how identity is itself a technology for organizing communities and value.[42] "Race itself is a kind of technology—one designed to separate, stratify, and sanctify the many forms of injustice experienced by members of racialized groups, but one that people routinely reimagine and redeploy to their own end," Ruha Benjamin writes; like algorithms, "racism is . . . a means to reconcile contradictions."[43] That said, no system is perfect. In the distance between users' identity and (un)predictable behavior, we can "relish the failure of the algorithm to entirely colonize relationality and imagination," Katherine Sender writes.[44]

Our histories with technology and data are deeply connected to the colonization and oppression of raced people, particularly Black and Indigenous people. We can connect Simone Browne's work on the technologies of surveillance in slavery, used to track and transform Black people into commodities,[45] to the digital surveillance and sorting of creators on platforms like Facebook or TikTok, as scholars from danah boyd to Chelsea Peterson-Salahuddin have uncovered in contemporary studies.[46] Scholars like John Cheney-Lippold, Nick Couldry, and Ulises Mejias write expansively on how contemporary data systems represent colonization's newest form, shaping social life and individual sovereignty.[47] Still, this is not new to the digital economy, as theorists like Oscar Gandy have for decades exposed capitalism's use of data to reinforce social inequalities.[48] If we know that humans struggle to cultivate connective spaces, how can we expect machines trained on unprocessed data and exploited labor to do the same?

Platforms devalue the human intelligence necessary to cultivate community and culture, so it makes sense that corporations developed AI using algorithmic large language models to colonize human expression. All publicly accessible information, including large amounts of "organic" data from our interactions on social media platforms, has trained AI. What knowledge does this process produce? Kate Crawford argues that AI is an *atlas*, a creative way of organizing information to achieve varied but specific ends. Corporations are *mapping* intelligence—as if human intelligence can be replicated and rendered "natural and distinct from social, cultural, historical and political forces."[49] The corporate impulse to digitize and automate all knowledge on the planet leads Crawford to characterize AI as an "extractive industry . . . exploiting energy and mineral resources from the planet, cheap labor, and data at scale."[50] From data extracted from our cultures to "ghost workers" in Kenya paid $2 an hour to detoxify ChatGPT, AI represents a continuation of the colonial impulse to control communities through global data regimes.[51]

Automating culture online has colonized our cultural data while underestimating the cultural specificity of place and the complex practices necessary for sustainable community engagement, which is what creates culture in the first place. Tech platforms push toward "binging" (whether on Netflix or TikTok) and refining the process of content delivery on purely technical terms while neglecting the social and cultural specificity of engagement and the ways communities come together. This leaves communities hungry for deeper engagement, having us feeling more divided as we watch in our private spaces.

Repair requires us to decenter our focus on technology and increase our focus on identity and culture, as Seeta Peña Gangadharan argues.[52] Creators are doing this work, but they need help. We need culturally informed, community-accountable digital platforms that can be intentional about why they are hosting, sharing hosting duties, and the information they are collecting. Locally rooted digital platforms have a lot to teach about how to do this. Both locally and digitally, we decentralized hosting while offering support and, eventually, tools for hosts to cultivate accountability. OTV engagements were all nonexclusive. We did not try to lock in creators or their communities to our platform. As a small platform, this would have been counterproductive.

Online, intimate, personal, and community connections fueled OTV's hosting strategy. Our audience started small, naturally. Even though it was theoretically global, practically our audience was local: Facebook and Vimeo data suggested that most users viewed OTV from the state of Illinois. As the elder millennial on the team and a Facebook user since 2004, I invited over one thousand of my friends to like the OTV Facebook page and, in the first three years, invited several hundred people I knew in Chicago to every single local event, publicized primarily via Facebook Events. Our creators shared their episodes, hosted on Vimeo. In later years, Instagram became more important to our exhibition strategy than Facebook, whereas Twitter never delivered high engagement.

In general, the four-year OTV data set suggests that the conditions for spreading complex narratives on corporate algorithmically run platforms is a high bar few creators can attain, at least not without paying platforms directly. We find evidence for this in the distribution of exposure of OTV's original programs, including thirty series and twenty-nine pilots or experimental pieces representing the intersections of race, gender, sexuality, ethnicity, religion, disability, citizenship status, and class from 2015 to 2019. Overall, exposure for OTV programs comprised 3.64 million loads (exposure to video embeds) on platforms and other sites. Yet only two "hit" shows in the first five years, *Brujos* and *Brown Girls*, accounted for over 80 percent of all OTV program views. Seen another way, just two projects (3 percent) represented around 66 percent of total viewership—even though many series released after the two shows benefited from how they grew OTV's exposure and social network connections.

We also see the prominence of these two shows released in 2017 in overall plays of our videos in the same period (figure 4.3). OTV inputted a diverse set of complex, artistic, and award-winning intersectional narratives into algorithmically driven platforms and found that most struggled to spread beyond the artists and their immediate local networks. Data from Netflix suggests this may not be unique to OTV or representative of our

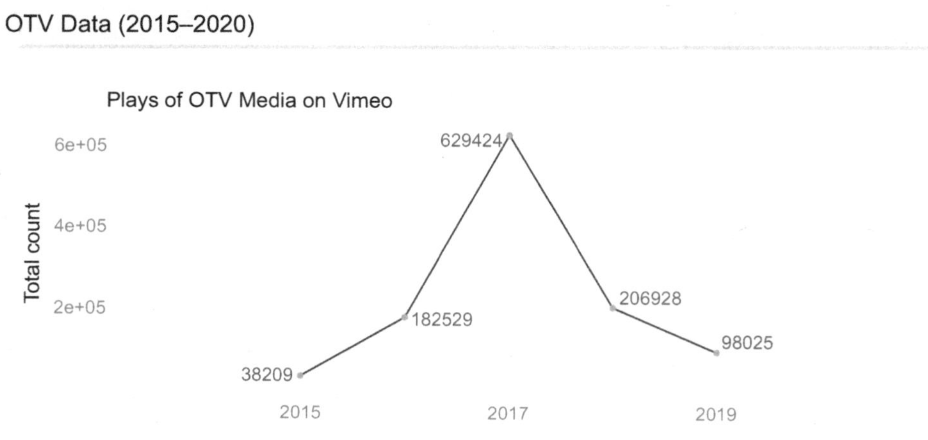

FIGURE 4.3
OTV viewership, 2015–2019.

program quality but rather to algorithms; in late 2023, following a WGA contract stipulating payments for "hit" shows watched by at least 20 percent of Netflix users, Netflix released data suggesting that only 4 percent of their programs are big hits.[53]

We used these social platforms because they were the only options available, except for our choice of video platform. We chose Vimeo over YouTube for a few significant reasons that speak to our hosting values. For one, Vimeo allowed us to hide viewership stats. I wanted our community to focus on the story, not the quantitative data it generated. More importantly, Vimeo did not censor videos like most ad-supported corporate hosts, as YouTube has been known to do. As an advertiser-supported platform, YouTube is notorious for taking down videos from queer creators; many queer creators do not use culturally specific words that are terms of art or endearment in our community because they are curse words when spoken by nonqueer people. YouTube's goal is to protect advertisers from ads appearing alongside videos that don't align with their "values," because ad placements are algorithmically generated rather than human curated. The platform has endured several waves of "demonetization" scandals, where large creators complained of explicit or implicit censorship of their videos for cultural or political reasons, highlighting challenges that smaller creators consistently face.

By contrast, Vimeo, supported by creators directly versus advertisers algorithmically, leveraged this difference as a core business strategy: "YouTube's revenue model continues to place narrative guard rails on creators. . . . In contrast, Vimeo—with no interruptive advertising anywhere on the platform—empowers creators with full creative control," a representative told Tubefilter.[54] Indeed, OTV's experiences with another ad-supported platform, Facebook, reveal how multiple videos could have been censored on YouTube. OTV was unable to publicize two experimental film projects, NIC Kay's *Bronx Cunt Tour* and Zackary Drucker's *Southern for Pussy*, because of their names, which Facebook deemed "pornographic" but in queer community are references to an art form ("cunt" is hyperfeminine performance in ballroom culture) and symbols to be deconstructed (Zackary's film engages hyperfeminine representation to destabilize the trans versus cisgender binary).

Corporate social media platforms were inhospitable hosts of our creators and stories, leaving us with mixed reviews from artists on our online exhibition efforts. Many artists appreciated that their work was hosted on OTV's curated website, no matter how low the views. Zackary Drucker, whose project grew quite popular online after it appeared on a Buzzfeed list about trans art, said, "I'm so happy that it's available on something that's not just like, my personal website, or on YouTube, but on a place that's curated and a part of a bigger community." Echoing this sentiment was Rashayla Marie Brown, creator of the pilot/short *Reality Is Not Good Enough*, a metacritique of Black women's representation on reality TV: "Once it was on Open TV, I think a lot more people took it seriously." Here we see the value of OTV as a host inviting specific people to our cookout, placing borders, however open and porous, around community as a way of valuing their presence. *Starving Artists* cocreator Aasia Bullock also appreciated the logistical support we put into releasing projects in person and online: "I was appreciative to whatever you guys were doing because it was like, thank you guys for taking care of that part because we were . . . just trying to make sure everything was done." NIC Kay noted how online engagement was sparse but had the opportunity to grow steadily over time, unlike in-person exhibitions, which are time-limited: "The videos themselves didn't get many comments . . . and then in person I had some people close to me say that they did get a chance to watch it and they thought that it was really cool. . . . The more time passes, I'm getting more reactions." NIC found evidence of people in their community watching the work online because they were telling NIC in person.

Creators consistently critiqued our online hosting efforts in those early years, with many feeling that OTV could have found more ways to market their shows to communities. Part of this was staff capacity. Fighting algorithms, our marketing team was not paid enough to create bespoke campaigns for each project, though they went above and beyond meeting and advising creators on how to do it themselves. Chris Walker noticed this in their social media marketing efforts: "Whenever you have niche content, you have stans and that's great for us. But I think in order to nurture that community, you need a very online social media person noticing what [artists are] talking about, what they need and, like, *gardening*." Here, Chris shows how cultivating online community is akin to cultivating anything you want to grow organically and how this is even more rigorous online than doing so in person because of the expansive, borderless nature of social media platforms compared to community gardens. We found ourselves trying to host community on lands we did not own and had no say in who was invited.

OTV struggled to establish a "brand" in a digital culture that conflates branding with cultural simplicity and a broader culture that does not value the work of distribution.[55] Our focus on hosting multiple, disparate communities as opposed to one single specific community inhibited our ability to create a unified, static brand perceived as authentic.[56] The deeper reason our online exposure was circumscribed was structural. As small local hosts cultivating specific complex stories, we could do little about it. There was a lot of passion for OTV online from our core audience, largely local. "We have people that are riders for OTV," Chris said, but "we are really feeling a huge gap." We struggled to raise awareness about OTV as a platform. Many people did not understand what we were. Indie distribution platforms, particularly those led by Black/queer people, are very rare compared to titans like Netflix or even BET: "People outside of the OTV universe don't understand that there are folks who are making beautiful work with very few resources and like, it looks good. And this is like where to find it," Chris said. Shea Couleé clearly identified this challenge in understanding the value of OTV's hosting: "People that were all closely . . . involved with the project, they have a great understanding of Open TV's role. But like, the broader audience did not. . . . There's so many production houses [and networks] that get mentioned and talked about . . . you don't really think about it. All you think about is like, you know, these blockbuster moments. . . . A lot of people, unless they're trained to pay attention to those things, don't. . . . People's attention spans are very short."

Here Shea points out the invisibility of smaller distributors like OTV, juxtaposed with the growth of larger streaming platforms like Netflix or TikTok offering "blockbuster moments" in a competitive attention economy. She also mentions the growth of indie producers and collectives at the same time, as creators race to serve audiences ready to binge. Both trends blur the boundaries between indie and corporate platforms and indie platforms and producers as hosts for stories. Online, anyone can host, so how can people easily distinguish the scale of work being done offline? Corporate platforms do not make these distinctions easy.

Offline, OTV had much more control over what stories we platformed and how. In our early Chicago events, Elijah, then head of marketing and design, took a decentralized, artist- and community-driven approach to engagement. Our strategy was artist first versus platform or brand first. "At that point, a lot of people weren't actually making work for OTV," Elijah said. "I think the goal was really, 'I just want to make work and have people engage with it. So how do I do that first?'" They met with nearly every artist individually to craft a specific strategy to engage their specific community in Chicago, so each release was different and not always hosted by OTV. They also encouraged creators to craft unique experiences for their communities, like hands-on interactive exercises or artisanal design elements: "Everyone was under resourced. And what I was wondering was, 'Why are there no collaborations? Why aren't there any partnerships? Why aren't you being more strategic with your engagement strategies?'" To help artists host community, Elijah asked them questions about their lives. When working with Sam Bailey for her first series (and OTV's first release) *You're So Talented*, they collectively brainstormed a specific engagement. Elijah said, "Sam was like, 'Where should we go?' And I was like, 'Well, where do you hang out? Where are you in community?' And she was like, 'In Logan Square' [where she grew up]. And I'm like, 'Where's that bar?' And that's when she reached out to the Whistler. So that was really the engagement strategy: *going to where people were*." We see here how Elijah employed a core tenet of Indigenous methodologies: "Start where you are, it will take you where you need to go."[57]

OTV launched with local hosts who were already cultivating communities without us. We can see the value of this artist-first approach to hosting through the work of Chicago's drag superstar Shea Couleé. Before OTV launched, I was already a fan of Shea, who at the time was hosting a weekly night of local drag performance called #FACE at Hydrate, one of the main bars in Chicago's gayborhood. I was drawn to Shea for what she characterizes as her unapologetically Black performance as "equal parts banjee and bougie" and for her polished fashion, emblematic of her degree in design from Columbia College Chicago. Because her night at Hydrate was in the middle of the week, it was not always the kind of packed, big-budget production she performs today. Still, queens like Shea bring incredible talent, social, and cultural capital to local bars, particularly their ability as hosts to curate art, space, and community: "Booking the girls. That's the most difficult. Everyone wants an opportunity, and I am always willing to give it. But . . . there are so many factors that go into booking a show. Does the bar management like the performer? Do the other performers like them? Does the crowd like them? Do they have a following? Do they fit well within the lineup of the show? Do they match the theme that week? I could go on for days."

Here, Shea identifies the community-based knowledge and skill it takes to host a platform for queer people. Hosts balance art, community, and the institutions between them (e.g., gay bars) that they do not own or control. "The whole process is completely collaborative," she added. "The main thing in creating a show is to identify which direction you want to take it in. Formulate a group of entertainers that fit the brief, and guide everyone to reach their full potential and to TOGETHER achieve a brilliant outcome."

Shea leveraged the community she cultivated to produce and exhibit a short film, *Lipstick City*, with the support of her partner and graphic designer Dan Polyak, producer/drag artist Kelly Boner, costumer designer Tiger Lily, and several other drag queens and Chicago queers. To fund the film, they tapped local networks, hosting a drag revue/fundraiser at Berlin nightclub, alongside an Indiegogo to leverage online support from fans. To produce it, Shea and her team called in favors to secure locations and other production resources. *Lipstick City* premiered at Gman Tavern, a bar next to Smartbar, home of the infamous weekly queer house/EDM dance party *Queen!* that Shea sometimes cohosted. At the premiere, they screened the film several times to a packed and excited crowd. It was profound how Shea proved not only her star power as an artist but also the power of her community ties, while screening at a venue where that community often finds itself. Within a year after *Lipstick City*, Shea was cast on season nine of *RuPaul's Drag Race*, where she was a finalist, and rocketed to stardom even before she won *RuPaul's Drag Race: All Stars* a few years later. I imagine few of her over one million social media followers knew all the work and connection it took to create global stardom.

Hosts' specific connections to spaces defined most of OTV's early releases. In our first set of releases in 2015 for *Nupita Obama*, we hosted three premieres in three neighborhoods where those artists lived or consistently worked. For Zackary Drucker's pilot, *Southern for Pussy*, we hosted an intimate screening in the offices of *Pose* star Angelica Ross's nonprofit, TransTech Social Enterprises, which advocates for trans people who are consistently discriminated against in tech and other professions. In fall 2015 and spring 2016, we partnered with Woman Made Gallery, which at the time had hired its first Black woman executive director, Sydney Stoudmire, for a pair of projects by artists exploring gender: Rashida Webb-Miller's *Let Go and Let God*, a short film about her resilience after an abortion, and NIC Kay's *Bronx Cunt Tour*, exploring gender beyond the binary. In 2016 we premiered Julie Keck and Jess King's drama *Full Out* (costarring *Star Trek: Deep Space Nine*'s Nana Visitor) at Reunion Chicago, a space cofounded by Elijah and Kristen Kaza, one of Chicago's most well-known party planners for queer-woman-focused events; and later that year, Shea Couleé hosted the premiere of *Lipstick City* at Gman Tavern.

In OTV's first couple of years, managing in-person events while also publishing and marketing works online was a lot of work for Elijah and me, so we quickly hired Chris. Chris was working for the Chicago Community Trust at the time but wanted a deeper connection to their community, which overlapped with OTV's (they cited Kristen Kaza's queer R&B slow jam party, Slo 'Mo, as a key site).[58] Even in a support role, Chris embodied OTV's community-based ethos, and their engagement with the platform was artist and community centered: "When I am talking about OTV events . . . inviting my friends and folks . . . what separates this from other work is that I feel deeply invested in what the artists are doing and how they're exhibiting that to the world. And so when I'm inviting people into that, it feels very personal as opposed to like, 'we need people to show up.' It's very much like, 'no, *this is really special*. I think you would get something out of it and you should come' . . . as opposed to like, '*well, we need numbers*.'" Here we see how Chris and Elijah prioritized the quality of engagement over its size. Indeed, all our engagements in 2015 and 2016 were relatively small, under one hundred people each and most under fifty. The focus on the intimate work of connection resisted the impulse in both local/nonprofit and corporate/digital exhibition to see people as "numbers" instead of unique contributors to a specific cultural moment.

Creators recognized the differences in OTV's local hosting versus corporate platform's global hosting, consistently privileging the local over the digital in dozens of post-release interviews in the first five years of OTV. Even as our screenings grew larger and less specifically curated in 2017, creators still found value in bringing people together in Chicago. *Starving Artists* cocreator Dewayne Perkins—later known for his 2023 feature film *The Blackening*—noted how screening his show for a live audience brought a sense of "realness," allowing him to get direct feedback not only from his friends but also from unbiased, potential audiences: "It felt more real because you saw people watching your stuff and they didn't have any loyalty to you. You're like, oh, I can get a good gauge of what these strangers think. Versus all the people that you know, so I felt like that was a good mix." The "mix" is what we can think of as community: the combination of the people we know and hold dear and those connected to them with whom we have looser relations.

Inertia creator Brandon Markell Holmes noted how he appreciated the opportunity to have a more nuanced conversation about his work in person, which also helped him understand his own identity more clearly: "It was a great conversation. I got to talk about really important issues that were surrounding the film, like civil rights and mental illness and premature joining of Black joy and the correlation of Blackness and religion and Black people in the future and being a part of the future, but not necessarily having a fully resolved reconciled past." For Brandon, screening an intimate film as a Black queer person, hosted by a Black queer platform, provided a space to explore the complexities and most healing aspects of his story.

Feedback after screenings stood out as a key benefit of local exhibition. Although it was challenging, the OTV team worked as much as possible to curate a meaningful, substantive discussion around the works. Having people in the audience who shared various identities made these easier and more intentional. For creators, this meant that even though attendance at in-person premieres was always smaller than online viewership in raw numbers, it was more meaningful and fostered connection and even future collaborations. *Geeta's Guide to Moving On* creator Puja Mohindra echoed this sentiment: "One person showing up to an Open TV screening, in my mind, is more powerful than a hundred people watching online. . . . Because I feel like there's nothing that replaces getting to meet you, people having the opportunity to have your face connected in person. There were people that I met that evening that I have continued to keep in touch with. . . . These new relationships and collaborations and creative partnerships [are] essential and hand in hand with everything that you're doing online." Here Puja connects physical presence as critical to building real relationships and receiving feedback.

Connections leading to deep collaboration happened consistently over the years. OTV is not the first or only digital platform to host local events. Several indie TV channels predating us inspired this idea, and Elijah brought this perspective from their prior experience as well. What was original was the scale at which we did it and the lens of intersectionality we brought to it. Showing every single project in Chicago before it went online was a lot of work, more than most other digital platforms do. Bringing together diverse communities similarly contributed to the breadth and depth of our audience.

Hosting locally reveals efficiencies. Simply put, every screening not only attracted traditional TV "viewers" but also the crew members, actors, writers, and directors of each piece. When OTV started to have enough projects to screen multiple films and series together, we cross-pollinated creators and indirectly kickstarted new collaborations and projects. Several times I would see two people from different projects speaking only to have them present with a collaboration years later. I remember attending a screening of Sam Bailey's *You're So Talented* in 2016 and meeting Zak Payne and Nathaniel Tenenbaum, who the following year would release their series *Kissing Walls*, a beautifully rendered drama about Black queer men seeking love in hookup culture. In another case, the screening for Rashayla Marie Brown's experimental pilot, *Reality Is Not Good Enough*, was incredibly underattended due to a failed experiment in scheduling screenings on weekend afternoons in the spring (figure 4.4). Still, because we paired her screening with a preview of Fawzia Mirza's film *Signature Move*, she was still able to connect with famed director Jennifer Reeder, executive producer of *Signature Move*, who years later produced a version of *Reality* with higher technical production value. Despite our fetishization of global audiences in the digital age, local connections have underestimated value for independent and historically excluded storytellers for whom meaningful relationships are more critical to their ability to tell their stories.

Our work shows how distributors are critical hosts and nodes for cultural change. It may take many years, even decades, for the public to understand how abundant and healing our culture would be if corporate platforms and government policy supported smaller, locally focused digital platforms as community-accountable hosts—not "brands"—for our stories.

WHERE ARE WE HOSTING?

It matters where we host the cookout. Spaces carry traces of years, if not generations, of congregation, just as soil carries nutrients from millennia of

FIGURE 4.4
Fawzia Mirza, Jennifer Reeder, and Rashayla Marie Brown at a screening of Rashayla Marie Brown's work. Credit: Jaclyn Rivas.

growth, death, and change. The right space builds trust and fosters community, but intentional space is increasingly rare. The fast pace of global capitalism has increased migration and destabilized local communities. Yet we still desire steady, sustainable relationships with our environments. Digital platforms have challenged this stability, pulling us away from our physical environments and onto our screens while constantly shifting the terms of engagement in digital space. Every year brings changes to platform rules about what they allow on and how they curate their spaces. The result is collective destabilization, a growing anxiety that challenges our ability to grow roots both in our local communities and online. In response, many of us go online and speak harshly, unsure of why we feel more disconnected from each other.

Part of our disconnection lies in how platforms subtly recreate real-world segregation to make it easier for advertisers to target us, as argued by Wendy Chun.[59] She writes, "This is because individuals and groups do not construct the digital environment in a social vacuum, but from positions situated within already existing structural formations shaped by factors such as gender, race and ethnicity, age, social class, and education, among others."[60] The digital environment emerges from our natural and urban environments.

In Chicago, OTV both resisted and succumbed to real-world segregation. The difference between us as a community-based platform and social media as corporate platforms is that we felt accountable to where we were hosting and took steps to mitigate segregation and bridge communities based on where and how we were exhibiting. Locally, OTV was always accountable to where we were and who we invited to these spaces, and our awareness of this only deepened and grew more conflicted as time passed. In the beginning, when we hosted every screening in small community spaces and sometimes homes, building trust and fostering community seemed easy. But as our audience grew, we faced similar issues with "scale" as global digital platforms, just with far less intensity.

In 2017, the year we debuted our season to an audience of nearly three hundred people at the MCA Chicago, we also received a residency at the Chicago Cultural Center, and for the next three years, we hosted premieres there for up to two hundred people. Some of our creators born or raised in Chicago associated these institutions with exclusivity because of their wealth and location downtown and on the North Side, inhospitable spaces for Black and Brown residents who largely live on Chicago's South and West Sides. In protest of premiering their show at the MCA, *Brujos* creator Ricardo Gamboa released their show online one week before the MCA premiere. This was technically against our never-enforced agreement to premiere exclusively with OTV, but we honored this subtle recognition of Chicago's spatial politics and how its legacy of policing and unequal investment affects our communities. When Ricardo showed up to the MCA for their premiere, they wore a T-shirt stating "The MCA Is Elitist" (figure 4.5). This was prescient. In 2020, the MCA Chicago lost the trust of Chicago's artist community, leaving OTV caught in between our need for a space large enough for our growing community and our need to be accountable to that community. More on that later.

Our small team could not produce these events in the same way we did earlier ones, but we needed larger spaces for our growing community. "It was creating more of a system or a formula that we can offer, similar to an entree," Elijah said, using the metaphor of how local restaurants standardize menus to offer the highest-quality products but still customize and adapt

FIGURE 4.5
Brujos codirectors Reshmi Hazra-Rustebakke (left) and Ricardo Gamboa at OTV Tonight at the MCA Chicago.

over time. "The MCA event is a lot different than the way that we show up at the Cultural Center versus the way that we showed up at Reunion," they added. For example, to decenter the MCA on the night of our first premiere, we partnered with Party Noire, a Black women-led collective, to throw an official after-party and screening of their documentary at our smaller community space in Humboldt Park on the West Side. It was one of our most *lit* and freewheeling events. "There was this complete, very synergy-fueled experimentation that was happening in terms of community building and partnerships," Elijah said of this time.

It was harder to experiment with cultivating space online. In 2018, after a year of growth in person and online, the team was near burnout. The project was clearly growing into a fully-fledged platform as opposed to a university experiment. Just like we streamlined our local in-person releases to maximize our internal capacity, Elijah and Chris streamlined the online releases and communicated with artists beforehand on how to talk about OTV and what they could expect from the platform. This increased local awareness that OTV was a distribution platform because artists were told to clearly communicate that. It also made it possible for the team to market every project but at the cost of our ability to tailor our engagement to each specific project. Elijah said,

> We said: "this is what you're going to get." And this is where we developed out the "one [social media] post pre-show," "one post show after release," all of that kind of stuff. And we were able to create a real marketing calendar that supported our capacity and also delivered on expectations. And we aimed really low so that we can over-deliver. And that's why I think a lot of people were very eager to be like, "Oh yeah, I'm on OTV." Because it was explained to them what they would get from the marketing perspective. And it wasn't much. So they were like, "Oh, shit I'm going to have to do more."

Here, Elijah shows how streamlining the way OTV exhibited our work online both gave creators a better sense of what it meant to be on our platform and incentivized them to put more thought into how to host their communities online. Indeed, we found that creators were always the best hosts of their work because they represent their specific identities better than we could as a platform designed for multiple communities.

During the first five years of OTV, the visibility of our little online cookout waxed and waned, often based on shifting moderation and algorithmic norms on corporate platforms (figure 4.6). After it launched its own streaming video service, Facebook minimized the spreadability of videos posted from other video platforms like Vimeo, cutting our views overnight. It also added new ways to react to our videos, changing how it calculated our data as well as how much of it we could access, making our efforts at research more difficult. Facing competition from new platforms like Snapchat, Instagram added new types of videos, stories, and livestreaming, increasing the number of digital assets we had to create. It changed how our videos appeared on platforms from chronological to algorithmic order, separating us from our community with opaque rules over which we had no control. Our community had to do more work to find us online.

To be sure, hosting on corporate platforms can generate incredible value to creators and their communities. In her thorough study of how musicians engage fans, Nancy Baym finds that social media erases some of the boundaries between performers and their fans that are reinforced in physical spaces: "Concert halls limit and constrain the norms and forms of communication, as well as the relational dynamics among those there. Social media unbind them, opening an array of relational possibilities while imposing constraints of their own."[61] Still, the constraints of social media platforms can prove quite vexing, Baym finds, including the difficulty in identifying true fans and platforms' loose and ever-changing content moderation policies. If OTV found more success locally, it could be because our

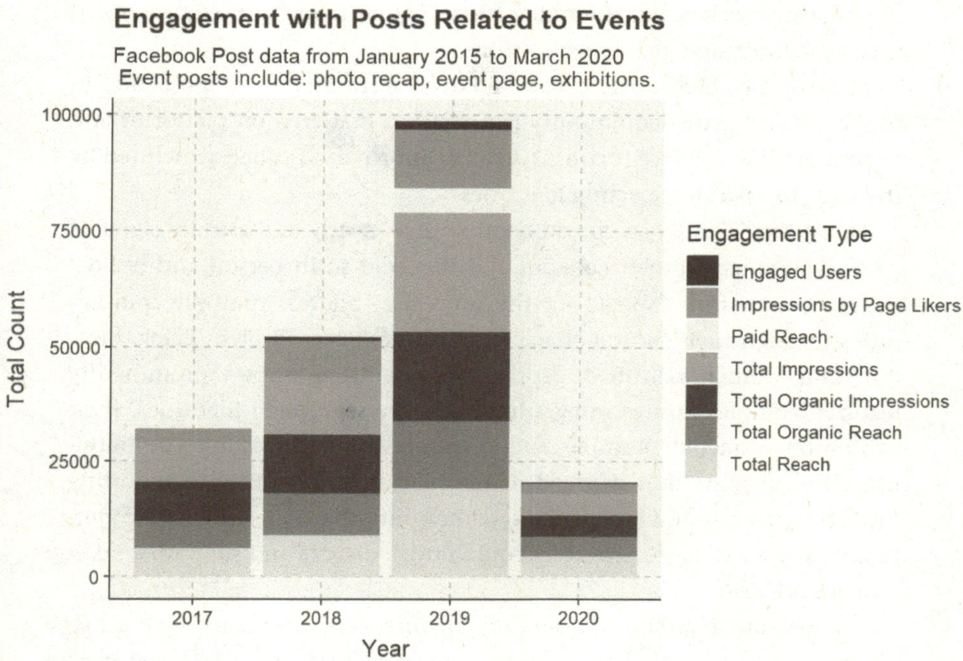

FIGURE 4.6

Data from Facebook, where we published all our local Chicago events, indicates a significant rise in interest after *Brown Girls* and *Brujos* and after the OTV team streamlined our marketing support, followed by a steep decline during the pandemic.

venues were generally more intimate and less rigidly structured than the standard concert halls, and our online audience emerged organically from our local one, both of which were by design.

As a distributor of complex yet underfunded stories that took years to write, fund, and produce, OTV was not a space from which many stories spread widely on corporate platforms. Yet some OTV stories did spread widely on platforms. Our two most popular programs, *Brown Girls* and *Brujos*, offer unique case studies on the differences hosting online versus in person.

Both *Brown Girls* and *Brujos* spread widely online. My simplest hypothesis is that by signaling race, ethnicity, and gender in their titles and sexuality in their beautifully executed trailers, both series were intelligible to algorithms and users. "Brown girls" can refer to Asian, Latinx, or Black women, all of whom were featured in the trailer, whereas "brujos" refers to male Latiné witches, but the trailer shows Latinx men of different ethnicities, sexualities, and gender expressions.

More deeply, both series connected diverse communities online and in the real world. Artist-community connections mattered on platforms and in person. These different contexts can reinforce each other, structured by the creators' own intersecting identities.

Brown Girls and *Brujos* spread because they clearly and artfully signaled who was invited to their cookout and then did so in person and online. Intersectional stories spread for the ways they address multiple communities through their central characters—Latiné, queer, Brown, Black, Muslim, and women-identified people. Because these shows prominently featured complex stories integrating normally segregated identities, their exhibition attracted multiple and disparate but intersecting communities. This suggests that if social media platforms focused on supporting intersectionality—and independent community-specific platforms for journalism and entertainment—they could bridge divides and support solidarity over division.

When we analyzed how *Brown Girls* and *Brujos* circulated on social media, we found an interesting conundrum: Although both series amassed hundreds of thousands of views, few came directly from social media platforms. Online, it is possible that these shows were able to resist networked segregation by extending their reach beyond social media platforms. Excluding Vimeo.com, where the videos were located, overall exposure on other social platforms was markedly smaller. Each series' spreadability was likely driven by factors outside of social media exhibition.

The most important online hosts for these series were identity-specific press websites and the artists themselves as sincere holders of those identities. Websites that regularly serve specific communities drove them to watch *Brown Girls* and *Brujos*. This does not completely negate the role of social media platforms. Indeed, it is likely that many viewers found out about *Brown Girls* and *Brujos* from social media shares of articles from identity-specific press. Yet there is strong evidence that coverage from publications that consistently covered specific identities indicated to viewers these shows were "for them." We saw this across projects, along different identity lines, but it worked best when the stories related to what communities wanted to see. For instance, the queer dance drama *Full Out* received well over ten thousand views for its pilot when StarTrek.com posted about it because

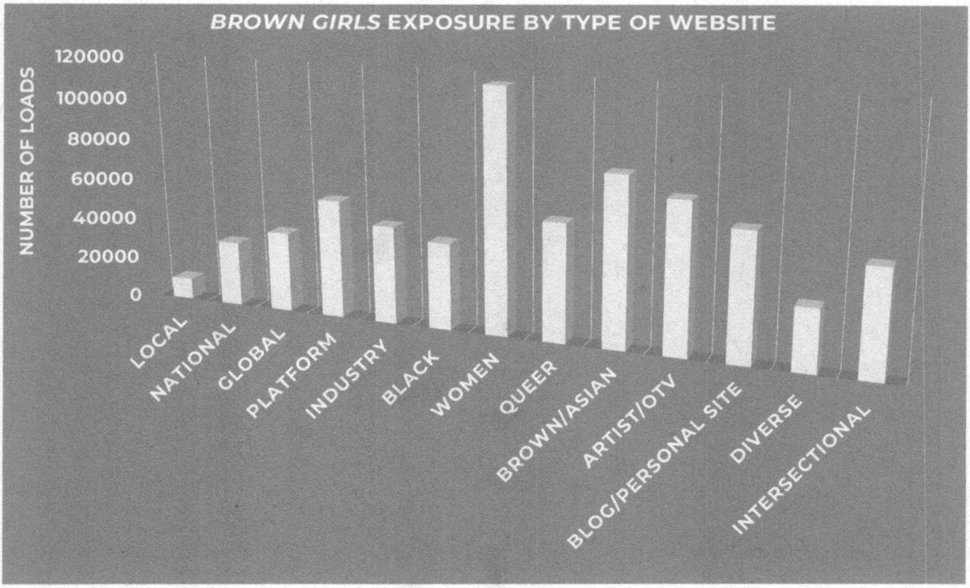

FIGURE 4.7
Exposure (page loads) of *Brown Girls* trailer by website target audience.

it starred Nana Visitor from *Star Trek: Deep Space Nine*. However, because *Full Out* was written for queer women and dance fans—not *Star Trek*'s sci-fi community—most of those views did not sustain across all episodes.

To understand where communities show up online, we categorized every website that embedded the *Brown Girls* and *Brujos* trailers by primary target audience across thirteen types and categories: local, national, global, industry (entertainment), Black, women, queer, Latinx/Asian/Asian American, artists/OTV, multicultural, intersectional, and platform (general social media, e.g., Facebook).[62]

Identity-specific exhibition was critical to the online circulation of these stories, at least equally valuable as social platforms (figures 4.7 and 4.8). For *Brown Girls*, Latiné, Asian, and women's media drove the plurality of views, driven by coverage first from *Remezcla* (covering Latiné culture) and then *Elle* (women), *Autostraddle* (queer women), NBC Asian America, and *Jezebel* (women). Fusion, an independent multicultural site, was also a strong driver. Meanwhile, for *Brujos*, *Remezcla* contributed more exposure than any site, followed by NewNowNext (queer), AfroPunk (Black), and *Out*

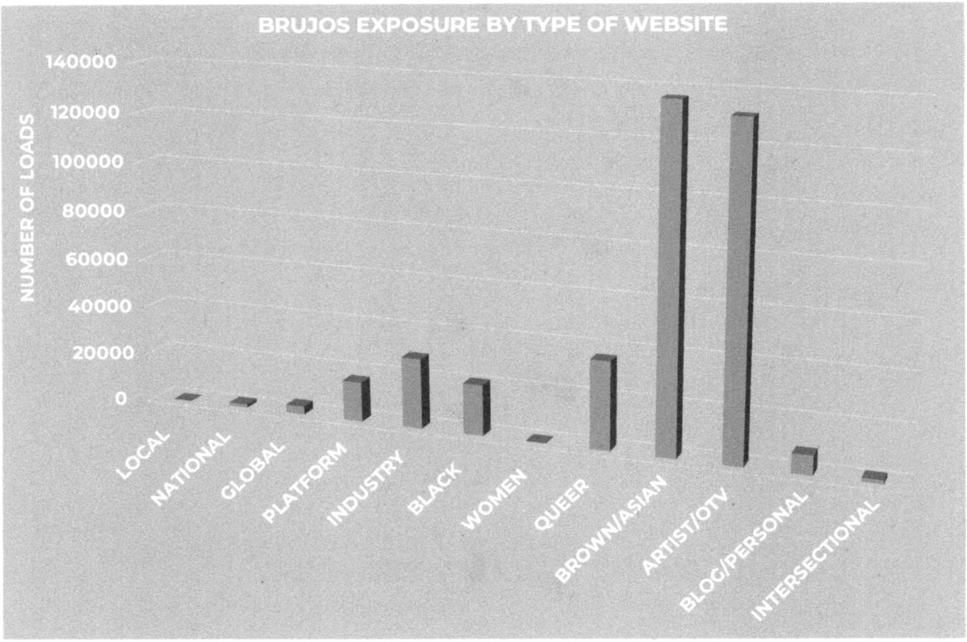

FIGURE 4.8
Exposure (page loads) of *Brujos* trailer by website target audience.

(queer); after those, Latino Rebels contributed almost as may views as *Vice*, a national site with a much wider reach. *Remezcla*, in fact, provided the most exposure to OTV programs overall because of its coverage of *Brown Girls* and *Brujos*, despite being a site without much mainstream recognition. Overall, the scale of exhibition from identity-specific sites constituted a strong plurality of *Brown Girls'* exposure, nearly equaling exposure on Vimeo and totaling over *five times* exposure on social platforms Facebook, Twitter, and Tumblr. For *Brujos*, identity-specific sites exceeded exposure over *ten times* than social media platforms.

The data also suggests that creators as online hosts were key drivers of engagement, as they are the most specific representatives of their intersecting identities. For *Brown Girls*, which received more press than most indie TV series at eighty-six articles from 2016 and 2017, and *Brujos*, which received twenty-two over the same period, their own websites and social media presences, alongside those of their collaborators, delivered a disproportionate amount of exposure: for *Brujos*, ranking second, and for *Brown*

Girls, fourth, among all exposure.[63] In their trailer, the *Brown Girls* team referred fans to their own website, and *Brujos*'s website amassed most of the exposure after *Remezcla* embedded it. We can also see the importance of intersectional artists' own efforts at self-representation in their overall social media reach: *Brown Girls* had 9,360 followers on Instagram and *Brujos* had 2,705 followers on Facebook, exceeding that of OTV, which had 2,009 followers on Instagram and 2,444 followers Facebook at the time.

Cultural identity matters online, in complicated ways. Tweets using #BrownGirlsTV and #BrujosTV show a sophisticated focus on intersectionality and the politics of representation, like what we see with engagement with legacy texts like *Scandal*.[64] The top tweeters (hosts) for *Brown Girls* prioritized specific, historically marginalized communities: Eve Ewing, a prominent Black feminist scholar, writer and poet in Chicago and the official host of the online premiere; the *Brown Girls* account; podcast host BlackGirlCheerleader; and the website Black Nerd Problems. For instance, several users used GIFs to highlight Leila's "coming out" scene by quoting her sister who says, "All that hiding is going to kill you" (hiding from her Muslim elders), "We have so much family that's not blood family" (referring to queer chosen family), and "Quit hiding." Two users reacted to the same scene with two different GIFs, one of Mariah Carey as a judge crying after an *American Idol* performance and one of Rihanna crying, published by Ewing. Here we see Black, Brown, femme, and queer users harnessing mainstream Black women's iconography to comment on a queer Muslim scene.

One user responded to the series' first scene revealing Leila's "fat femme" Latina lover in bed using an image of Pepperidge Farm's "Very Thin" *white* bread, using it to describe what queer representation "usually" is. These moments, retweeted dozens of times, show most fans commenting specifically around moments tied directly to struggles around race, gender, and sexuality. Ewing and the lead artists were critical nodes in these reparative conversations, highlighting the importance of community leaders and artists surviving specific intersections in curating and spreading these conversations and discourses. These tweets are a soft form of #hashtagactivism: "Twitter hashtags" became "an important platform for historically disenfranchised populations to advance counternarratives and advocate for social change."[65] We see in these tweets that #hashtagactivism was often communicated through GIFs that platform algorithms or AI may not be able to understand given their complex significations.[66]

Creating porous borders around spaces of engagement is critical for creating brave spaces. On corporate social media platforms, conversations can be derailed when digital networks spread to people who do not identify or act in solidarity with those communities surviving challenging intersections. When *NowThis News* promoted *Brown Girls* on Facebook with an original video about the show, it produced the show's most caustic commenting environment, with white men decrying the show's focus on diversity behind the camera. Many of the comments came from viewers of the trailer who did not understand the story and the importance of representation for queer women of color; this fact was pointed out by the commenters and sparked discourse around identity politics in the first year of Donald Trump's presidency. Overwhelmingly, the response the video was positive, as nearly all the 16,000 reactions were "like" or "love"; only 10 people reacted "angry" or "sad." Representative of that tiny minority, one commenter posted, "Imagine the reaction if there was a video boasting that a TV crew was 95% straight white males," in response to the video stating that "95% of the [*Brown Girls*] crew is female." This comment sparked a debate resulting in 110 comments, disproportionately focusing 10 percent of the total 1,500 comments on the video on white heteropatriarchy, the source of harm that the show resists.

Now that we see how different communities come together online, and how corporate platforms both enable and disable this engagement, we can ask how hosts steward their communities in real life. Hosts hold cultural, emotional, physical, and virtual space as healers, moderators, elders, and storytellers. In local engagement, community leaders find it easier to intentionally bring communities together and deepen understanding than on platforms. Through in-person engagements, we see how embodied performance and pedagogy are ritual forms of ancestral intelligence. Performances establish the values of a space and cultivate a vibe where different people feel encouraged to come together.

On one night in February 2017 the *Brown Girls* team brought together roughly 1,000 people in Chicago, New York, Detroit, Atlanta, Seattle, Los Angeles, Providence, Baltimore, London (UK), Puerto Rico, Boston, Oakland, Richmond, Miami, Montreal, and Williamstown. *Brujos* had four premieres, three in Chicago from 2017 to 2018 and one in Boston, with around 430 people in attendance across all three. Many of the people exhibiting *Brown Girls* outside of Chicago were friends of its cocreator Fatimah Asghar, who inspired hosts when she made a request to support *Brown Girls* on Facebook. Many of these organizers were poets and writers like her, and not all were Black, Brown, Muslim, queer, or woman-identified, though many shared at least one intersection.

These community engagements reveal how culture drives online engagement in ways invisible to large social media platforms. Hosting these events did more than create "buzz" for online premieres. Interviews with event producers suggest that local artists and activists used *Brown Girls* and *Brujos* to provide rare opportunities for women and queer people of color to come together; solidify bonds between communities of varying racial and ethnic identifications; celebrate and promote original art by women of color across the fields of music, fashion, visual art, comedy, dance, and poetry; inspire and educate young storytellers; engage in discussions around local political issues related to their communities; and allow communities to engage culture through embodied, interdisciplinary performance. In Atlanta, Jovan Julien, whose friend tagged him on Fatimah's Facebook request, knew of *Brown Girls* beforehand and was present for filming. "It only felt natural to support my friend's work in more ways than posting it online," he said in an interview, indicating the significance of off-platform engagement. As a regional organizer for Project South, which advances social justice and governance, new economies, changing paradigms, and narratives around the US South, Julien said the *Brown Girls* screening fit within a local series of events to cultivate community and bring awareness to the group's efforts. "The work we do works to promote safety for brown and Black communities," he said, making *Brown Girls'* intersectional representation especially potent given the dearth of mainstream programming that bridges Black and Brown representation.

A similar dynamic occurred at the *Brujos* screening in Boston, organized by Tufts University professor Kareem Khubchubdani for the Men of Melanin Magic community group: "It was a really great occasion to show up somewhere where people could actually talk and hang out," as opposed to bars were the group typically meets. The *Brujos* screening offered the group rare programming for queer people of color: "There isn't a queer of color performance scene or creative scene [in Boston], so I think this was a really great opportunity for people to know the possibilities of working together," he said. In Miami, Marci Calabretta Cancio-Bello, who knew Fatimah from an Asian American poetry retreat and works for the Miami

Book Fair, wanted to organize a screening through the fair, but it fell apart, so she convened five or six of her students at Florida International University. Although small, the screening had deep value for those who attended, many of whom went back to their homes to rewatch it with friends who didn't attend: "I think it was important for the people that showed up that they were able to watch it with other people . . . who might be struggling with being a queer brown girl in Miami. It can be very isolating," Cancio-Bello said. The screening inspired burgeoning, young storytellers, new cooks for the cookout: "Having it be that this was written by someone who was young and women of color, it was a new idea for them. They were used to seeing that you have to be 40 and established to do something like this."

Local engagement deepens connections through participatory performance, long understood by performance studies scholars to be a form of embodied knowledge: "Performance helps me see. It illumines like good theory. . . . Like good theory, performance is a blur of meaning, language, and a bit of pain," D. Soyini Madison wrote.[67] The *Brown Girls* premieres in Chicago and New York exhibited interdisciplinary arts from women and nonbinary people of color (figure 4.9). In Chicago, as prologue to the screening, the stars of the show danced to Bollywood classics (Nabila Hossain) and performed stand-up (Sonia Denis), whereas Jamila Woods, a Chicago-based singer-songwriter, performed original music she curated for

FIGURE 4.9
Brown Girls premiere in Chicago: vimeo.com/206437359. Credit: VAM Studio.

the series. Black burlesque performers Jeez Loueez and Po Chop, both leaders in the form, also performed. Local venders from activist group Assata's Daughters to jeweler Mashallah, healer Samantha Jo, and bath and body brand Sugar & Scrub sold their wares, connecting TV fans to local, small businesses run by artists from the communities represented. New York featured similar arts, including live body painting by nonbinary artist Anuva and stand-up from people like Aparna Nancherla.

Brujos had two premieres two weeks later. After a sold-out premiere at the Chicago Cultural Center, we traveled to Pilsen, a historically Mexican American neighborhood facing gentrification, to premiere the show in a Latiné-owned bar where series composer Sadie Woods DJ'd in between episodes, allowing fans to dance to the music connected to the cultures onscreen. Even without a DJ, attendees embodied the representations. As *Brown Girls'* Seattle organizer noted, "People were laughing. People were clutching the heart, dancing to the music." Omi Osun Joni L. Jones writes that "people learn through participation," and "through participation, the audience can contrast their own culturally inscribed bodies with those from the community being shared."[68] Such deep, embodied connection to stories has been invisible to platforms and their algorithms.

Broadly, across all the events we hosted, OTV found that local audiences desire cultural specificity and value intersectionality. An analysis of 1,529 survey responses to Chicago screenings of OTV series in 2017 and 2018 provide ample support for the power of cultural specificity.[69] Intersectional representation was not only appreciated but also seen as one of the most important parts of what these stories offered. For instance, one viewer at a screening of *Brown Girls* noted that their favorite part of the series was seeing an honest representation of their community: "the beauty of queer woc [sic.] *(women of color)* on screen! And unapologetically queer people." Similarly, a Latiné man at a screening of *Brujos* wrote that what stood out to him was "the inclusion of a very large spectrum of the black and brown queer community." A Black cisgender woman noted that she appreciated "the emphasis on gender non-conforming characters." Some respondents also commented on how unabashed representation of intersectional identities allowed for the stories to build discussions around greater societal harms. For example, one survey respondent said their favorite part of *Seeds* was "Black women's friendships and solidarity in the face of racism and sexism."

OTV's process of serving community-based stories shows how and where identity matters both on *and* outside of social media. Focusing on local engagement alongside online engagement shines a brighter light on what platforms obfuscate and the conditions for networked solidarity. Because identity is more specific, complex, interdependent, and interpersonal than platforms can account for, it is important to examine how communities engage them across different contexts. For example, we could see, very closely and intimately, how successful we were in combating segregation in Chicago. When we opened applications to our Fellows program for the first time, we mapped where storytellers lived (figure 4.10). We found significant interest in OTV across the north (predominantly white) and south (predominantly Black) sides of the city. (We were aided by promotion by the Mezcla Media Collective, an active online and Chicago-based community group of women and trans/nonbinary filmmakers of color in the city.) This suggests we were actively resisting segregation even if, due to our low resources, we struggled to fund projects from communities that have seen decades of disinvestment.

Many OTV events and screenings featured rituals, interdisciplinary engagements highlighting cultural specificity. Over 40 percent, or twenty-nine out of sixty-nine events in Chicago (and abroad in Mexico and South Africa produced by Elijah), featured engagement beyond screening film or television. These served as rituals that set the tone for the space, expanding how we represented communities through music, dance, poetry, stand-up comedy, culinary arts, messages from community organizers, interactive artmaking, and other forms of storytelling. Each of these forms is highly culturally specific and decenters cinematic visibility as representative of a particular community, thereby lessening the burden of representation for OTV's storytellers and allowing their stories to speak for themselves. Music always set the proper tone. For example, Brandon Markell Holmes is an incredible Grammy-nominated singer-songwriter and performed songs at the screening for his video art piece, *Inertia,* demonstrating the layers of how he represents himself. We screened the Brooklyn series *195 Lewis* about a community of Black queer women and invited KC Ortiz, a local hip hop artist and Black transwoman who happened to be on their soundtrack. Darling Shear, a brilliant Black trans choreographer and dancer who appeared in multiple OTV projects, including her own series, performed at Andre Perez's *Been T/Here* docuseries premiere and Ruby Western and Kayla

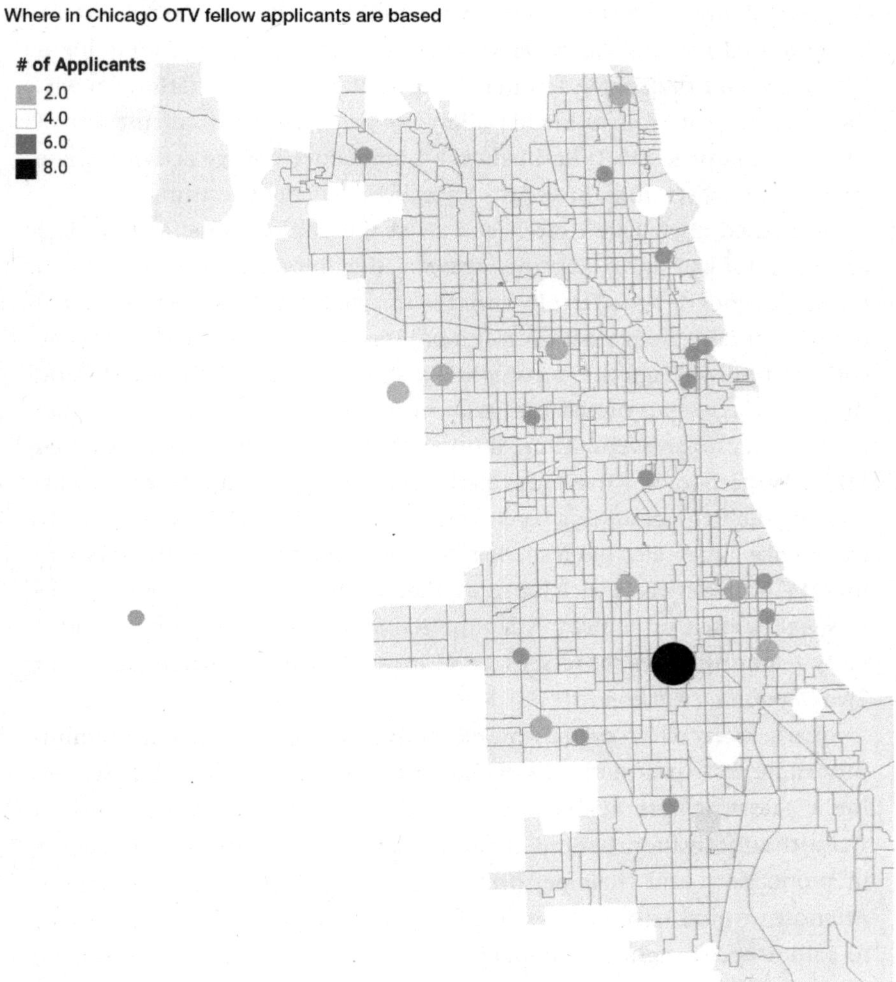

FIGURE 4.10
Where in OTV applicants live in Chicago.

Ginsburg's *Afternoon Snatch*, both in which she was featured. Rashida Webb-Miller hosted a special dance class where we also screened her film to highlight the theme of dance as trauma therapy critical to the narrative. For NIC Kay's premiere at Woman Made Gallery, we partnered with Art Institute of Chicago curator Kamilah Rashied for an interactive collage activity where guests remixed art from queer artists across the gender spectrum.

A talented chef, Elijah often embraced the culinary arts, as food is a key ritual for gathering. For three seasons, they produced *Two Queens in a Kitchen*, a series designed to platform the storytellers behind and connected to OTV's project. Each artist became a host on the show and had an organic conversation with another artist while making a meal. For the second and third seasons, Elijah filmed the series in front of a live audience, turning production into an event. At the third season's taping, Elijah commissioned Mister Wallace to do a live music performance with backup dancers, transforming the light, charming cooking shows into a powerfully sonic, sweaty experience. Elijah also did a smaller version of the show as a "friendraiser" for OTV hosted by E. Patrick Johnson, then professor at Northwestern, who was well-known on Chicago's South Side as a host of an iconic holiday party featuring ancestral recipes he showcased in two separate tapings of *Two Queens in a Kitchen*.

Nearly every OTV event featured conversation, a ritual our community came to expect and creators came to appreciate. After each screening, creators, writers, actors, and directors would have an opportunity to share the motivation behind their story, their triumphs and challenges in production, and their perspectives on the politics of representation. Attendees would have an opportunity to ask questions of what they saw, to gain deeper insight to the images they witnessed. Creators would have an opportunity to hear how viewers were interpreting their stories and get intimate or public feedback, while attendees would have an opportunity to see how their friends, neighbors, and strangers responded to these unique stories. To further our intention to promote community connection, we invited a "community representative" to present before each screening during our three-year residency at the Chicago Cultural Center. For the *Brujos* screening, we invited a group of organizers in Chicago's Latiné community responding to the rise in hate post-Trump by distributing posters for guests to display in their homes, offices, and businesses, proclaiming their acceptance of immigrants and other marginalized communities. For *Afternoon*

Snatch, which featured the local queer theater About Face in their series, a representative from the theater came to speak to raise awareness of their work. In stark opposition to online commenting cultures or "thumbs up/thumbs down" metrics on corporate platforms, local exhibitions promoted exchanges of ideas and solidarity.

WHAT CHALLENGES SUSTAINABLE HOSTING?

At the cookout, everyone's responsible for the vibe, and the hosts are accountable to every guest they invite. Some guests bring a generous vibe by offering various rituals—music, dance, prayer—and others by mediating conflict if it arises. Guests come with an offering: a dish they cooked or the gift of one's energy or spirit, sharing love with others. At the cookout, guests try to avoid triggers that may throw off their mood and increase the potential for violence, but conflict and harm are inevitable in any ecosystem. Hosts are ultimately most responsible for handling conflict and harm organically so as not to upset the delicate balance of energies. Reparative platform development requires both specificity and care, both for the hosts and the attendees.

Hosting at OTV was ever-evolving. I hosted most of the events in the early years. While I was competent at it, I never had much capacity to focus on the vibe, safety, and protection because of my responsibilities supporting research and story development. It was not until several years after that when I started regularly offering land acknowledgments to honor the land stolen from Indigenous people on which we exhibited. It took a couple years for us to have enough time, capacity, and resources to focus on accessibility, including offering American Sign Language interpretation and subtitles for our deaf and hearing disabled community. It was not until 2017 that we started to clearly list space constraints and considerations in our event descriptions. This helped guests with wheelchairs and other physical disabilities and space needs, people across the gender spectrum who wanted to know how bathrooms were labeled, and our deaf community for whom the Chicago Cultural Center had assistive technologies. Doing this in person encouraged us to do so in online exhibition, where we guaranteed subtitles, issued content advisories, and even experimented with audio description for Aquarius Ester's *ambivert* through a collaboration with Kevin Gotkin's accessibility class at NYU. Attending to these different ways of hosting our media was important for "upending universalism" and showing how "media's access, use, and meaning occur in diverse contexts and infinite variations."[70] As Elizabeth Ellcessor writes of media access, "A public sphere founded upon exclusions is capable of gross oppressions. This is why it is imperative to consider the place of access and inclusion in emergent media cultures."[71]

By 2018, I realized that my limited capacity for holding space and the team's decreasing capacity for event planning restricted our platform's accessibility. For various reasons explored in greater depth in the final chapter, I hired Jenna Anast in 2019 as OTV's first head of community and exhibition. Inspired by Chicago's abolitionist collectives and Jenna's own journey of radical self-acceptance, Jenna conducted a series of workshops to create "Brave Space Agreements" for our artists, community, and partners, in addition to producing the 2019 season. These agreements set the tone for when we invited people to engage or work with us, "to be fearless when entering this new world we are creating together," Jenna said. Jenna wanted to offer a map to help us navigate our identities and values when coming together: "It was being in that space, working with people where they're at, and really wanting to create agreements that not only I and us as a staff believe are the way to go, but really diving into the actual needs and finding the flexibility." The agreements encouraged people to speak up for their needs while allowing the hosting organization to be flexible in how it responded. Through Jenna, OTV continued to deepen our understanding of sustainable online and local engagement.

What does it mean to take best practices for holding space in real life and translate them online and vice versa? Reading our Brave Space Agreements, I imagine how healing our experiences on social media platforms would be if users had to consent to them before signing on:

I agree that my gifts bring value to this space, and I receive the gifts that this space offers me.

I agree to be nourished to my best abilities in this space and ask for what I need.

I agree to be playful if my spirit allows, and I agree to do this with energetic consent.

I agree to honor different people's communication styles to the best of my abilities.

I agree to honor each other's IP, both copy-written and not.

I agree to step up and step back in conversations, breakout sessions, and workshops.

I agree to resist and disarm against racism, ableism, sexism, classism, homophobia, transphobia, xenophobia, shame, and other harmful systems of oppression.

I agree to maintain the confidentiality of unrecorded, off-the-record discussion.

I agree that no one is disposable.

I agree to make space for additional agreements to be added to this list to ensure that my needs and the needs of my community are met with bravery.

We featured these agreements at the beginning of all our 2020 livestreams on Facebook and our app to ensure online discussions aligned with our values, the vibe we were cocreating. We also used them in our in-person and online workshops, like when we partnered with the Sundance Institute to support emerging writers. Brave Space Agreements are adaptable. For instance, we added the line about respecting IP for the Sundance event because writers were sharing story ideas with each other.

Our hosting in partnership with larger institutions like the Chicago Cultural Center and the MCA Chicago exposed deeper needs for safety and solidarity. In one instance, a trans/nonbinary guest at the Cultural Center was harassed in a bathroom, not for violating gender norms but because the building was closing (our screenings always lasted after building hours, and so staff worked overtime to serve us). This rattled our guest and prompted us to call for accountability from the city's staff, with little success. We were never able to change the signage on the Cultural Center's bathroom to gender-neutral, even though we knew that up to 20 percent of our community identified as trans or nonbinary.

Hosting at the MCA became precarious after 2020's COVID lockdowns and Black Lives Matter protests. That year, the institution faced a slew of demands for accountability and repair based on harmful actions, including a call to divest from police from staffers for its teen program; a call to keep the museum closed during the pandemic and compensate frontline workers, many of whom were also Black and other people of color disproportionately at risk for COVID; and rehiring dozens of workers laid off purportedly for budget reasons.[72] At the same time, the museum was organizing an exhibition of Chicago artists, *The Long Dream,* to which OTV was invited to contribute a video. *The Long Dream* artists stood in solidarity against the MCA; several pulled their work and launched an Instagram campaign, @MCAccountable, to raise awareness of the MCA's actions and raised $35,000 for frontline workers. *The Long Dream* closed after just two weeks.

All of this transpired while OTV was planning our fifth premiere at the MCA. Changing our plans and pulling work that we invested time and resources into making did not feel aligned with our values, nor with the partnership agreements developed by our head of community Jenna Anast. Elijah and I wrote a letter "calling in" the MCA and asking for transparency on their process; a public livestream with MCA leadership, which we offered to host; and a capital campaign led by the MCA's board to raise the funds to hire and compensate staff, stating, "We believe a commitment to equity must involve the redistribution of capital to those most in need."[73] As a result, a representative from the MCA reached out in support and opened up a communication channel. We ultimately hosted a virtual premiere of our season at *The Long Dream* and intentionally had a conversation on the complexities of institutional accountability. Live at the MCA, I spoke with Zackary Drucker about how institutions, including the MCA, have failed our communities and yet how they continue to assert their importance in our livelihoods.

Yet in the end, the MCA did not fully meet our asks, only inviting us and a few other arts leaders to a semi-closed meeting with the museum director and staff to explain how they were still ahead of their museum peers in terms of diversity and the specifics of their tight budget.

Cultivating community-accountable hosts is challenging even at the local level. But we need to continually engage in this process of asking for and demanding care and accountability. As our online spaces outsource these tasks to machines trained on data extracted from us, we must work together to experiment with new and ancestral ways of listening to and supporting each other. It sounds kumbaya, but anyone who has practiced this work knows it is among the rigorous, challenging, and thought-provoking but rewarding efforts we can pursue.

5 PRACTICING REPARATIONS: HEALING OURSELVES, COMMUNITIES, AND INDUSTRIES

How can we heal conflict and harm at the cookout? Can we scale our strategies to heal systems?

We are strong but tender beings. Life is a fleeting, rigorous journey where the prospect of pain and death never fully subsides. Black, Brown, and Indigenous disabled, queer, trans, men, women, nonbinary people, and others face specific aggressions, both from each other and from people who are different from us. We are rarely handled with care by our people, organizations, institutions, or systems. Many of us move through the world just waiting for the next betrayal or hurt. We learn to anticipate it. Our defenses are up. Chicago drag icon The Vixen famously said, "Don't poke the bear," referring to herself, but many felt the same, particularly the Black community she serves. The slightest poke can yield a powerful response, but because we face resistance nearly every day, not every poke gets a response. Many times, we suppress our feelings, concerns, and dissent because we cannot fight every harm. We are owed so much—care, resources, time—and given too little. Many of us retreat from engaging with each other on interpersonal, communal, or organizational levels as a form of protection.

At the cookout, we meet each other, our beauty and brokenness. Because of this, it was impossible for OTV to avoid harm or repair. In a harmful society, reparative strategies are impossible to execute perfectly. We *practiced* repair strategies, and this chapter explores what we learned from this experiment. Centering harm and its survivors, we paved paths to justice on interpersonal, communal, and systemic levels. And still, we are far from justice.

Community organizers and writers are embracing the inevitability of harm in our capitalist society. Many of these writers are trans/people of color developing frameworks to help us manage this disabling reality. The idea that we must be healthy and well to pursue justice is an ableist fantasy. Because harm is so pervasive, it manifests in different ways for different people. Mariame Kaba, leader in restorative (interpersonal) and transformative (systemic) justice movements and organizations,[1] writes about the importance of being nonjudgmental or prescriptive in justice movements, balancing care for survivors and perpetrators of harm: "I had to work with the survivor of the harm and let them tell me what the harm is. Also, the person who harmed has to come up with their definition of the terms, and then you have to figure out a way to bridge the gap between those realities."[2] This gap is hard to fill. It takes so much time and care that few people have in a corporate-capitalist world that demands so much of our labor.

The challenges we face in healing and thriving may not only be inevitable but also necessary for justice. Writing about what he calls "trans maladjustment," Cameron Awkward-Rich grapples with the struggles trans people have being seen and cared for. He questions why trans people are expected to conform to a culture that for so long denied their existence, beauty, and right to self-identify. He rejects the idea "that sanity/health indexed by the absence of bad feeling should be necessary to secure the authority of minoritarian subjects and thought in the first place."[3] Embracing the inevitability of maladjusting to a harmful society opens a space for centering those in pain and practicing repair. Hil Malantino suggests "we may be rushing too quickly toward the reparative" and that community organizers "might do well to ground themselves in the realities, the givenness, of negative affect."[4] Instead, Rebecca Wanzo, reading Black feminist writer Bernice Johnson Reagon, argues for an "ethics of uncare." She asks us to consider what would be possible if we stop expecting care from every space we enter and instead distinguish between "the necessary nurturing spaces that sustain us and the conflicted, challenging spaces of coalitional work."[5] In other words, why do we expect others to care when we know there are some wounds that either cannot be healed or, if they can, require tremendous amounts of self-care, or time away from others and with close friends and family? These scholars provoke us to consider that others may never fully care for our wounds, but we can still collaborate with others to repair the systemic or root causes of our pain.

Many of us move through the world incredibly lonely in our pain, not realizing that our pain connects us to each other; that sometimes when our own people hurt us, it is often because they need healing too; and that when people outside our community hurt us, it is because they are unfamiliar with what we are going through because systems have been designed to promote and reward their ignorance.

Being vulnerable and brave in sharing our pain is the first step to achieving accountability and care. But our cultural environment, increasingly experienced through capitalist media and tech, is inhospitable. If I show my vulnerability, are the people and systems around me structured to help me seek justice? The answer is often no.

And yet, every year, circumstances arose to push me and my collaborators to try to cultivate care through radical vulnerability.

Working to repair systemic harm requires a tremendous amount of patience, empathy, and humility for our collective unwellness. To work intimately with people who are different from you—and we're all differently impacted by systems—requires recognizing boundaries and triggers, even when others may not clearly show that lines have been crossed. As someone living in a body perceived as Black and male, with fancy degrees and an exclusive job, I increasingly felt as though the people around me treated me as if I did not and could not care: It took some people months or years to let me know that they felt *some type of way* about something I did, assuming the worst intentions on my part. As someone who grew up mired in violence and studying its patterns, I came into this project feeling that I had developed the skills to navigate harm and conflict. OTV tested that belief at every turn. I had to accept my own and others' inevitable shortcomings while embracing strategies for repairing them, even if healing could not be achieved.

Just as there is no single cure for psychic and cultural pains, so too is there no single medicine for systemic healing. Practicing reparations means engaging both our enduring pain and potential strategies for healing, simultaneously, at every level of existence, from the most personal to broadly systemic.

PRACTICING REPAIRING OURSELVES

Less than three years into the OTV experiment, it felt like everyone around me was, as Black folks say, *on one*. Months after *Brown Girls'* sale to HBO and

Emmy nomination, I could feel the stakes going up. People were coming up to me congratulating me like I had cracked the code, the pipeline from Chicago to Hollywood. I knew that my work was only one part of a complex ecosystem, but I could not avoid the perception that I was a charismatic trailblazer and local powerbroker—aided, no doubt, by some media recognition, like when *Filmmaker* listed me in its 2018 "25 New Faces of Independent Film" as "the Midwest's great connector for a diverse generation of web series innovators."[6] My presence in local Chicago media triggered a few collaborators, showing the power of media representation to both exalt and distort. This perceived power did not sit right with me because as a media scholar I know that very, very few people have power in entertainment, let alone someone Black, queer, and living in Chicago.

One big mistake was my lack of transparency about the severe limits I faced experimenting with reparative R&D in media, tech, and academia, as I wrote throughout this book. The lean budget of the project did not align with my commitment to saying "yes" to nearly everyone who came to me looking for support. This meant that my own and my team's capacity was being stretched thin, undermining our collective efficacy. Some conflicts revealed my misunderstanding of the project's scale and my inability to stop it from growing. I feared erecting borders on what was supposed to be an "open" network, which could cause even more conflict. As a result, the two years following the success of *Brown Girls* and the rising expectations from those around me were the most mentally, emotionally, and professionally difficult years of my adult life.

"That year is when I was about to murder you," a collaborator later told me about 2018. They were speaking figuratively, but I understood the intent. I felt the intensity at the time. My closest collaborators deserved more care but also more money, agency, power, and recognition, most of which I could not promise.

As our community expanded, we were being made aware of more conflict and harm that needed our increasingly limited time and attention. Revelations of conflict and harm highlighted the pain in our communities. It forced me to experiment with ways to decenter myself and cultivate the organization's capacity to center healing.

That year, if I was The Vixen's proverbial bear, I felt people poking me. In retrospect, I believe people were poking me to see if I cared; I did, too much, but struggled to show it because of the complexity of the situations and my overlapping, contradictory roles as community member, researcher, participant (director, producer, etc.), and principal investigator working for a university as opposed to an independent organization. For that reason, the poking felt painful, amplified by my own trauma, whose effects manifest as conflict aversion, as I discuss in the acknowledgments.

The first poke was in 2017 after the revelation of hurt feelings of marginalization from my collaborators following the local publicity I received, explored in chapter 2. Months later, we came together to resolve the issue, but in the meantime others started to poke. In 2018 an artist called me one day asking if I could support the development of a music video. They mentioned wanting to hire a cis male director who I knew had an extended track record of violence toward women and nonbinary people. This person had stalked, harassed, and mistreated three of my friends, including an artist with a project on OTV. I was so surprised that I did not mention this on the call, and I wanted to take the time to consider a strategy. My first instinct was to contact two of the survivors and make sure I was properly remembering their stories (the third survivor I knew well as a very close friend who had shared the situation in detail when it happened). It was important to capture these two stories accurately because I remembered that the incidents occurred during a film production directed by the person doing the harm. The two artists consented to an anonymous interview where I took detailed notes of the harm they experienced. I told them I would not share their names with anyone and asked for permission to share their anonymized stories with the person who wanted to hire the director. They consented. Before I could, however, a few weeks later the artist called me to say they had changed their mind and selected a different director, saying they were a better fit. I was so relieved, but both situations revealed to me the need to build capacity for restorative justice within OTV.

The following months brought more conflict, deepening my conviction to center healing in OTV's practice. In one case, conflict emerged with an artist who I had selected to fund a pilot concept of a series they had been writing and sending to me for feedback for over a year. I'd reserved 10 percent of the retention funding I received from Northwestern to give to two creative teams to green-light short narratives, less than ten minutes. I saw in previous years how filming an excerpt or concept of a story helped artists secure funding for the full project. Before I was about to disburse the funds to the creator, I consulted OTV's then head of production Stephanie Jeter, who quite reasonably requested to see a budget and schedule for the production. When the artist sent it, Stephanie expressed concerns about the project's ambitions, which was about double the recommended amount, and I agreed with her expert assessment, ashamed I had not asked for it earlier. I had seen in other projects that when artists decide to produce too much story for too little time and money, conflict and harm can emerge in the stress of production.

I informed the creator that we needed to schedule a meeting to go over their plan and see if we could scale it down. The creator called me on a Sunday night *furious*. For over thirty minutes, they yelled and cussed me out. I stayed calm even as my partner in the other room told me I should have stood up for myself and our process more vigorously. To be honest, I was calm because I was shocked and triggered as someone with early memories of violence and screaming. I was also caught between multiple roles. As a human, I felt attacked and disrespected. But as a researcher, I had to pay attention to what the artist was saying and take notes because conflict is important data. As a development executive, I saw their anger as a natural response to fearing I was going to pull funding altogether, which I knew I would not. I said I would not, but they did not believe me in that moment, probably because there are many Black men who do not keep their word to women, trans, and nonbinary femmes. I suspected I had probably stepped on a trigger of theirs. That week, Stephanie and I met with the production team, offered suggestions on how to trim down the project, and I released the funding soon after. A year later when the project was completed, I discovered that the artist did not take our suggestions, and there was, predictably, conflict in the production (to make it more complicated, they did an incredible job and it's one of my favorite projects, so much so that I wrote the creator recommendations for grad school). But by that time, I had cultivated limited capacity at OTV for mediation, and so the team had support in mediating that conflict. More on that soon.

There were other interpersonal conflicts at this time forcing me to develop internal systems for repair, knowing that the number of roles I was performing was not conducive to holding the care I needed to show. I had close collaborators who were dealing with deep traumas, fighting with me and with each other. At one point during a production I was directing, I was in another room reviewing previous takes and heard yelling from the main cast room. Two cast members were fighting, one was visibly angry and yelling and the other was more measured. The more measured person was someone I knew who would go on to be involved in a lot of disagreements that year, including with me, for reasons that were unclear to me at the time but I later found out resulted from harmful self-medicating practices. The more visibly angry person would later tell me they felt undervalued and underused in my project and threatened to pull out (which would make it impossible to release) and that they were nervous their IP would be stolen (as of this writing, it has not been, to my knowledge). Field notes from my research assistant suggest the fight could have started with a scheduling issue, but I still don't have a clear sense of what the fight was about as the people involved don't want to talk about it. Among the crew, there was also some conflict. In general, we finished every production day on time, sticking to an eight-hour day, and we got a great final product, in my opinion. However, both my on-set assistant and I noticed different expectations among the crew about their jobs, broadly related to different levels of experience (in my first book *Open TV* I found that crew roles in indie series are often blurred because productions lack resources to hire all roles and enforce hierarchies, which can lead to conflict[7]).

Indeed, I was not the best director both days. I took on the responsibility of housing and driving cast members to set each day, before sunrise, and some of them worked late, causing me to not get enough sleep and arrive late. My assistant mainly observed how different factions of production interacted with one another inefficiently. The process by which different individuals were communicating with one another seemed to be a constant work in progress. For instance, when we first started filming, there seemed to be a bit of frustration over how and where the script department should be communicating with the camera department. Different people chimed in, based on their level of experience. Because I was tired and lack corporate production experience, I could not mediate, and there were no other systems in place for mediation at the time.

On another production, I was furiously reprimanded by a nonbinary director for complimenting them and mentioning an upcoming production. I thought I was being encouraging, but the mention of an upcoming production in the middle of a current production understandably triggered stress and anxiety. It also made the person feel as though I was demanding more work from them, at a time when they had taken on a lot of responsibility, not all of which was at my direction. (OTV never instructed an artist to do a project, because we could never fully fund them; we only partnered with artists on stories they came to us wanting to tell.) The dynamic of being a man appearing to put pressure on someone who was not added pain to the whole situation. The person and I met a couple weeks later. I apologized, and it was accepted. But I was thoroughly shaken. The rageful reaction to a compliment was concerning because I knew this person was also having conflict with other people in our community that year. It also was another reminder that as a man "in charge," I was not always going to be the best person to mediate conflict or navigate harm.

All of 2018 I feared that I was in over my head, struggling to care for myself, let alone others, and needed to act. But restorative justice takes time, skill, and resources. People need to be paid to do this difficult work, as it's time-consuming to execute equitable processes for restoration. After these incidents, I had the idea to hire a "head of community" for OTV whose job would be to hold space for intra-community conflict and harm. I did not have any funding for it—I was confronted with the reality that the systemic underinvestment in my communities results in our continued subjugation. Thankfully, Angelique Williams-Power, then head of the Field Foundation, restructured that nonprofit to focus its giving on organizations based in and led by people in Chicago's underinvested South and West Sides. OTV was programming largely out of Humboldt Park on Chicago's West Side, and I had incorporated OTV as a nonprofit in early 2018 in the hopes that I could sustain it outside of Northwestern.[8] That fall, I applied to the Field Foundation to support OTV's first head of community. I initially reached out to a prominent restorative justice consultant for the contract, but after consulting with the OTV team, I realized they most needed support with producing our Chicago events, which by 2018 was around ten screenings a year, plus more in partnership with local organizations. So, the role became "head of community *and exhibition*," and I hired Jenna Anast, a local organizer and artist who was eager to bridge their experience in film with restorative justice after experiencing both harm and liberation on set, in Chicago's activist community, and in their everyday life as a Black nonbinary person.

Jenna joined OTV after having worked on the set of *Brujos* and knowing many other artists who'd worked on OTV projects. They had a generally favorable view of the platform. Their impression was that the OTV team was great at "dreaming, scheming and execution" but perhaps at the expense of building deeper, human connections, which can cause tension: "There's a lot of love for each other and a lot of tight bonds that are created that sometimes we can fall short of that line of sight. . . . Sometimes because I think there's a little bit of fragility with egos and communication, I feel like more transparency and more team building is something that we don't prioritize. . . . I would say that a weakness is not prioritizing building together as a team . . . really investing in each other, where we're at, what we're really doing together." Jenna's statement resonated with me. I had a lot of love for everyone in OTV, particularly the team, but also felt the increasing intensity of maintaining that care alongside the consistency needed for production and output, especially when no one was getting paid much to do so. This is a persistent problem in nonprofits, where organizers doing the work of systemic transformation burn out before they have the funding to keep the work going. It is a dynamic that Jenna noticed in activist spaces and in several restorative circles they conducted with OTV creators: "I cultivated a space in which they could communicate with each other and having someone there to be a mediator for everyone to hear what they were saying. That's my shit, and I love doing that."

Reviewing my field notes, I noticed that so many people were struggling to care for themselves. It took me years to realize the ways I wasn't caring for myself and how this impeded my ability to care for others. I lived by the researcher's code—do no harm—but I was harmful to myself. I binged on high-sugar foods and coffee to manage the stress, which I later learned worsened a handful of conditions in my body affecting digestion, cognition, and muscle tension. I was always uncomfortable. I did not sleep consistently, nor did I have consistent physical exercise. I worked weekends and weeknights. In my head, I was always working. There was so much to do and process, I could not stop thinking about OTV and our community. The project completely took over my life. Without any staff for operations or fundraising, I had a lot of responsibility and few people to hold me accountable or support me in building capacity for the project. My to-do list and email were a daily source of anxiety. I could never keep it short for very long. By 2019, I was drowning.

"There were moments where we tried to share things and just: the look in your eyes. You were so burnt out," Elijah told me in late 2019 after they had assumed leadership of the OTV nonprofit, allowing me to exhale. "All of the things that you had going on impacted us. And that's the thing that

I realized specifically with OTV is that: this is a thing that is wrapped in our identities, and you cannot separate. And I think that's why at the beginning of the cycle, I was able to hold that capacity for Jenna and Chris, because I was like, 'I'm sober. I'm not working as hard as them because I refused to do that,'" they continued.

During the early days of OTV, I felt I did not have the luxury of refusing to labor. I was accountable to so many people, building an entire platform with less than $50,000 each year to pay a team of four and dozens of artists. Had I stopped, the project would have fallen apart, and my collaborators would have labored and underpaid, without ever experiencing what the work could be with adequate support, as they did after I handed it over. I don't believe there was an easy solution to this, a "right" answer that I somehow missed. The truth is that overworking myself unpaid helped OTV reach the place where Elijah had the resources to make the organization more care centered. This reality is common among leaders starting organizations in a capitalist system and reflects the persistent paradox of harm/repair and care/uncare in our pursuit of justice.

Part of my healing journey has been realizing that although I was too often blind to the full effects of my actions and made mistakes, I was not my circumstances. I was not always treated with care, but the fact that I experienced conflict was often unavoidable because I was not the only person in the situation in need of greater awareness or care. I learned that how we respond to conflict and harm is as important as trying to avoid it all together. Acting with integrity, embracing transparency, and taking accountability are essential, but objectivity when faced with harm is a fiction. Community-based researchers are also participants and therefore not neutral. I am a subject of this book too. My feelings are valuable data, but I wish I'd had more capacity to be more open about them with those around me in the moment instead of fearing it would create "bias." This may not have avoided conflict, but responding more honestly and openly might have eased the path to repair and invited the people around me deeper into the process of cocreation.

In retrospect, peaceful communion feels like a fantasy. Our systems offer an inhospitable environment for it. This is especially true for people whose identities are caught in a matrix of intersecting oppressions structured by this capitalist system. We are working hard, and systems are not distributing support evenly or competently. So many of my peers working to reform academia, media, and tech have struggled navigating the tenure track, starting nonprofits, or codesigning platforms; why did I believe myself immune? We lack reparative systems that can hold our pain and help us witness it in our ourselves and in each other. These pains may never subside but must be acknowledged so we can tap into whatever collective agency we have to address them.

Cultural reparations are still a dream worth pursuing. Reparation is a daily practice or, as adrienne maree brown writes, an emergent strategy.[9] Indeed, through the aforementioned efforts, I have maintained healthy, productive relationships with almost everyone involved. I must believe it is because I care.

In 2020 and 2021, small cracks in OTV's foundation started to be exposed, publicly and privately, within the OTV team and our broader community. As I witnessed it, I was so grateful to have had Jenna on the team and to have handed over leadership to Elijah, who is also trained in restorative justice. We were prepared, even if full repair or justice eluded us.

PRACTICING REPAIRING COMMUNITY

The year 2020 was one of reckoning, with the COVID-19 pandemic making us more aware of systemic harm, and the world shouting "Black Lives Matter," igniting arguably the largest protest movement in world history. The year also brought a wave of pain and demands for accountability in all fields, from the law, medicine, and across culture industries. Labor movements called for justice everywhere. In the art world, workers initiated a wave of unionization efforts to stop labor exploitation, including successfully at the Art Institute of Chicago. Art workers launched campaigns like Change the Museum (@changethemuseum), an Instagram account with over fifty thousand followers that for years exposed bias and inequality in art institutions. In theater, We See You White American Theatre (@weseeyouwat) similarly launched an accountability campaign around racial discrimination in their industry.

In Hollywood, writers and actors launched campaigns to #ChangeHollywood, with #Hollywood4BlackLives and #EndLatinXclusion calling for more jobs for people of color, an end to stereotyping, divesting from police, and more. Started by Color of Change, #ChangeHollywood quickly expanded to a #ChangeIndustries initiative to advocate for equity in music, fashion, and more. The Black Lives Matter movement had global effects on television: streamers Netflix, Hulu, BBC, Channel 4 (UK), and ABC (Australia) removed episodes from over a dozen series featuring blackface and brownface, some released as recently as 2015 and most after 2000.[10] The WGA's Committee of Black Writers released its first open letter, shining a light on rampant employment discrimination. Kendrick Sampson's BLD PWR organization partnered with Black Lives Matter cofounders Patrisse Cullors and Melina Abdullah to call the industry in for not working to uplift the Black community, enlisting over three hundred Black stars including Viola Davis, Chadwick Boseman, Issa Rae, and Michael B. Jordan.

Community calls for reparation also swept through Chicago. In many cases, white male for-profit and nonprofit leaders faced swift accountability for not caring or actively harming the Black artists who participated in their programming and helped them raise millions of dollars. As mentioned in the previous chapter, Chicago's drag community banded together to demand accountability from the mostly white owners of bars and businesses in Chicago's gayborhood. Chicago's arts and media organizations did not avoid accountability. First came Young Chicago Authors, a decades-old institution known for mentoring some of Chicago's most celebrated Black artists through its Louder Than a Bomb poetry festival including Chance the Rapper, Jamila Woods, Noname, Ric Wilson, Saba, and Nate Marshall. Young Chicago Authors founder Kevin Coval stepped down following accusations that he dismissed multiple accusations of a mentor from the organization sexually assaulting young people in the organization. Free Write Arts and Literacy, a nonprofit that supported incarcerated, court-involved young people in the arts, faced similar accusations and eventually folded after a year-long accountability process. Meanwhile, alums of another youth media organization, Free Spirit Media, organized a months-long successful campaign to oust founder Jeff McCarter, publishing a wave of stories of labor exploitation and hostile work environments.

OTV was not spared in this wave of accountability, though neither the organization nor our team were called out directly. On a Friday in July 2020, I received a text from a community leader, who shared a public Instagram post featuring the story of a sexual assault by an OTV creator. Sol Cabrini, a young Black transwoman and brilliant artist I had known for years, accused this OTV creator of sexual abuse in brave, uncompromising detail. What made this even more heartbreaking was the respect I had for Sol, an actor, video artist, musician, poet, and scholar: a polymath whose gifts blessed Chicago's culture.

To their credit, the creator admitted to the assault within hours. Over the next week, I checked Instagram obsessively as more survivors, including artists I had worked with for years, published similar stories. My soul sank and anxiety grew as I realized that harm ran deeper in the OTV community than I had known.

Through the community leader, I was told that Sol saw OTV as partly accountable for platforming the creator to such a degree that it made it more challenging for her to acknowledge the harm that was done. Sol later told me that the creator dangled the promise of featuring her music in their OTV show right before the assault. The OTV creator became a bit of a local celebrity, not solely but in small part from my own personal help, which was substantial compared to other artists.

Feeling culpable, I posted a personal statement to Instagram in support of Sol and taking accountability for the ways in which I supported the creator, who, with another creator, cocreated one of OTV's most critically acclaimed series. Other Chicago artists and arts leaders saw my post, alerting them to their own responsibility in elevating the creator's status in Chicago, and they reached out to me asking if they could support Sol.

We cannot always avoid harm in our communities, but we can control how we respond. Acknowledging my role in perpetuating harm was just the first step in an ongoing, collective process of healing. The platform elevated someone who at the same time was harming the most vulnerable people in our community. *All* survivors of the creator's actions were Black.

In our capitalistic, liability-averse society, we fear accountability and repair because we fear the cost and the risk to profits. But OTV did not have the luxury of neutrality, nor the burden of profit and loss. We were embedded in our community. Black queer, trans/nonbinary and femme-identified artists, some survivors, were also leaders in the organization. In July 2020, amid seemingly endless #BlackLivesMatter protests and videos of anti-Black police violence, my collaborators were tired and several triggered by the revelation of sexual assault between an OTV creator and an artist in our community. They knew this would take time. Both Elijah and Jenna were trained in restorative justice and knew the long arc of healing. An organic development process responds to the whole environment, not just our own aims and desires.

We needed to take our time, but I wanted to act—perhaps too soon, revealing how healing ourselves is critical to healing community. I was nervous, fearful, and triggered but likely for different reasons. In my fear I pushed for OTV to address the issue within hours of the revelation, later realizing this was a trauma response. I spent most of my childhood amid conflict. Watching people I care about fight became a trauma; I vividly remember trying to intercede in their fights to stop the violence. My impulse was to resolve conflict as quickly as possible, a response to stop the trauma. When I give myself space to think and breathe, I remember harm takes time to heal—and that I have seen this healing happen in my life. My earliest memories are me fearing for the lives of loved ones, who, along with my aunties, all educators, and my grandmother, a nurse and healer, showed me Black women's resilience. I had to remind myself that, as traumatizing as this was, the violence stopped and healing happened. I realize all of this in the following months, as I also started therapy and yoga, forms of self-care I had no time for in the intense four years of building OTV. Researchers are trained to see the effects of experiments on participants. We are not trained to see the effects of our research on ourselves.[11] My history was affecting the study: The thought of my research in any way contributing to a Black transwoman's pain had me pushing for new interventions too quickly.

Thankfully, how OTV responded to this harm was not up to me, despite my vigorous calls for immediate response. Because I hired Jenna as an internal restorative justice healer, we were able and willing to respond. The OTV team told me to slow down, to "allow," the only word healer Jade T. Perry uttered to me during OTV's subsequent staff retreat organized by Jenna in response to our need for team building. It's a word I carried with me in the years to come as I transitioned leadership over to Elijah: *allow*.

Healing takes time, and it must be led by survivors. At the time, we did not have a formalized process in place for handling sexual assault in our community. We had "community standards" that broadly promised a commitment to restorative justice. Still, I gave up my push for publishing a beta restorative justice process and realized we did not need one. Our restorative justice process was organic. Within two weeks, before the end of July, our team drafted a statement and plan for ways OTV could facilitate justice for Sol, but our first meeting with Sol and her partner at the time did not happen until September, two months later. Not until our second meeting in October did we start to clarify concrete actions. Over several months of deep and sometimes tearful discussions, led by Jenna and including me, Sol and her partner bravely and beautifully communicated their feelings, histories, hopes, and boundaries, while I listened and shared ways OTV could support them. Our organic restorative justice process was Black queer people listening to each other's needs and trying our best to meet them, centering the needs of the people who have survived great harm. We rejected the criminal justice system to redefine justice on our own terms.

Complicating our process was the fact that the perpetrating creator's relationship to OTV was a show in which they shared 50 percent ownership. They split every role in the project, including acting, writing, directing, producing, and music supervision, raising tens of thousands of dollars to make the show. Making an indie show is incredibly difficult, and any calls for accountability for the creator would necessarily impact their collaborator, who didn't do anything wrong and worked really hard for their success. All accountability has implications beyond those directly harmed, so after many meetings with Sol, I checked in with the collaborator, who was understandably hurt by not being part of discussions.

In the end, six months later, OTV released "a public call to support restorative justice for Sol Cabrini."[12] The statement focused on what OTV was doing to support Sol as well as encouraged the Chicago arts community to take similar actions, a gesture to transformative justice. OTV's statement showed how critical the arts, media, technology, community, and our organic development process were to repair. It included the following:

- Sharing Sol's story on Instagram and other social media by OTV and the organizations that had supported the perpetrating creator.
- Deplatforming the show on OTV. Out of deference to the collaborator, we did not remove the show entirely from the platform, but we removed the show and related images from all marketing and publicity (basically, someone had to actively search for the show to find it).
- Supporting Sol's artistic career, including possible distribution of her beautiful video art work on OTV and development support from the organizations that had supported the creator.
- Providing financial support for Sol.
- Calling for Chicago-based arts organizations to act in solidarity, deplatforming the creator, and investing in Sol.

Each of Sol's requests pointed to the areas OTV had been developing for five years: (1) television and video distribution, key to Sol's art practice; (2) social media, critical to raising awareness for stories of harm and healing; (3) community in Chicago; and (4) economic justice.

Sol's bravery showed me how OTV could use art, media, and technology as tools for healing, restorative and transformative justice. We could open our platform to an artist we excluded. Our openness to repair made us a better platform, closer to our communities, truer to our values, and furthering our mission through groundbreaking art, including Sol's incredibly rich, complex and thought-provoking video work.

I am forever indebted to Sol for her bravery and strength in revealing her pain, which opened the door for others to share and opened OTV and I to our capacity to facilitate healing, however imperfectly. I cannot claim this is a process that will work for every situation. There is no formula to harm reduction or healing, yet trans/people of color have historically innovated strategies to "do it" anyway. As Tourmaline writes, "It's always been us—queer and trans sex workers, friends, organizers, healers, drug users, those of us who are disabled, without health insurance, reliant on systems that extract value from us without offering anything in return—who figure out what needs to be done to make one another's lives more livable, and who proceed to *do it*."[13] Repairing cultural systems means opening ourselves to new ways of creating and distributing our stories that address harm in every aspect of the development process. We do not police each other. We organically develop and experiment to restore and hopefully transform what justice looks like in our ecosystems, beyond systems that exclude us.

Our process has no end. In community, at any cookout, we confront our personal and collective wounds. These take time to heal, if they ever do. Yet there is value in trying because if we do, we might find our pain a little easier to hold, because we know we are not alone. In her art, Sol shows an understanding of the transformative power of pain, not as a necessity for progress but as a fact of living in bodies that will die. Carrying pain is both an individual and collective endeavor. In her book of poems, *Tgirl.jpg,* she writes

> we don't outlast it we don't surpass it we don't transcend it   we don't
> reprimand it we carry it together willingly   all over to the ground
>   watching
> over each other[14]

Outside of our communities, industries and other systems make our wounds harder to carry. We owe it to ourselves to not just assume that this harm is inevitable but also to help each other hold it.

PRACTICING REPAIRING SYSTEMS

At the same time, OTV was in a leadership transition. In early 2019, I asked the OTV team if anyone was interested in becoming the organization's executive director and cofounder. Thankfully, Elijah answered the call. As you've seen throughout the book, they performed a lot of work for the organization: producing programs and running our marketing. Of course, I had thoughts on how the organization should be run during the tumultuous times of COVID and racial pandemics, but I learned to check my "founder's syndrome" and allow OTV's Black women, trans, and nonbinary team members to lead.[15] In this transition, I developed a deeper appreciation for *allowing*, ceding what little power and control I had.

It's not easy to build a foundation for a Black liberatory nonprofit organization in the fields of entertainment and digital technology. The so-called nonprofit industrial complex is real and historically as resistant to Black leadership as it is to funding media entertainment. I remember in 2019 an exchange with a large nonprofit foundation in its fifth year supporting a media grant in Chicago. Over those years, OTV creators were applying to a white-led local nonprofit that administered the grant and winning consistently (supported in part by my coaching). Nearly every year since 2016, OTV's most popular show was funded by this grant even though the white-led nonprofit was not offering artists any support for their projects beyond funding. In fact, artists consistently complained to me that the grant's administration made it harder for them to finish their projects.

For a five-year assessment of the program, the foundation asked the local nonprofit for data on how projects were doing, including quantifying viewership, which OTV kept hidden from the public. I started receiving emails from artists asking for viewership counts. I got mad because quantitative viewership data, as shown in chapter 4, is not the most important metric for community media. Instead, my grad students and I wrote a thirty-page report offering quantitative viewership metrics as well as qualitative assessments of success, including press, festival exhibitions, and testimonials from creators about how the project shaped their career opportunities. I emailed the foundation directly, knowing the local nonprofit would only report the numbers (I was right). The foundation seemed surprised that a Black-led organization in Chicago was doing all this research and artist support, so they asked for a meeting. I told them that they should be funding OTV directly because we were fulfilling the fund's goals of promoting social justice and offering artists better support than the white-led organization they were funding. The foundation told me they could not do that for unspecified reasons. Meanwhile, the white nonprofit received hundreds of thousands of dollars in more funding and updated their website with all the data I collected on the programs they funded—data I only had because I had such close relationships with the artists with whom they did not. They took our research and the funding we deserved.

Years later, OTV is still trying to raise a production fund to support our creators, who struggle to raise enough money to produce their projects, causing all kinds of harm. Lacking a production fund also inhibits OTV's ability to mentor, train, and support our artists in producing in more sustainable, care-centered ways.

At least now OTV has funds for general operations. Elijah, with my support, has since raised well over $4 million to sustain operations through 2026. While these numbers sound large, it is far from the level of reinvestment needed to counteract corporate extraction. Consider that $1–3 million is roughly the average cost of *one episode* of narrative television. Netflix alone reportedly spent between $50 and $100 *billion* on developing and producing programming in the 2010s, whereas, according to Media Impact Funders, nonprofits gave only $27 billion in media grants over the same period, spread across over sixty-five thousand organizations globally and likely to mostly white-led organizations.[16]

Still, the nonprofit industry is slowly embracing Black and Indigenous leadership, representing the nascent emergence of a reparative philanthropy.[17] OTV benefited from forward-thinking foundation program officers who trusted our vision and expertise: Javier Torres from Surdna, Jen Humke from MacArthur, Tempestt Hazel and Lolly Bowean from Field, and Bridgit Antoinette Evans and Tracy Van Slyke from Pop Culture Collaborative. These program officers took the time to understand OTV's unique model—community-based digital distribution of entertainment—and our dual theory of change—reforming corporate systems while cultivating alternatives. They then trusted us and gave us time to work toward our lofty goals.

Foundations are embracing more risk and trust, over longer periods, to deepen impact. Nonprofit leaders like former Ford Foundation President Darren Walker and Mellon Foundation President Elizabeth Alexander are great examples of how this transformation is happening. Disparities in gender, race, sexuality, and disability persist in foundation funding. The MacArthur Foundation specifically found this to be the case in its portfolio, disproportionately represented by majority white and male-led boards of white-led organizations.[18] In an analysis of forty-four reports from foundations, organizations, and research reports released from 2018 to 2022, my lab found that 85 percent of reports by foundations explicitly stated the need for investment in organizations led by and supporting Black, Indigenous, and people of color, moving away from color-blind investment practices and instead having a race-based lens to develop solutions in philanthropy. Whether this survives fresh attacks on race-conscious organizational policies has yet to be seen.

Nonprofit funding alone cannot heal the harms of a corporate-capitalist economy. Seeing the limits of nonprofit, I sought to bridge for-profit and nonprofit funding as an experiment in systemic reparations. In winter 2020, right before the COVID lockdown, I was in Los Angeles with Stephanie Jeter and Julie Keck, cofounders of what I thought would be a for-profit arm of the OTV nonprofit: OTV Studio (figure 5.1). In addition to hosting a brunch for OTV writers, directors, and actors now working in Los Angeles, we were meeting with executives who had expressed interest in supporting our work, including at Sony Pictures Television, Bron Studios, FX, WarnerMedia, Gamechanger Films, and other small production companies and agencies. It was my hope that the company would both provide both opportunities for emerging writers looking to sustain their careers in the industry and an ancillary revenue stream for the OTV nonprofit: leveraging Hollywood's interest in buying and producing our artists' IP to sustain a distribution platform that could support more emerging creators.

I was dreaming of a new model for systemic reparations: siphoning funds from the exclusionary Hollywood system to support a new one led by historically excluded leaders.

I'd spent years researching and developing this new path to repairing Hollywood's supply chain for stories and storytellers. In 2017, after *Brown Girls'* Emmy nomination, I received an email from an agent at WME, the agency representing the most TV writers. It was from the late Maxwell

FIGURE 5.1
OTV Studio trip to Hollywood (clockwise from left): CEO and cofounder Stephanie Jeter, me, and Julie Keck at Sony Pictures; Theo Germaine, Jen Richards, and Fawzia Mirza at our brunch; me and Karan Sunil; Ashley Ray, Big Dipper, and me; just me.

"Max" Saines, who wrote, "Such exciting news for *Brown Girls*!! Couldn't be prouder to be a former student." Max was my brilliant Northwestern student turned enterprising agent who'd savvily worked his way from the mail room to literary agent in a just a couple years by taking on extra work. We hopped on a call, and he said that "people are talking about you" and that he could set me up with meetings if I was ever in LA. I flew to LA that September to attend an Emmys reception, and by that time, Max had shifted from WME to Endeavor Content, a production company founded by WME to give it access to TV's lucrative IP market.

I was skeptical Max would be able to get me—a professor with a small nonprofit—any meaningful meetings. A month before I arrived, he told me that HBO, Amazon, FX, Hulu, Netflix, Showtime, and STARZ all wanted to meet with me. One month later, I'd return to LA for a conference, and he added Netflix, YouTube Red, and Apple (shortly before they launched Apple

TV+). I was gobsmacked and nervous. I wasn't prepared for these meetings, some of which were very serious. For most, I met with only a couple junior executives, but some platforms took it more seriously. For STARZ, which had used Black and queer programming to build its streaming audience, I met with most of the entire programming team, including Carmi Zlotnik, president of programming.

I now see why. Since *Brown Girls'* HBO deal, at least five other OTV artists have received offers to develop their projects. By my count, over two dozen have earned writing, directing, and acting credits for Netflix, NBC, Showtime, CBS, Hulu, and more.

I had tapped into Hollywood's thirst for diverse storylines as the conglomerates launched new streaming platforms—just as I had predicted before launching OTV. As a scholar, I had theorized this thirst for IP as a neocolonial project, a way for mostly white corporations to own what Black and other racialized creators produce for their own profit. In this period, few people—of any race—owned IP for long before a conglomerate bought them out.

In person, the Streaming Studio System's interest in our stories did not feel as sinister. The Hollywood system is run on smiles and sunshine until the contracts come in. From 2017 to 2020, I met with no fewer than sixty-seven executives at cable and streaming channels, studios, production companies, agencies, management companies, and start-ups. The list includes almost every company releasing diverse stories in that period, including large teams of executives at Netflix and WarnerMedia; the head of Bad Robot (*Star Wars*, *Star Trek*, *Westworld*); streamers starting original programming at Hulu, YouTube, and Facebook; emergent indies SeeSaw, Gunpowder & Sky, and MACRO; managers and agents at 3Arts and CAA; and smaller streamers that never took off, like El Rey, SuperDeluxe, Topic, and, yes, even Quibi. Most of those interested were junior executives who were younger and more diverse than company leadership. Every meeting was lovely, and Max would often send me post-meeting emails with positive reviews from contacts.

I learned that I was going on a "general meeting," which I was ashamed to have not heard of before. Indeed, in decades of researching Hollywood, I had never read scholarship about the general meeting, but it is the lubricant of the Hollywood system. Few studio film or television shows get greenlit without a general meeting at some point. The general meeting—or just a "general" as it is more often called—is an introductory meeting that allows storytellers and executives to get to know each other and decide on whether to enter one another in their "rolodex." It is a very LA thing. People want to see your vibe—experience who you are and learn what motivates you—while assessing your ability to talk about your work in a business context. It is *not* a pitch meeting, though ideas may come up, and sometimes creators end up soft pitching ideas. Instead, the goal is to entice interest in a future meeting that could become a pitch. I learned later that seasoned writers and directors come to generals with a clear, effortless, and seemingly unrehearsed but very polished answer to the prompt "tell me about yourself." I quickly caught on and unspooled a narrative about researching YouTube in grad school while learning the basics of production before coming to Chicago to repair issues in the web TV market, only to stumble upon a thriving intersectional arts community. I also learned that I probably needed a more personal touch about my background and upbringing.

It took me a little over a year and three rounds of meetings to realize I was quietly failing. I came to this realization in my third round of meetings in the spring of 2018 in a meeting with then president of Bad Robot Brian Weinstein. I started the meeting with my usual story, mentioning that OTV was in the process of incorporating as a nonprofit. The studio head interrupted: "Stop right there. Don't ever say 'nonprofit' in Hollywood." I was taken aback, but in retrospect, it was good advice. I was meeting with for-profit corporations with a ravenous interest in IP. Especially as streaming distribution was destroying the syndication market, everyone wanted a piece of IP to make money from production.

I realized in that moment these meetings were a waste of everyone's time—myself, the executives, and the artists I was trying to support—if I did not create an entity that could retain some IP. At the time, several people on OTV's advisory board were telling me I was foolish for not taking a cut of the IP we were spending so much time developing. I resisted vigorously: As a professor, I did not want to create a conflict of interest in my research, and all my research has been a critique of corporate IP ownership. But after the meetings in Hollywood, I saw the flip side: In years of interviews with OTV artists, the vast majority stated an interest in Hollywood, and my principles were standing in their way. OTV was perceived by the industry as a pathway to emerging artists, and IP was the best way to secure this path.

In the spirit of symbiotic, regenerative economics, I decided to slowly, deliberately explore a for-profit arm of OTV but only on the condition that I not receive any profit from it. Instead, I planned for the OTV nonprofit to take my share of the company, funneling profits from Hollywood to a Black-owned distribution platform that could develop IP outside of the corporate system. Meanwhile, the nonprofit would support a for-profit entity by developing artists and projects they could sell.

I felt passionately about this experiment in reparations. I also needed help crafting a business model. Luckily, a Kellogg MBA student with experience in Silicon Valley, Oscar Dang, saw a presentation I gave at Northwestern and agreed to help. During my next two rounds of LA meetings, I flipped the script on executives and started to ask them questions on what models they believed would work, turning their development meeting into my research meeting. Throughout 2018, Oscar and I developed an incubator model that would offer mentorship and management to artists and invest in a smaller number of projects to sell. This model combined what most executives told me—the need for IP interest—with OTV's values of artist development—the role best typified by managers, who support storytellers' careers for the option of securing a percentage of IP or production credit.

I had no intention of quitting my job as a professor and running a company, and so that same year I asked Stephanie if she was interested. She said she was, so long as I promised she would have control. I agreed, believing we were aligned on the vision. OTV Studio was launching.

In early 2019 Stephanie, Oscar, and I presented the plan and asked for feedback from artists OTV had supported. At an in-person meeting at OTV's Humboldt Park location with over fifty OTV artists (a majority), I gave a lengthy presentation on how the idea arose, how the model would work, and what I saw as the challenges. I surveyed everyone in attendance so they could offer anonymous feedback, which were coded by my grad student at the time, Chelsea. Creators expressed ideas, issues, and concerns around OTV's role in helping them to broaden their audience and expose their work to potential stakeholders. Many of the artists saw their partnership with OTV as an opportunity to gain exposure to general audiences, audiences outside of Chicago, and to the media industry. Several expressed that we could be a good partner by providing guidance, support, and resources to them on everything from script writing to project development and distribution. Others noted how they looked to their relationship with OTV (chiefly, me) to help guide them throughout various parts of the development process and would like to see this continue. One wrote that "I appreciate the idea that OTV will have much more hands on when it comes to managing and supervising deals." This sentiment was also felt strongly around the idea of management and OTV's ability to help artists navigate potentially tricky and difficult partnerships within the media industry: "OTV will help by acting as a mentor for myself and for my production throughout the development/production process."

There were concerns, many revolving around confusion regarding whether the for-profit would replace the nonprofit distribution platform because at the time, the nonprofit did not yet have funding to continue. Others were concerned about being left behind in the incubator, since the model suggested that not all projects would be pitched and not all artists would receive representation. Creators saw funding as a potential challenge in the OTV sustainability model. They seemed unclear about how funding and payment to artists and staff would work under this new model, if certain projects would be paid and funded over others, and if so, how these decisions around financing would be made. Speaking to many of these concerns in their response to potential challenges, one artist wrote, "Funding and Financing! I'm not clear on this exactly. Would all future OTV projects be funded by OTV provided they have equity in the project? Or would some still [be required] to find their own financing, and OTV would have equity in those in exchange for the service of shopping the project?" These were all legitimate concerns and ones that would only have answers once funding came in to support the project, as different investors and partners have different needs.

I saw many of these concerns as roadblocks OTV could overcome with the right partners and leadership on board, particularly impact investors who were more interested in our mission than profits. So we moved forward knowing we had broad support from our community and also a good sense of the concerns they had that we needed to keep in mind. That spring, I released a call for pitches from every person I'd met with over the years, including those without a project on OTV, several hundred. We received around seventy submissions, and the OTV team worked through them to collectively pick the top twenty. We signed those artists to management contracts—representing the artist by working to develop their creative output—and shopping agreements—giving us the right to pitch their projects to partners—for a commission. Stephanie and I brought on Julie Keck, who we'd known for years as a tireless supporter of diverse indie artists and a writer of many web series herself, to support business development.

We flew to LA in early 2020 for a round of meetings that concluded just days before the pandemic lockdowns. The pandemic delayed our progress significantly, but we still managed to get some meetings for writers that year, including with Hulu and HBO. Then, by the end of that year, Lilly Wachowski (*The Matrix*, *Sense8*, and more) who had been following OTV for years—including attending our premiere of *the T*, our only one to receive a standing ovation—signed on to help OTV Studio. By 2021, it looked like we might have a shot.

In 2023 OTV Studio rebranded as Breaking Light Studio and entered a partnership with the studio arm of Circle of Confusion, the management company that has represented Lilly since the beginning of her career. Breaking Light Studio has a roster of incredibly talented writers, a strong partner in Lilly and her managers, and passionate, capable leadership in Stephanie. I pulled away in 2022 to avoid potential conflicts of interest and gave my ownership stake to Stephanie to do with what she pleased. By 2022, I also felt I had done the most I could to support the company's development: helping develop a values-aligned business model; introducing the leadership to more than fifty executives I knew from my meetings; introducing leadership to every funder I knew who might support the company, including one that did eventually offer funding; writing grant and award applications with Stephanie and Julie; reading and giving notes on scripts, though far less than Stephanie; advising artists on career strategy; and advising on business strategy alongside Oscar and Julie.

I also stepped away from OTV Studio because I was not able to give my ownership stake to the OTV nonprofit. Spending four years working for and developing a company without ever getting paid sounds like a failure to some, but it was always part of my plan. Practicing reparations requires personal sacrifice. If I have any regrets, it's the loss of a vision of siphoning Hollywood profits to a nonprofit that works to repair Hollywood's exclusions—the original vision for experimental reparations. It didn't happen because I spent too much time trying to build *economic* capacity for the OTV for-profit and nonprofits and not enough on the *social* and *cultural* work of cultivating trust and care among the many leaders it would take to cultivate such a grand vision. The bonds between us were not strong enough for such a complex undertaking.

By practicing reparations, I have learned how integral my own healing journey and the healing journeys of my community are to my vision for systemic healing. As mentioned throughout the book, the early years of OTV were not ones where I could take care of myself, let alone fully account for how my actions or inactions might be shaping the dozens of relationships I was managing. I realized this too late. I have so many regrets, but I take solace in knowing our work is still valuable. Both OTV and Breaking Light have promising futures and strong leadership. I am forever in debt to Stephanie and Elijah for their work, a debt they never have to forgive. They will always have my support. At the same, I credit myself for what I have already given. I put in a lot of unpaid labor for these organizations,[19] and I continue to offer it freely. In fact, as a Black queer man working for an exclusive institution, I need my work be as nonextractive as possible. I largely resisted incentives to extract value that are pervasive in media, tech, and research. We were poised to raise millions in grants, and the university system incentivizes researchers to funnel that money into our research accounts to reduce teaching loads and increase productivity using grad student labor, instead of supporting communities that need it most. There were dozens of executives in Hollywood interested in the project, and the media system incentivizes selling artists' IP to corporations and cutting a deal with a major studio or network. Executives told me that's exactly what I should have done. The tech system incentivizes platform owners to seek investors to grow audiences rapidly and globally, undercutting the value of deep community relations. I resisted these incentives to extract, and I am proud that my labor went to support leadership by brilliant Black women and nonbinary people who can pay themselves through organizations I helped build. This process of redistributing power and repairing relationships, of refusing to settle my debts, is ongoing and ever refreshing.

Repairing systems requires leaders with resources, time, or privilege to offer it freely to support other leaders who need it. This process is messy. We cannot assume perfection from leaders—this ultimately reinforces colonial narratives that power is absolute and inaccessible except for the privileged few. We all need to see ourselves as leaders who are accountable to others and our own actions and inactions. To do this, we must heal from the ways systems have devalued us, shaped how we value ourselves and how others value us. Having lacked so much systemic support or care—abundant access to resources, food, shelter, mental and physical healthcare as children or adults—many find it challenging to identify where the hurt is and who it comes from. In our pain and fatigue, we can struggle to hold ourselves accountable to each other. Repair cannot thrive in these contexts.

Our great challenge is healing ourselves, our communities, and our institutions in a climate that rewards harm and blocks repair. We cannot resolve this tension. We must engage it—consistently. We cannot let systems and institutions off the hook, but denying accountability from ourselves, our peers, and our communities also allows harm to continue, just on a smaller scale.

Still, all failure is productive. Even if things fall apart, our labor has value. We can learn from mistakes but only if we take accountability. We can create value for ourselves and our communities, but we must check in with each other as we do. We must move at the speed of trust, as adrienne maree brown and others have written.

Individuals and communities need consistent healing practices and redistributive organizations to cultivate systemic reparation. We are all connected: our efforts with our dreams, our relationships with our organizations, our stories with our platforms, our individual freedom and collective liberation.

EPILOGUE: AN INVITATION TO THE COOKOUT

Dear creator of art or community—

I'm honored to invite you to *The Cookout*, a groundbreaking new protocol and film series. You have been selected because we believe your practice celebrates Black or Indigenous liberation and healing. You have been recommended by people we trust who affirm that you are truly 'bout that life.

Your invitation is for life, and you are free to do with it what you wish, at any time. We know you because of your creating, curating, or producing of music, filmmaking, writing, dance, video games, community, etc., but what you do with this invitation is up to you, so long as you are willing to collaborate, combining your individual vision with our collective vision.

We have a team of curators and a budget to help you share a message of liberation and healing to the world. We will help you find collaborators so that you can cook the most delicious, innovative, and healthy cultural meal for our community to consume.

Your invitation includes the following:

(1) An invitation to the Cookout protocol to connect with others working toward liberation

(2) A segment in an episode of *The Cookout*, at a length we will mutually decide upon

(3) An ownership stake in your episode, split with all collaborators in that episode

(4) Ownership of your segment in the episode, split with any collaborators you choose

(5) The right to distribute, sell, or develop your segment outside of *The Cookout*

(6) A vote and voice in future episodes

(7) Access to restorative justice practitioners should conflict and harm arise

We hope you honor this invitation to cook something beautiful for our community.

* * *

I have a vision for a platform and series of films as a cookout, called *The Cookout*.

I have a vision for an app that intentionally invites community members to cocreate this show and other knowledges, where users own their data, share in the wealth of its monetization, and cultivate their own AI (ancestral/artificial intelligences). I want this app to serve as a tool for organizing for our collective liberation from oppressive systems.

I resist our desire to talk about who is *not* invited to the cookout. I want to focus on who *is*.

I want a platform and show that invites artists and audiences to cocreate a community vibe.

I want a show that breaks the boundaries of established film/TV formats (late night, variety, etc.) and the boundaries of time, with episodes as long as they need to be.

I want an uncensored platform and show that platforms the histories and lived experiences of those who powerful institutions forget or fear. I want a Black-led app and series that invites people of other identities to *The Cookout* who have demonstrated their commitment to Black life, particularly our Indigenous American and African friends who deeply understand the impact of colonialism and what it means to be in deep relationship with the earth.

I want a platform and show that showcases all art forms outside of competition. I want to see music, film, dance, drag, comedy, theater, performance, poetry, visual art, costume design, graphic design, makeup, video games, VR, social video, conversation, information, and even culinary arts produced to inspire and inform.

I want a show that is owned by the people who make it *and* by the users who watch it, whose profits go toward sustaining the series itself along with its creators and the organizations our communities need.

I want a show released nonexclusively on large streaming platforms to support its distribution independent of the corporate system.

I want a show exhibited not only on digital platforms but also in community cookouts around the country and world, a platform for deep, local community engagement.

I want a platform and series programming released with the cycles of the earth, not of capital. I want to watch *The Cookout* at the start of every season, even every new moon, with each episode themed to help us set intentions via natural rhythms.

I want a show that embraces new technologies in community-accountable ways, honoring collective human intelligence over, but not against, AI, blockchain, computer-generated images, interactivity, and decentralized distribution.

I want a platform and show that centers healing in all aspects and scales of production. I want them to deplatform those causing harm and not actively healing, with clear protocols for how they can be invited back.

I want these projects to honor ancestors: Maya Angelou, Ellis Haizlip, R. J. Watkins, and the many other Black and Indigenous series creators who used media to bring artists and communities together.

There are so many ways to cultivate and grow this vision. I want it done sustainably.

If you want this too, you know where to find me!

In solidarity, Aymar

NOTES

ACKNOWLEDGING WHO I COME FROM: HEALING OVER CENTURIES

1. Gad J. Heuman, *Between Black and White: Race, Politics, and the Free Coloreds in Jamaica, 1792–1865* (Greenwood Press, 1981), 38.

2. Heuman, *Between Black and White*, 38.

3. Heuman, *Between Black and White*, 41.

INTRODUCTION

1. Media ecology studies informs my view of culture as an ecosystem. However, I differ in foregrounding cultural identity, particularly race, as structuring media and technology versus media ecologists' prioritizing technology as structuring our identities. Nevertheless, I am inspired by its critique of the role of corporate capitalism as hazardous to our culture. See Neil Postman, *Amusing Ourselves to Death: Public Discourse in the Age of Show Business* (Penguin, 1986); Douglas Rushkoff, *Program or Be Programmed: Ten Commands for a Digital Age* (OR Books, 2010).

2. Donella Meadows, *Thinking in Systems: A Primer* (Chelsea Green, 2008), 2.

3. Viktor Pickard, "Another Media System Is Possible: Ripping Open the Overton Window, from Platforms to Public Broadcasting," *Javnost—The Public* 30, no. 2 (2023): 284–297. On platform cooperativism, see also Trebor Scholtz, *Platform Cooperativism: Challenging the Corporate Sharing Economy* (Rosa Luxemburg Stiftung, 2016).

4. My reclaiming of "diversity" throughout this book resists its co-optation by corporations (for-profit and nonprofit) in ways that understate how power structures our differences. Grounding diversity in ecology critiques how institutions limit diversity by viewing differences as bureaucratic problems to be resolved rather than natural

phenomena to be liberated from the constraints of human-made structural inequalities. I concur with Ralina Joseph that "if we embrace difference without striving for equity, we re-create inequality through forces that pretend sameness." In nature, diversity sustains life through differences in power equitably distributed, where all participants can thrive and where nobody evades accountability. See Ralina Joseph, "What's the Difference with 'Difference'? Equity, Communication, and the Politics of Difference," *International Journal of Communication* 11 (2017): 3306–3326.

5. Jessica Clark has written about the concept of "regenerative media" in relation to journalism. See Jessica Clark, "From Extractive to Regenerative," Nieman Lab, December 2021, https://www.niemanlab.org/2021/12/from-extractive-to-regenerative; "Regenerative Agriculture 101," Natural Resources Defense Council, November 29, 2021, https://www.nrdc.org/stories/regenerative-agriculture-101.

6. Miriyam Aouragh, inspired by Indigenous activists, writes that radical kinship is insurgent, compassionate, and reproductive: "Don't come to help me, but come to join your struggle to mine." See Miriam Aouragh, "Towards a Theory of Radical Kinship," *Race & Class* 65, no. 1 (2023): 39–41.

7. The series brings to television a queer tradition of Afro-Asian collaboration with extensive history in music and activism, what Elliott Powell calls an "understanding of African and Asian (diasporic) comparative racialization as a site of kinship and anti-imperial, anti-capitalist, and anti-racist alliances." See Elliott Powell, *Sounds from the Other Side: Afro-South Asian Collaborations in Black Popular Music* (University of Minnesota Press, 2020), 7.

8. Thomas Poell, David Nieborg, and Brooke Duffy, *Platforms and Cultural Production* (Polity Press, 2022), 5.

9. "Platform," Encyclopedia.com, updated May 18, 2018, https://www.encyclopedia.com/humanities/dictionaries-thesauruses-pictures-and-press-releases/platform-0.

10. Tarleton Gillespie, *Custodians of the Internet: Platforms, Content Moderation, and the Hidden Decisions That Shape Social Media* (Yale University Press, 2018), 7.

11. Aldon Morris, *The Scholar Denied: W. E. B. Du Bois and the Birth of Modern Sociology* (University of California Press, 2017).

12. Kim Gallon, "Making a Case for the Black Digital Humanities," in *Debates in the Digital Humanities 2016*, ed. Matthew K. Gold and Lauren F. Klein (University of Minnesota Press, 2016); Tara McPherson, "Why Are the Digital Humanities So White? or Thinking the Histories of Race and Computation," in *Debates in the Digital Humanities*, ed. Matthew K. Gold (University of Minnesota Press, 2012).

13. In my own field, Roopali Mukherjee argues that "a disgraceful white boys' club persists in the field of Communication." For evidence of exclusion in my field of communication, see Roopali Mukherjee, "Of Experts and Tokens: Mapping a Critical Race Archaeology of Communication," *Communication, Culture and Critique* 13, no. 2 (2020): 152–167; Paula Chakravartty, Rachel Kuo, Victoria Grubbs, and Charlton

McIlwain, "#CommunicationSoWhite," *Journal of Communication* 68, no. 2 (2018): 254–266.

14. Olúfẹ́mi Táíwò, *Reconsidering Reparations* (Oxford University Press, 2022), 74.

15. Khadijah Costley White and Aymar Jèan Escoffery, *Media Reparations* (Polity Press, forthcoming).

16. adrienne maree brown, *Emergent Strategy: Shaping Change, Changing Worlds* (AK Press, 2017).

17. Chelsea Mikael Frazier, "Black Feminist Ecological Thought: A Manifesto," in *Ecofeminism: Feminist Intersections with Other Animals and the Earth*, ed. Carol J. Adams and Lori Gruen (Bloomsbury, 2022); Alexis Pauline Gumbs, *Undrowned: Black Feminist Lessons from Marine Mammals* (AK Press, 2020).

18. Cameron Awkward-Rich, *The Terrible We: Thinking with Trans Maladjustment* (Duke University Press, 2022); Ruha Benjamin, *Viral Justice: How We Grow the World We Want* (Princeton University Press, 2021); Meredith D. Clark, "The Year Journalism Starts Paying Reparations," Nieman Lab, December 2020, https://www.niemanlab.org/2020/12/the-year-journalism-starts-paying-reparations; Jenny Davis, Apryl Williams, and Michael Yang, "Algorithmic Reparation," *Big Data & Society* 8, no. 2 (2021), https://doi.org/10.1177/20539517211044808; Hil Malatino, *Trans Care* (University of Minnesota Press, 2020); Chelsea Peterson-Salahuddin, "Repairing the Harm: Toward an Algorithmic Reparations Approach to Hate Speech Content Moderation," *Big Data & Society* 11, no. 2 (2024), https://doi.org/10.1177/20539517241245333; Leah Lakshmi Piepzna-Samarasinha, *Care Work: Dreaming Disability Justice* (Arsenal Pulp Press, 2018); Eve Kosofsky Sedgewick, *Touching Feeling: Affect, Pedagogy, Performativity* (Duke University Press, 2003); Apryl Williams, *Not My Type: Automating Sexual Racism in Online Dating* (Stanford University Press, 2024).

19. André Brock Jr., *Distributed Blackness: African American Cybercultures* (NYU Press, 2020), 10.

20. Lisa Henderson, *Love and Money: Queers, Class, and Cultural Production* (NYU Press, 2013), 164.

21. Ramzi Fawaz, *Queer Forms* (NYU Press, 2022), 336.

22. Activists and scholars are taking an expansive view of disability and embracing its inevitability to help us see how the work of systemic repair is in everyone's interest. See Piepzna-Samarasinha, *Care Work*; Sam Schalk, "Coming to Claim Crip: Disidentification with/in Disability Studies," *Disability Studies Quarterly* 33, no. 2 (2013), https://doi.org/10.18061/dsq.v33i2; Sam Schalk, *Black Disability Politics* (Duke University Press, 2022).

23. Afropessimism challenges the possibility of liberation within systems of capital generation. Productivity requires the degradation, exploitation, and death of Black and Indigenous lives, most sharply seen in the work of Frank Wilderson and Orlando Patterson, though there is considerable variation in the discourse on the

depth of this determinism, particularly among Black queer and feminist scholars. See (in film) Frank B. Wilderson III, *Red, White & Black: Cinema and the Structure of US Antagonisms* (Duke University Press, 2010); Frank B. Wilderson III, *Afropessimism* (Liveright, 2021).

24. Nathan Hare, "Black Ecology," *The Black Scholar* 1, no. 6 (1970): 2–8; J. T. Roane, Megan Femi-Cole, Preeti Nayak, and Eve Tuck, "'The Seeds of a Different World Are Already Alive in the Everyday Practices of Ordinary Black and Indigenous People': An Interview with J. T. Roane," *Cultural Inquiry* 52, no. 2 (2022): 129–138; Leanne Betasamosake Simpson, *As We Have Always Done: Indigenous Freedom Through Radical Resistance* (University of Minnesota Press, 2017).

25. Adrian Miller, *Soul Food: The Surprising Story of an American Cuisine, One Plate at a Time* (University of North Carolina Press, 2013).

26. Miller, *Soul Food*, 10.

27. Paul Fehribach, *The Big Jones Cookbook: Recipes for Savoring the Heritage of Regional Southern Cooking* (University of Chicago Press, 2015), xiv–xv.

28. adrienne maree brown, "Four Insights for Radical Organizing from the Mysterious World of Mushrooms," Truthout, May 1, 2023, https://truthout.org/articles/four-insights-for-radical-organizing-from-the-mysterious-world-of-mushrooms.

29. Robin Wall Kimmerer, *Braiding Sweetgrass: Indigenous Wisdom, Scientific Knowledge, and Teachings of Plants* (Milkweed Editions, 2015).

30. Stanley Deetz, *Democracy in an Age of Corporate Colonization: Developments in Communication and the Politics of Everyday Life* (SUNY Press, 1992), 2, 3.

31. Deetz, *Democracy in an Age of Corporate Colonization*, 10.

32. MACRO Lab, University of California San Diego, accessed September 26, 2024, https://macrolab.ucsd.edu.

33. Thomas Tufte, *Communication and Social Change: A Citizen Perspective* (Polity Press, 2017), 167; Todd Gitlin, *Media Unlimited, Revised Edition: How the Torrent of Images and Sounds Overwhelms Our Lives* (Henry Holt, 2002); Robert W. McChesney, *Rich Media, Poor Democracy: Communication Politics in Dubious Times* (University of Illinois Press, 1999); Victor Pickard, *America's Battle for Media Democracy: The Triumph of Corporate Libertarianism and the Future of Media Reform* (Cambridge University Press, 2015).

34. A critical context is the power of large firms that own and finance both media and tech corporations. See Andrew DeWaard, "Financialized Hollywood: Institutional Investment, Venture Capital, and Private Equity in the Film and Television Industry," *Journal of Cinema and Media Studies* 59, no. 4 (2020): 54–84.

35. The relationship between race, colonization, and capitalism is the subject of many books. For a start, see Cedric J. Robinson, *Black Marxism: The Making of the Black Radical Tradition*, 3rd ed. (University of North Carolina Press, 2020).

36. Jennifer Holt, *Empires of Entertainment: Media Industries and the Politics of Deregulation, 1980–1996* (Rutgers University Press, 2011); Tanner Mirrlees, *Hearts and Mines: The US Empire's Culture Industry* (UBC Press, 2016).

37. Miriyam Aouragh and Paula Chakravartty, "Infrastructures of Empire: Towards a Critical Geopolitics of Media and Information Studies," *Media, Culture & Society* 38, no. 4 (2016): 559–575; Paula Chakravartty, "Media, Race and the Infrastructures of Empire," in *Media & Society*, 6th ed., ed. David Hesmondhalgh (Bloomsbury, 2019).

38. Ben H. Bagdikian, *The New Media Monopoly* (Beacon Press, 2004).

39. Marwan Kraidy, "Hybridity in Cultural Globalization," *Communication Theory* 12, no. 3 (2002): 316–339; Tanner Mirrlees, *Global Entertainment Media: Between Cultural Imperialism and Cultural Globalization* (Routledge, 2013); Hebert I. Schiller, *Culture Inc.: The Corporate Takeover of Public Expression* (Oxford University Press, 1989).

40. The increasing pace of corporate ownership in media from the beginning of broadcast television to its deregulation in the late twentieth century has been well-documented by scholars like Thomas Streeter and Patricia Aufderheide. See Patricia Aufderheide, *Communications Policy and the Public Interest: The Telecommunications Act of 1996* (Guilford Press, 1999); Thomas Streeter, *Selling the Air: A Critique of the Policy of Commercial Broadcasting in the United States* (University of Chicago Press, 1996).

41. Andrew deWaard and Ashley Bui, "Cumulative Mergers and Acquisitions in Top Media Companies, 1985–2023," MACRO Lab, March 13, 2024, https://macrolab.ucsd.edu/research/mergers-and-acquisitions-media.

42. Carter Moulton uses the term "franchise lands" to describe studio theme parks, but it is an apt metaphor for the colonial tendency to own vast swathes of IP. See Carter Moulton, "Pay (to Pay) to Play: Drillable Immersion at Transmedia Theme Parks," *Communication, Culture and Critique* 15, no. 4 (2022): 479–488.

43. Shawna Kidman, "The Disneyfication of Authorship: Above-the-Line Creative Labor in the Franchise Era," *Journal of Film and Video* 73, no. 3 (2021): 3; Shawna Kidman and Ho-Hsin Wang, "Number of Franchise Films Released Annually, 1960–2023," MACRO Lab, March 13, 2024, https://macrolab.ucsd.edu/research/franchise-frequency.

44. Andrew deWaard, "Total Television Series in US by Type, 2002–2022," MACRO Lab, March 13, 2024, https://macrolab.ucsd.edu/research/television-series-us-format.

45. Aymar Jèan Escoffery and Jamie Cooley, "How Do Black Lives Matter to Hollywood? Marketing Black Trauma and Joy on Streaming Platforms" *Television & New Media* (2025), https://doi.org/10.1177/15274764251320075.

46. Kristen J. Warner, "In the Time of Plastic Representation," *Film Quarterly* 71, no. 2 (2017), https://filmquarterly.org/2017/12/04/in-the-time-of-plastic-representation.

47. Soraya Giaccardi, Eun Jung (Kristin) Jung, Dana Weinstein, Shawn Van Valkenburgh, and Erica L. Rosenthal, *A Balancing Act for Asian Representation in Streaming*

Visibility Doesn't Always Mean Cultural Specificity (Media Impact Project, USC Norman Lear Center, 2023), https://www.mediaimpactproject.org/asianrepresentation; Darnell Hunt, *Race in the Writers' Room: How Hollywood Whitewashes the Stories That Shape America* (Color of Change, 2021), https://hollywood.colorofchange.org/wp-content/uploads/2019/03/COC_Hollywood_Race_Report.pdf; Al-Baab Khan, Katherine Pieper, Dr. Stacy L. Smith, Marc Choueiti, Kevin Yao, and Artur Tofan, "Missing & Maligned: The Reality of Muslims in Popular Global Movies," USC Annenberg Inclusion Initiative, June 2021, https://assets.uscannenberg.org/docs/aii-muslim-rep-global-film-2021-06-09.pdf; Erica L. Rosenthal, Adam Amel Rogers, Emily Peterson, Erica Watson-Currie, and Heesung Shin, *Change the Narrative, Change the World: How Immigrant Representation on Television Moves Audiences to Action* (Define American/Media Impact Project, USC Norman Lear Center, 2020), https://defineamerican.com/research/change-the-narrative.

48. Soraya Giaccardi, Adam Rogeres, and Erica L. Rosenthal, *A Glaring Absence: The Climate Crisis Is Virtually Nonexistent in Scripted Entertainment* (Media Impact Project, USC Norman Lear Center, 2022), https://learcenter.s3.us-west-1.amazonaws.com/GlaringAbsence_NormanLearCenter.pdf.

49. Rebecca Pardo, Tracy Wheeler, and Shoshana Ungerleider, *Death on Television: Flipping the Script* (End Well, 2023), https://endwellproject.org/pdf-death-on-tv.

50. John Thornton Caldwell, *Production Culture: Industrial Reflexivity and Critical Practice in Film and Television* (Duke University Press, 2008); Michael Curtin and Kevin Sanson, eds., *Precarious Creativity: Global Media, Local Labor* (University of California Press, 2016); Vicki Mayer, *Below the Line: Producers and Production Studies in the New Television Economy* (Duke University Press, 2011).

51. Aymar Jèan Christian and Chelsea Peterson-Salahuddin, "Rage Against the Streaming Studio System: Worker Resistance to Hollywood's Networked Era," *Information, Communication & Society* 26, no. 5 (2023): 923–940.

52. Jeff Yang, "Hollywood's Picket Line Confronts Its Color Line," *Capital & Main*, September 4, 2023, https://capitalandmain.com/hollywoods-picket-line-confronts-its-color-line.

53. Axelle Asmar, Tim Raats, and Leo Van Audenhove, "Streaming Difference(s): Netflix and the Branding of Diversity," *Critical Studies in Television* 18, no. 1 (2023): 24–40.

54. Ramon Lobato, *Netflix Nations: The Geography of Digital Distribution* (NYU Press, 2019), 71.

55. Olivia Khoo, "Picturing Diversity: Inclusion Strategy and the Netflix Recommender Algorithm (NRA)," *Television & New Media* 24, no. (2023): 281–297.

56. Karin van Es, "Netflix & Big Data: The Strategic Ambivalence of an Entertainment Company," *Television & New Media*, ahead of print, September 26, 2022, https://doi.org/10.1177/15274764221125745.

57. Blake Hallinan and Ted Striphas, "Recommended for You: The Netflix Prize and the Production of Algorithmic Culture," *New Media & Society* 18, no. 1 (2016): 117–137.

58. Lulu Garcia-Navarro, "The Interview: The Netflix Chief's Plan to Get You to Binge Even More," *New York Times*, May 25, 2024.

59. Mareike Jenner, "The Quantification of Diversity: Netflix, Visibility Politics and the Grammar of Transnationalism," *Convergence*, ahead of print, August 9, 2024, https://doi.org/10.1177/1354856524126.

60. Since 2019, tech mergers and acquisitions have peaked at over one thousand annually. See DeWaard and Bui, "Cumulative Mergers and Acquisitions."

61. However, algorithmic systems are not purely automated and rely on underpaid human labor in poorer nations. For more information on labor conditions for training AI, see Josh Dzieza, "AI Is a Lot of Work," The Verge, June 20, 2023, https://www.theverge.com/features/23764584/ai-artificial-intelligence-data-notation-labor-scale-surge-remotasks-openai-chatbots; Casey Newton, "The Trauma Floor: The Secret Lives of Facebook Moderators in America," The Verge, February 25, 2019, https://www.theverge.com/2019/2/25/18229714/cognizant-facebook-content-moderator-interviews-trauma-working-conditions-arizona; Billy Perrigo, "Exclusive: OpenAI Used Kenyan Workers on Less Than $2 Per Hour to Make ChatGPT Less Toxic," *Time*, January 18, 2023, https://time.com/6247678/openai-chatgpt-kenya-workers.

62. This is particularly true for youth. danah boyd (2014), one of the earliest scholars of social media among youth, has found both positive and negative impacts of social media. More recently, the American Psychological Association found that social media use can have numerous negative developmental impacts, much of it based on what platforms show to youth; it encourages parents to intervene to mitigate these effects. See "Health Advisory on Social Media Use in Adolescence," American Psychological Association, May 2023, https://www.apa.org/topics/social-media-internet/health-advisory-adolescent-social-media-use; danah boyd, *It's Complicated: The Social Lives of Networked Teens* (Yale University Press, 2014).

63. Andre Brock, "From the Blackhand Side: Twitter as a Cultural Conversation," *Journal of Broadcasting & Electronic Media* 56, no. 4 (2012): 529–549; Meredith Clark, "Hashtag: Social Media as a Source for Developing Community," in *Presumed Incompetent II: Race, Class, Power, and Resistance of Women in Academia, New York*, ed. Yolanda Flores Niemann, Gabriella Gutiérrez y Muhs, and Carmen G. González (Peter Lang, 2020); Rachel Kuo and Sarah J. Jackson, "The Political Uses of Memory: Instagram and Black-Asian Solidarities," *Media, Culture & Society*, ahead of print, July 26, 2023, https://doi.org/10.1177/01634437231185963; Sarah J. Jackson, Moya Bailey, and Brooke Foucault Welles, *#HashtagActivism: Networks of Race and Gender Justice* (MIT Press, 2020).

64. For studies on algorithmic discrimination, see Safiya Noble, *Algorithms of Oppression: How Search Engines Reinforce Racism* (NYU Press, 2018); Cathy O'Neil, *Weapons*

of Math Destruction: How Big Data Increases Inequality and Threatens Democracy (Broadway Books, 2016).

65. Emily Bender, Timnit Gebru, Angelina McMillan-Major, and Shmargaret Shmitchell, "On the Dangers of Stochastic Parrots: Can Language Models Be Too Big?," in *FAccT '21: Proceedings of the 2021 ACM Conference on Fairness, Accountability, and Transparency* (ACM, 2021), 610–623, https://doi.org/10.1145/3442188.3445922.

66. Nicholas Diakopoulos, "Algorithmic Accountability," *Digital Journalism* 3, no. 3 (2015): 398–415.

67. Fred Turner, *From Counterculture to Cyberculture: Stewart Brand, the Whole Earth Network, and the Rise of Digital Utopianism* (University of Chicago Press, 2006).

68. I will discuss this more in chapter 4, but here are some important sources: danah boyd, "Friends, Friendsters, and Top 8: Writing Community into Being on Social Network Sites," *First Monday* 11, no. 12 (2006), https://firstmonday.org/article/view/1418/1336; Catherine Knight Steele, *Digital Black Feminism* (NYU Press, 2021); Charlton McIlwain, *Black Software: The Internet and Racial Justice, from the AfroNet to Black Lives Matter* (Oxford University Press, 2020).

69. Nancy K. Baym, *Tune In, Log On: Soaps, Fandom, and Online Community* (Sage, 2000); Henry Jenkins, *Fans, Bloggers, and Gamers: Exploring Participatory Culture* (NYU Press, 2006); Howard Rheingold, *The Virtual Community: Homesteading on the Electronic Frontier*, rev. ed. (MIT Press, 2000).

70. Jean Burgess and Joshua Green, *YouTube: Online Video and Participatory Culture*, 2nd ed. (Polity, 2018); Anatoliy Gruzd, Barry Wellman, and Yuri Takhteyev, "Imagining Twitter as an Imagined Community," *American Behavioral Scientist* 55, no. 10 (2011): 1294–1318; Tim Weninger, Xihao Avi Zhu, and Jiawei Han, "An Exploration of Discussion Threads in Social News Sites: A Case Study of the Reddit Community," in *2013 IEEE/ACM International Conference on Advances in Social Networks Analysis and Mining (ASONAM 2013)* (IEEE, 2013).

71. David Craig and Stuart Cunningham, *Social Media Entertainment: The New Intersection of Hollywood and Silicon Valley* (NYU Press, 2019); Brooke Erin Duffy, *(Not) Getting Paid to Do What You Love: Gender, Social Media, and Aspirational Work* (Yale University Press, 2017).

72. Here I was inspired by Tim Wu's theory of the "master switch," which argues that there is a pattern in US media history of open beginnings to more controlled, extractive systems across radio, film, and television. I agree with Tarleton Gillespie and T. L. Taylor that there is no "inherent openness" to platforms and that this is a "fantasy." Indeed, my first book shows how producers and distributors' efforts to leverage platform openness were rarely successful. See Aymar Jèan Christian, *Open TV: Innovation Beyond Hollywood and the Rise of Web Television* (NYU Press, 2018); Gillespie, *Custodians of the Internet*, 9; T. L. Taylor, *Watch Me Play: Twitch and the Rise*

of Game Live Streaming (Princeton University Press, 2018), 218; Tim Wu, *The Master Switch: The Rise and Fall of Information Empires* (Vintage Books, 2010).

73. This focus on popularity and one's status in the system is part of the culture of Silicon Valley. See Alice E. Marwick, *Status Update: Celebrity, Publicity, and Branding in the Social Media Age* (Yale University Press, 2013).

74. G. Elijah Dann and Neil Haddow, "Just Doing Business or Doing Just Business: Google, Microsoft, Yahoo! and the Business of Censoring China's Internet," *Journal of Business Ethics* 79 (2008): 219–234; Gerry Shih and Anant Gupta, "Facing Pressure in India, Netflix and Amazon Back Down on Daring Films," *Washington Post*, November 20, 2023.

75. Sareeta Amrute, "Twitter, Facebook, and Google All Have a Trust Problem," *Interactions*, 29, no. 6 (2002): 70–71.

76. Consider that most platforms only allow for the like/dislike binary to speed engagement. Speed shapes our late capitalist culture; see Judy Wajcman, *Pressed for Time: The Acceleration of Life in Digital Capitalism* (University of Chicago Press, 2014).

77. Noble, *Algorithms of Oppression*, 14.

78. Ruha Benjamin, *Race After Technology: Abolitionist Tools for the New Jim Code* (Polity, 2019).

79. Wendy Chun, *Discriminating Data: Correlation, Neighborhoods, and the New Politics of Recognition* (MIT Press, 2021), 41.

80. Chun, *Discriminating Data*, 35–74; Tukufu Zuberi, *Thicker than Blood: How Racial Statistics Lie* (University of Minnesota Press, 2001).

81. Beth Coleman, "Race as Technology," *Camera Obscura* 24, no. 1 (2009): 177–207.

82. Craig S. Wilder, *Ebony and Ivy: Race, Slavery, and the Troubled History of America's Universities* (Bloomsbury Press, 2013), 9.

83. Caine Jordan, Guy Emerson Mount, and Kai Perry Parker, "'A Disgrace to All Slave-Holders': The University of Chicago's Founding Ties to Slavery and the Path to Reparations," *Journal of African American History* 103, no. 1–2 (2018): 163–178.

84. Anemona Hartocollis, "Harvard Details Its Ties to Slavery and Its Plans for Redress," *New York Times*, April 26, 2022, https://www.nytimes.com/2022/04/26/us/harvard-slavery-redress-fund.html; Rina Torchinsky, "University of California Will Waive Tuition and Fees for Many Native American Students," NPR, April 28, 2022, https://www.npr.org/2022/04/28/1095209856/university-of-california-native-american-tuition-fees-waive

85. Roderick A. Ferguson, *The Reorder of Things: The University and Its Pedagogies of Minority Difference* (University of Minnesota Press, 2012), 13.

86. Ferguson, *The Reorder of Things*, 13.

87. Eli Meyerhoff, *Beyond Education: Radical Studying for Another World* (University of Minnesota Press, 2019); la paperson, *A Third University Is Possible* (University of Minnesota Press, 2017).

88. Ernest Boyer, *Scholarship Reconsidered: Priorities of the Professoriate* (Princeton University Press, 1990).

89. Stefano Harney and Fred Moten, *The Undercommons: Fugitive Planning and Black Study* (Minor Compositions, 2013), 38.

90. In Herman Gray's *Watching Race*, he identifies various representational strategies TV writers employed to portray Black representation on screen—assimilationist, pluralist, multiculturalist—offering a convincing argument that there was variability in how to be Black on TV. However, only multiculturalist series center Black culture and still are "contained within the larger hegemonic terms of the dominant US discourse on race and race relations driven by the narrative of inclusion" (92). While he finds some engagement with gender and sexuality on *A Different World*, he finds it preoccupied with "happy endings" (as was the norm on all broadcast TV) that foreclose narrative possibilities (111). *In Living Color* featured regular Black gay characters in the *Men on . . .* segment, but Gray finds it "ambivalent about gayness in the black community even when it satirizes effeminate black gay men" (131). This is not to engage in the positive/negative binary that scholars like Raquel Gates and Cael Keegan write is overly simplistic because, indeed, seeing *Men on . . .* offered some pleasure to me as a child. Rather, I argue that the constraint and ambivalence in Black representation in my formative years related deeply to my own feelings of ambivalence and limitations about who I was. See Herman Gray, *Watching Race: Television and the Struggle for Blackness*, 2nd ed. (University of Minnesota Press, 2004).

91. Beretta Smith-Shomade identifies limits to Black female TV representation in the 1990s, writing that "although wearing the proper skin, however, Black women failed to benefit substantially from the colorized onslaught of 1990s comedies. . . . Whether talking about its articulations as reality, its ability to parody itself, its location as uniquely feminine, or its commonsense understanding of our daily lives, television comedy process a critical battleground for women—even Black ones." See Beretta E. Smith-Shomade, *Shaded Lives: African-American Women and Television* (Rutgers University Press, 2002), 31.

92. We can also look to the work of Donald Bogle and Stuart Hall, who provided frameworks and typologies of stereotypes during the twentieth century. See Donald Bogle, *Toms, Coons, Mulattoes, Mammies, and Bucks: An Interpretive History of Blacks in American Films* (Bloomsbury, 2001); Stuart Hall, "The Spectacle of the 'Other,'" in *Representation: Cultural Representations and Signifying Practices*, ed. Stuart Hall, Jessica Evans, and Sean Nixon (Sage, 1997). Even outside of the positive/negative, scholars have identified a limited range of representations due to the dual effects of capitalism and legacies of colonialism. See Ed Guerrero, *Framing Blackness: The African American Image in Film* (Temple University Press, 1993); Wilderson III, *Afropessimism*.

93. Mark A. Neal, *New Black Man* (Routledge, 2005).

94. bell hooks, *We Real Cool: Black Men and Masculinity* (Routledge, 2004), xi.

95. Alfred Martin, *The Generic Closet: Black Gayness and the Black-Cast Sitcom* (Indiana University Press, 2021).

96. Lisa Bowleg, "When Black + Lesbian + Woman ≠ Black Lesbian Woman: The Methodological Challenges of Qualitative and Quantitative Intersectionality Research," *Sex Roles* 59, no. 5 (2008): 312–325.

97. Jennifer C. Nash, *Black Feminism Reimagined: After Intersectionality* (Duke University Press, 2018).

98. Kimberlé Crenshaw, "Demarginalizing the Intersection of Race and Sex: A Black Feminist Critique of Antidiscrimination Doctrine, Feminist Theory, and Antiracist Politics," *University of Chicago Legal Forum* 1989, article 8 (1989): 139–169, https://chicagounbound.uchicago.edu/uclf/vol1989/iss1.

99. Catherine Squires, *bell hooks: A Critical Introduction to Media and Community Theory* (Peter Lang, 2013).

100. Collins expounds on the power of controlling images in Patricia Hill Collins, *Black Feminist Thought: Knowledge, Consciousness, and the Politics of Empowerment*, 30th anniversary ed. (Routledge, 2022); bell hooks theorizes Black feminist resistance in, among others, bell hooks, *Talking Back: Thinking Feminist, Thinking Black* (South End Press, 1999); bell hooks, *Black Looks: Race and Representation*, 2nd ed. (Routledge, 2015).

101. Moya Bailey, *Misogynoir Transformed: Black Women's Digital Resistance* (NYU Press, 2021), 2.

102. Patricia Hill Collins, *Intersectionality as Critical Social Theory* (Duke University Press, 2019).

103. Collins, *Intersectionality as Critical Social Theory*, 3–4.

104. Linda Tuhiwai Smith, *Decolonizing Methodologies*, 3rd ed. (Bloomsbury, 2021), 5.

105. Max Liboiron, *Pollution Is Colonialism* (Duke University Press, 2021).

106. Whitney Phillips and Ryan M. Milner explore this in the area of political communication: *You Are Here: A Field Guide for Navigating Polarized Speech, Conspiracy Theories, and Our Polluted Media Landscape* (MIT Press, 2021).

107. Táíwò, *Reconsidering Reparations*, 75.

108. Ernest L. Boyer, "The Scholarship of Engagement," *Bulletin of the American Academy of Arts and Sciences* 49, no. 7 (1996): 27–28.

109. Sasha Costanza-Chock, *Design Justice: Community-Led Practices to Build the Worlds We Need* (MIT Press, 2020), https://design-justice.pubpub.org.

110. An additional six programs were screened by OTV in Chicago but not distributed, either because artists found distribution elsewhere or because they were not made in Chicago.

111. OTV annual development reports (2015–present), http://weareo.tv/development.

112. OTV artist and community research reports (2015–2020), http://weareo.tv/research.

113. OTV appeared as an official host of over 69 engagements, which include those 52 screenings we produced in Chicago and others produced in partnership with other organizations in Chicago and globally including Mexico and South Africa. Most screenings included the showcase of multiple projects, which is why the number of surveys exceeds the number of screenings.

114. Favianna Rodriguez, "Culture Is Power," posted October 17, 2023, by Color Congress, YouTube, 31:14, https://www.youtube.com/watch?v=Yoo2X0q1PFQ.

CHAPTER 1

1. Toni Cade Bambara, *Deep Sightings and Rescue Missions: Fiction, Essays, and Conversations* (Vintage Books, 1996), 139.

2. bell hooks, *All About Love: New Visions* (William Morrow, 2018), 215.

3. Raven Maragh-Lloyd thoroughly analyzes the politics and history of the racial draft. See *Black Networked Resistance: Strategic Articulations in the Digital Age* (University of California Press, 2024), 118–133.

4. Patricia Aufderheide, "The Video in the Villages Project: Videomaking with and by Brazilian Indians," *Visual Anthropology Review* 11, no. 2 (1995): 83–93; Deirdre Boyle, *Subject to Change: Guerrilla Television Revisited* (Oxford University Press, 1997); DeeDee Halleck, *Hand-Held Visions: The Uses of Community Media* (Fordham University Press, 2001); Clemencia Rodriguez, *Fissures in the Mediascape: An International Study of Citizens' Media* (Hampton Press, 2001), 2–3.

5. Kevin Howley, *Community Media: People, Places, and Communication Technologies* (Cambridge University Press, 2005), 2.

6. Howley, *Community Media*, 2.

7. Faye Ginsburg, "Indigenous Media: Faustian Contract or Global Village?," *Cultural Anthropology* 6, no. 1 (1991): 94.

8. Nick Couldry, "Alternative Media and Voice," in *The Routledge Companion to Alternative and Community Media*, ed. Chris Atton (Routledge, 2015).

9. Leah Lievrouw, *Alternative and Activist New Media* (Polity, 2011).

10. Chris Atton, *Alternative Media* (SAGE, 2002), 42.

11. Atton, *Alternative Media*. Atton's alternative media theory has resonances with Roman Lobato and Julian Thomas's formulation of the "informal media economy," which shares some similarities with various community and reparative media projects, though Lobato and Thomas do more to highlight the interdependencies between the informal and formal (more often commercial) media system, particularly in the digital age. See Ramon Lobato and Julian Thomas, *The Informal Media Economy* (Polity, 2015).

12. Other countries, including Canada, Australia, and many in South America and Europe, have much more robust histories of community-driven and Indigenous media. This literature is too exhaustive for this text, which narrowly focuses on the US, but please see the aforementioned work of Kevin Howley and Clemencia Rodriguez, in addition to Coco Fusco and Lorna Roth: Coco Fusco, *Young, British, and Black: The Work of Sankofa and Black Audio Film Collective* (Hallwalls, 1998); Lorna Roth, *Something New in the Air: The Story of First Peoples Television Broadcasting in Canada* (McGill-Queen's University Press, 2005).

13. The history of public access, noncommercial, or "guerilla" television outside of documentary tends to focus on large European or European-descended people with proximity to the even more exclusive art world of galleries and museums, dating back to at least the 1960s led by artists like Gerry Schum, Richard Serra, and others who aimed to "decentralize and decommodify the work of art and in turn to reclaim the agency of artists and audiences from the institutional confines of a gallery or museum." See Robyn Farrell, "Network(ed) TV: Collaboration and Intervention at Fernsehgalerie Gerry Schum and Videogalerie Schum," *Afterimage* 43, no. 3 (2015): 12.

14. Christina Dunbar-Hester, *Low Power to the People: Pirates, Protest, and Politics in FM Radio Activism* (MIT Press, 2014), 176–177.

15. Increasingly, scholars of journalism are finding the blending of news and entertainment revealing either biases for presenting information in entertaining ways on social media (Peterson-Salahuddin 2023) or a possible "shift away from audiences characterizing media as *either* news *or* entertainment" (Edgerly and Vraga 2019, 813). See Chelsea Peterson-Salahuddin, "News for (Me and) You: Exploring the Reporting Practices of Citizen Journalists on TikTok," *Journalism Studies*, ahead of print, December 21, 2023, 1–19; Stephanie Edgerly and Emily K. Vraga, "News, Entertainment, or Both? Exploring Audience Perceptions of Media Genre in a Hybrid Media Environment," *Journalism* 20, no. 6 (2019): 807–826.

16. Clemencia Rodríguez, Benjamin Ferron, and Kristin Shamas, "Four Challenges in the Field of Alternative, Radical and Citizens' Media Research," *Media Culture & Society* 36, no. 2 (2014): 152.

17. Tarleton Gillespie, *Custodians of the Internet: Platforms, Content Moderation, and the Hidden Decisions That Shape Social Media* (Yale University Press, 2018).

18. Oliver L. Haimson, Daniel Delmonaco, Peipei Nie, and Andrea Wegner, "Disproportionate Removals and Differing Content Moderation Experiences for Conservative, Transgender, and Black Social Media Users: Marginalization and Moderation Gray Areas," *Proceedings of the ACM on Human-Computer Interaction* 5, no. CSCW2 (2021): 1–35, https://doi.org/10.1145/3479610.

19. Akilah Hughes, "YouTube Rarely Promotes Black YouTube Stars, Even During Black History Month," Fusion, April 8, 2015, https://www.splinter.com/youtube-rarely-promotes-black-youtube-stars-even-durin-1793846967; Sharon Pruitt-Young, "Black TikTok Creators Are on Strike to Protest a Lack of Credit for Their Work," NPR, July 1, 2021, https://www.npr.org/2021/07/01/1011899328/black-tiktok-creators-are-on-strike-to-protest-a-lack-of-credit-for-their-work.

20. Lori Kido Lopez, *Micro Media Industries: Hmong American Media Innovation in the Diaspora* (Rutgers University Press, 2021).

21. More of this will be discussed in chapter 5. See Mark Deuze, "Ethnic Media, Community Media and Participatory Culture," *Journalism* 7, no. 3 (2006): 262–280; Roland Edgar Wolseley, *The Black Press, USA*, 2nd ed. (Iowa State University Press, 1990).

22. Miya Williams Fayne, "The Great Digital Migration: Exploring What Constitutes the Black Press Online," *Journalism & Mass Communication Quarterly* 97, no. 3 (2020): 704–720.

23. Sarah Banet-Weiser, Cynthia Chris, and Anthony Freitas, *Cable Visions: Television Beyond Broadcasting* (NYU Press, 2007); Beretta E. Smith-Shomade, *Pimpin' Ain't Easy: Selling Black Entertainment Television* (Routledge, 2012).

24. danah boyd, "Social Network Sites: Definition, History, and Scholarship," *Journal of Computer-Mediated Communication* 13, no. 1 (2007): 210–230; Dara Byrne, "Public Discourse, Community Concerns, and Civic Engagement: Exploring Black Social Networking Traditions on BlackPlanet.com," *Journal of Computer-Mediated Communication* 13, no. 1 (2007): 319–340.

25. Adrienne Massanari, "Never Alone (Kisima Inŋitchuŋa): Possibilities for Participatory Game Design," *Well-Played: A Journal on Video Games, Value and Meaning* 4, no. 3 (2015): 85–104.

26. Julia Jacobs, "With 'Molly of Denali,' PBS Raises Its Bar for Inclusion," *New York Times*, July 15, 2019.

27. Adrienne Shaw, *Gaming at the Edge: Sexuality and Gender at the Margins of Gamer Culture* (University of Minnesota Press, 2015), 5.

28. Anna Anthropy, *Rise of the Videogame Zinesters: How Freaks, Normals, Amateurs, Artists, Dreamers, Drop-Outs, Queers, Housewives, and People Like You Are Taking Back an Art Form* (Seven Stories Press, 2012).

29. Adrienne Shaw, "What's Next? The LGBTQ Video Game Archive," *Critical Studies in Media Communication* 34, no. 1 (2017): 88–94.

30. Jason Lewis and Skawennati Tricia Fragnito, "Aboriginal Territories in Cyberspace," *Cultural Survival Quarterly* 29, no. 2 (2005): 29.

31. Lewis and Fragnito, "Aboriginal Territories in Cyberspace," 30.

32. Karin Chien, "A New Distribution Future from the Ground Up," posted October 24, 2023, by Color Congress, YouTube, 25:22, https://www.youtube.com/watch?v=RXTcNWvhIBQ.

33. Angel M. Hinzo and Lynn Schoefeld Clark, "Digital Survivance and Trickster Humor: Exploring Visual and Digital Indigenous Epistemologies in the #NoDAPL Movement," *Information, Communication & Society* 22, no. 6 (2019): 791–807; Susan Shay, "Challenging Political Agendas Through Indigenous Media: Hawai'i and the Promotion and Protection of Cultural Heritage," in *Cultural Heritage Communities: Technologies and Challenges*, ed. Luigina Ciolfi, Areti Damala, Eva Hornecker, Monika Lechner, and Laura Maye (Routledge, 2018).

34. Brock Jr., *Distributed Blackness*; Maragh-Loyd, *Black Networked Resistance*; Joshua D. Miner, "Informatic Tactics: Indigenous Activism and Digital Cartographies of Gender-Based Violence," *Information, Communication & Society* 25, no. 3 (2022): 431–448.

35. Mary L. Gray and Siddharth Suri, *Ghost Work: How to Stop Silicon Valley from Building a New Global Underclass* (Houghton Mifflin, 2019); Julian Posada, "The Coloniality of Data Work: Power and Inequality in Outsourced Data Production for Machine Learning" (PhD diss., University of Toronto, 2022), ProQuest (29394279).

36. Anika Collier Navaroli, "Black in Moderation," *Columbia Journalism Review*, October 21, 2023.

37. Frances Haugen, *The Power of One: How I Found the Strength to Tell the Truth and Why I Blew the Whistle on Facebook* (Little, Brown, 2023), 257.

38. Chun argues that we need to shift our understanding of social media's problem from personalization to community-based discrimination.

39. Pablo Boczkowski and Eugenia Mitchelstein, *The Digital Environment: How We Live, Learn, Work, and Play Now* (MIT Press, 2021), 10.

40. Chun deconstructs linear regression as an underlying tool here: "The logistic regression models (designed to predict dichotomous values) presumed the existence of separate and opposed binary categories (male vs. female, Christian vs. Muslim)." See Wendy Chun, *Discriminating Data: Correlation, Neighborhoods, and the New Politics of Recognition* (MIT Press, 2021), 45.

41. Safiya Noble, *Algorithms of Oppression: How Search Engines Reinforce Racism* (NYU Press, 2018); Limor Shifman, "An Anatomy of a YouTube Meme," *New Media & Society* 14, no. 2 (2012): 187–203.

42. Brooke Erin Duffy and Colten Meisner, "Platform Governance at the Margins: Social Media Creators' Experiences with Algorithmic (In)Visibility," *Media, Culture & Society* 45, no. 2 (2022): 3, 17.

43. Zhasmina Tacheva and Srividya Ramasubramanian, "Challenging AI Empire: Unraveling the Interlocking Systems of Oppression in Generative AI's Global Order," *Big Data & Society* 10, no. 2 (2023), https://doi.org/10.1177/20539517231219241.

44. Casey Fiesler, Jialun Jiang, Joshua McCann, Kyle Frye, and Jed Brubaker, "Reddit Rules! Characterizing an Ecosystem of Governance," *Proceedings of the International AAAI Conference on Web and Social Media* 12, no. 1 (2018), https://doi.org/10.1609/icwsm.v12i1.15033.

45. Casey Fiesler, Shannon Morrison, and Amy S. Bruckman, "An Archive of Their Own: A Case Study of Feminist HCI and Values in Design," in *Proceedings of the 2016 CHI Conference on Human Factors in Computing Systems*, ed. Allison Druin and Jofish Kaye (ACM, 2016), 2574–2585; Zachary J. McDowell and Matthew A. Vetter, *Wikipedia and the Representation of Reality* (Taylor & Francis, 2022).

46. V. Jo Hsu, "T4t Love-Politics: Monica Roberts's TransGriot and Love as a Theory of Justice," *Transgender Studies Quarterly* 9, no. 1 (2022): 101–108.

47. Hil Malatino, *Trans Care* (University of Minnesota Press, 2020); Jennifer Nash, "Practicing Love: Black Feminism, Love-Politics, and Post-Intersectionality," *Meridians* 11, no. 2 (2013): 1–24.

48. Kate M. Miltner, "'There's No Place for lulz on LOLCats:' The Role of Genre, Gender, and Group Identity in the Interpretation and Enjoyment of an Internet Meme," *First Monday* 19, no. 8 (2014), https://doi.org/10.5210/fm.v19i8.5391; Sulafa Zidani, "Messy on the Inside: Internet Memes as Mapping Tools of Everyday Life," *Information, Communication & Society*, 24, no. 16 (2021): 2378–2402.

CHAPTER 2

1. Jack Halberstam, *The Queer Art of Failure* (Duke University Press, 2011).

2. Snorton's work presents compelling cases for the inherent queerness of Blackness throughout over a century of historical work and case studies. See Cathy J. Cohen, "Punks, Bulldaggers, and Welfare Queens: The Radical Potential of Queer Politics?," in *Black Queer Studies: A Critical Anthology*, ed. E. Patrick Johnson and Mae G. Henderson (Duke University Press, 2005); Roderick A. Ferguson, *Aberrations in Black: Toward a Queer of Color Critique* (University of Minnesota Press, 2004); E. Patrick Johnson and Mae G. Henderson, "Introduction: Queering Black Studies/'Quaring' Queer Studies," in *Black Queer Studies: A Critical Anthology*, ed. E. Patrick Johnson and Mae G. Henderson (Duke University Press, 2005); E. Patrick Johnson, ed., *No Tea, No Shade: New Writings in Black Queer Studies* (Duke University Press, 2016); C. Riley Snorton, *Nobody Is Supposed to Know: Black Sexuality on the Down Low* (University

of Minnesota Press, 2014); C. Riley Snorton, *Black on Both Sides: A Racial History of Trans Identity* (University of Minnesota Press, 2017).

3. Patricia Hill Collins, *Intersectionality as Critical Social Theory* (Duke University Press, 2019), 5.

4. This was before HBO ordered *Insecure*, so there were very few series centered on characters who could be associated with intersectionality, with rare exceptions like ABC's *Scandal* and Netflix's *Orange Is the New Black*.

5. Aldon Morris, *The Scholar Denied: W. E. B. Du Bois and the Birth of Modern Sociology* (University of California Press, 2017).

6. Morris, *The Scholar Denied*, 22.

7. Martin Bulmer, *The Chicago School of Sociology: Institutionalization, Diversity, and the Rise of Sociological Research* (University of Chicago Press, 1984).

8. Morris, *The Scholar Denied*, 45.

9. In her analysis of Hurston, Hazel Carby identifies contradictions in the writer as an intellectual at the center of the Harlem Renaissance, where Black middle-/upper-class artists claimed relationship to community or "folk" without necessarily being embedded within the particular constructions of the Black social life they imagined in fiction. However, Carby argues that Hurston's seminal novel, *Their Eyes Were Watching God*, written in between two books of anthropology, offered Hurston a critical outlet to expose and explore the tensions she could not when writing within the discipline of anthropology: "In her fictional return, Hurston represents the tensions inherent in her position as an intellectual . . . in antagonistic relation to her construction of the folk as community. . . . In this novel we can see how Hurston brings into being a folk consciousness that is actually in contradictory relation to her sense of herself as intellectual" (31). See Hazel V. Carby, "The Politics of Fiction, Anthropology, and the Folk: Zora Neale Hurston," in *Bloom's Critical Interpretations: Zora Neale Hurston's Their Eyes Were Watching God*, ed. Harold Bloom (Bloom's Literary Criticism, 2008), 31.

10. Audre Lorde, "Poetry Is Not a Luxury," *Chrysalis: A Magazine of Female Culture*, no. 3 (1977).

11. *Audre Lorde: The Berlin Years 1984 to 1992*, directed by Dagmar Schultz (Salzgeber, 2020).

12. Whitney Battle-Baptiste and Britt Rusert, eds., *W. E. B. Du Bois's Data Portraits: Visualizing Black America* (Princeton Architectural Press, 2018).

13. Craig Steven Wilder, *Ebony and Ivy: Race, Slavery, and the Troubled History of America's Universities* (Bloomsbury, 2013).

14. Collins, *Intersectionality as Critical Social Theory*.

15. Arts-based research is more common outside of the United States, particularly in Canada, where it is state supported and codified in promotion rubrics, even though,

as Natalie Loveless argues, it is under threat in Canada, the UK, and Australia as universities corporatize. See Owen B. Chapman and Kim Sawchuk, "Research Creation: Intervention, Analysis and 'Family Resemblances,'" *Canadian Journal of Communication* 37, no. 1 (2012): 5–26; Natalie Loveless, *How to Make Art at the End of the World: A Manifesto for Research-Creation* (Duke University Press, 2019); Stephanie Springgay, *Feltness: Research Creation, Socially Engaged Art, and Affective Pedagogies* (Duke University Press, 2022).

16. George Villanueva, *Promoting Urban Social Justice Through Engaged Communication Scholarship: Reimagining Place* (Routledge, 2021), 8.

17. Kara Keeling, *Queer Times, Black Futures* (NYU Press, 2019); José Esteban Muñoz, *Cruising Utopia: The Then and There of Queer Futurity* (NYU Press, 2019).

18. José Esteban Muñoz, *The Sense of Brown* (Duke University Press, 2020), 2.

19. Muñoz would say "feeling brown, feeling down." See José Esteban Muñoz, "Feeling Brown, Feeling Down: Latina Affect, the Performativity of Race, and the Depressive Position," *Signs: Journal of Women in Culture and Society* 31, no. 3 (2006): 675–688.

20. Kara Keeling, "Queer OS," *Cinema Journal* 53, no. 2 (2014): 154.

21. Margaret Kovach, *Indigenous Methodologies: Characteristics, Conversations, and Contexts* (University of Toronto Press, 2010), 10.

22. Kovach, *Indigenous Methodologies*, 10.

23. Ellie Rennie, *Community Media: A Global Introduction* (Rowman & Littlefield, 2006), 16.

24. Katherine Cizek and William Uricchio, *Collective Wisdom: Co-Creating Media for Equity and Justice* (MIT Press, 2022), 7–8.

25. Vicki Mayer, "Pedagogies of Paradox in Media Studies and Media Labour," *Synoptique* 8, no. 2 (2019): 9–10.

26. Vicki Mayer, "Small Data Theorizing," *Communication Theory* 31, no. 4 (2021): 1002–1021.

27. Moya Bailey writes about how the IRB, though important, paternalizes research subjects, whereas her work works with participants to achieve consent and ensure that research outputs are also useful to them. See Moya Bailey, "#transform(ing) DH Writing and Research: An Autoethnography of Digital Humanities and Feminist Ethics," *Digital Humanities Quarterly* 9, no. 2 (2015), https://www.digitalhumanities.org/dhq/vol/9/2/000209/000209.html.

28. Jesse Fox, Katy E. Pearce, Adrienne L. Massanari, Julius Matthew Riles, Łukasz Szulc, Yerina S. Ranjit, et al., "Open Science, Closed Doors? Countering Marginalization Through an Agenda for Ethical, Inclusive Research in Communication," *Journal of Communication* 71, no. 5 (2021): 764–784.

29. Robin M. Boylorn and Mark P. Orbe, eds., *Critical Autoethnography: Intersecting Cultural Identities in Everyday Life*, 2nd ed. (Routledge, 2021), 6.

30. Ruth Behar, *The Vulnerable Observer: Anthropology That Breaks Your Heart* (Beacon Press, 1997).

31. John Jackson, *Real Black: Adventures in Racial Sincerity* (University of Chicago Press, 2005), 163.

32. Jackson, *Real Black*, 163.

33. Kovach, *Indigenous Methodologies*, 12.

34. Springgay, *Feltness*.

35. Tanja Dreher, "Speaking Up or Being Heard? Community Media Interventions and the Politics of Listening," *Media, Culture & Society* 32, no. 1 (2010): 85.

36. I was inspired by the ethnographic, network, and anticipatory approaches to action research in new media. See Greg Hearn, Jo Tacchi, Marcus Foth, and June Lennie, *Action Research and New Media* (Hampton Press, 2009). For an in-depth analysis of how I used these methodologies in the first years of OTV, see Aymar Jèan Christian, "The Value of Representation: Toward a Critique of Networked Television Performance," *International Journal of Communication* 11 (2017): 1552–1574.

37. Villanueva, *Promoting Urban Social Justice*, 7.

38. Lisa Bowleg, "When Black + Lesbian + Woman ≠ Black Lesbian Woman: The Methodological Challenges of Qualitative and Quantitative Intersectionality Research," *Sex Roles* 59, no. 5 (2008): 317.

39. There is another aspect of the work only I could perform that I didn't fully understand how much time it would take: project administration. Paying people was the biggest time drain. University bureaucracies are not set up to pay working artists, who rely on payment to come on time and are not always banked. In a couple of cases, my relationships with artists were strained by delays in university payment processing, sometimes a result of me being overworked and forgetting to follow-up to ensure checks were sent. This was in addition to all the administration in running the project itself, including uploading videos to our Vimeo platform; getting and adding credits to videos and the website; running screenings from my laptop, including securing final cuts, assembling playlists, and running tech at venues; and contributing to website updates. Once it was clear that OTV needed to be its own organization, a new crop of work found me. After another "Open TV" threatened to sue us for trademark infringement, I had to find a "low bono" lawyer, formally create an LLC, trademark the new name (OTV), and register as a charitable organization. Then I had to develop a board, host regular meetings, and increase my fundraising and grant writing efforts. It is hard to convey the mental strain of all this work, performed on top of teaching, research, and service to the university, knowing that if I didn't do it, the project could fall apart and strain my relationships with artists and community members.

40. Tobias Dienlin, Niklas Johannes, Nicholas David Bowman, Philipp K. Masur, Sven Engesser, Anna Sophie Kümpel, et al., "An Agenda for Open Science in Communication," *Journal of Communication* 71, no. 1 (2021): 1–26; Tamarinde L. Haven and Leonie Van Grootel, "Preregistering Qualitative Research," *Accountability in Research* 26, no. 3 (2019): 229–244; Marcus R. Munafò, Brian A. Nosek, Dorothy V. M. Bishop, Katherine S. Button, Christopher D. Chambers, Nathalie Percie du Sert, et al., "A Manifesto for Reproducible Science," *Nature Human Behavior* 1, no. 0021 (2017), https://doi.org/10.1038/s41562-016-0021.

41. Mohan Dutta, Srividya Ramasubramanian, Mereana Barrett, Christine Elers, Devina Sarwatay, Preeti Raghunath, et al., "Decolonizing Open Science: Southern Interventions," *Journal of Communication* 71, no. 5 (2021): 804.

42. Dutta et al., "Decolonizing Open Science," 806.

43. See our research reports at http://weareo.tv/research and the organization reports at http://weareo.tv/development.

44. For the latter, see my blog post on collaboration, which resulted from tracking common problems and conflicts I noticed in the community over the first five years of the project: "Artist Development Blog #1: On Collaboration," OTV, September 6, 2021, https://www.weareo.tv/community/artist-development-blog-1-on-collaboration.

45. Sheena Erete, "Using Black Feminist Epistemologies and Activist Frameworks to Counter Structural Racism in Design," *Interactions* 28, no. 5 (2021): 56.

46. Erete, "Using Black Feminist Epistemologies," 58.

47. Jennifer Pierre, Roderic Crooks, Morgan Currie, Britt Paris, and Irene Pasquetto, "Getting Ourselves Together: Data-Centered Participatory Design Research & Epistemic Burden," in *Proceedings of the 2021 CHI Conference on Human Factors in Computing Systems*, ed. Pernille Bjørn and Steven Drucker (ACM, 2021), 1–11, https://doi.org/10.1145/3411764.3445103.

48. Pierre et al., "Getting Ourselves Together."

49. Karma Chàvez, "Bridge Work: A Radical Subject in the Community and New Ways of Knowing," *Journal of Autoethnography* 2, no. 1 (2021): 120.

50. Kevin Michael Foster, "Taking a Stand: Community-Engaged Scholarship on the Tenure Track," *Journal of Community Engagement and Scholarship* 3, no. 2 (2010): 1–11.

51. Maggie Berg and Barbara K. Seeber, *The Slow Professor: Challenging the Culture of Speed in the Academy* (University of Toronto Press, 2016), 57.

CHAPTER 3

1. Saidiya Hartman, "Venus in Two Acts," *Small Axe* 26 (2008): 1–14.

2. William Barlow, *Voice Over: The Making of Black Radio* (Temple University Press, 1999).

3. Aaron Cohen, *Move On Up: Chicago Soul Music and Black Cultural Power* (University of Chicago Press, 2019); Jack Halberstam, "Queer Voices and Musical Genders," in *Oh Boy! Masculinities and Popular Music*, ed. Freya Jarman-Ivens (Routledge, 2007); Robert Pruter, *Chicago Soul* (University of Illinois Press, 1991); Micah Salkind, *Do You Remember House? Chicago's Queer of Color Undergrounds* (Oxford University Press, 2018).

4. Clemencia Rodriguez, *Fissures in the Mediascape: An International Study of Citizens' Media* (Hampton Press, 2001), 2–3.

5. An argument made by Black entrepreneur Byron Allen, who unsuccessfully sued the major telecommunications companies for not carrying Black-owned channels on cable. The US Supreme Court's ruling on the case upended over a century of contract law that protected racial minorities from discrimination, showing how lax US media policy can have widespread ramifications beyond the media industry. See Ann Cullen, "Justice Could Blunt Racial Bias Cases with Comcast Ruling," *2019–2020 Supreme Court Preview*, September 13, 2019, 588–591.

6. Nina Metz, "Illinois Hopes Cinespace Helps Build on Big 2010," *Chicago Tribune*, May 11, 2011, section 3, 4c.

7. "Illinois Shatters Record for Film Revenues with $630 Million in 2021," Reel Chicago, June 17, 2022, https://reelchicago.com/article/illinois-shatters-record-for-film-revenues-with-630-million-in-2021.

8. Michael Phillips, "Coaxing Film from a Former Steel Plant," *Chicago Tribune*, September 2, 2012, section 4, p. 5.

9. Greg Hinz, "Pritzker Renews State's Film Tax Credit," *Crain's Chicago Business*, August 1, 2019, https://www.chicagobusiness.com/greg-hinz-politics/pritzker-renews-states-film-tax-credit.

10. Hinz, "Pritzker Renews State's Film Tax Credit."

11. Greg Braxton, "Slow Burn, but 'Fire' Ignites Strong Following," *Chicago Tribune*, April 24, 2013, section 4, p. 6c.

12. "About," Chicago Police Consent Decree, Illinois Attorney General, accessed June 17, 2022, http://chicagopoliceconsentdecree.org/about.

13. The most difficult aspect of the reparations agreement has been the monument to the survivors, a telling example of how culture, and how we tell stories of our history and ourselves, is critical to repairing state-sanctioned violence.

14. Melissa Brown, Rashawn Ray, Ed Summers, and Neil Fraistat, "#SayHerName: A Case Study of Intersectional Social Media Activism," *Ethnic and Racial Studies* 40, no. 11 (2017): 1831–1846.

15. Charlene Carruthers, *Unapologetic: A Black, Queer and Feminist Mandate for Radical Movements* (Beacon Press, 2018), 13.

16. Mayor Rahm Emanuel's suppression of the Laquan McDonald evidence was widely considered a significant factor in him losing reelection.

17. Darnell Hunt, *Race in the Writers' Room: How Hollywood Whitewashes the Stories That Shape America* (Color of Change, 2021), https://hollywood.colorofchange.org/wp-content/uploads/2019/03/COC_Hollywood_Race_Report.pdf.

18. Hunt, *Race in the Writers' Room*, 22.

19. Hunt, *Race in the Writers' Room*, 22.

20. Tanja Dreher, "Listening Across Difference: Media and Multiculturalism Beyond the Politics of Voice," *Journal of Media and Cultural Studies* 23, no. 4 (2009): 445–448.

21. Harvey Young and Queen Meccasia Zabriskie, *Black Theater Is Black Life: An Oral History of Chicago Theater and Dance, 1970–2010* (Northwestern University Press, 2014).

22. Miranda Banks, *The Writers: A History of American Screenwriters and Their Guild* (Rutgers University Press, 2015), 6–8.

23. Jess King, *Inclusive Screenwriting for Film and Television* (Routledge, 2022), 17.

24. Caldwell calls this form of collaborative capitalist production "industrial auteur theory," whereas Johnson finds a matrix of creative agents in the administration of high-value franchises. See John Caldwell, *Production Culture: Industrial Reflexivity and Critical Practice in Film and Television* (Duke University Press, 2008); Derek Johnson, *Media Franchising: Creative License and Collaboration in the Culture Industries* (NYU Press, 2013).

25. Several reports have since confirmed Henderson's analysis using survey data, also finding barriers to promotion and harassment amid tokenization. See Hunt, *Race in the Writers' Room*; Felicia D. Henderson, "The Culture Behind Closed Doors: Issues of Gender and Race in the Writers' Room," *Cinema Journal* 50, no. 2 (2011): 145–152; Felicia D. Henderson, "*South Central*: Black Writers and the Responsibility and Burden of Creating Black Characters for a Black Audience," *Emergences: Journal for the Study of Media & Composite Cultures* 11, no. 2 (2001): 237–248.

26. Maeve Connolly, *TV Museum: Contemporary Art and the Age of Television* (Intellect Books, 2014); Jason Mittell, *Complex TV: The Poetics of Contemporary Television Storytelling* (NYU Press, 2015); Michael Z. Newman and Elana Levine, *Legitimating Television: Media Convergence and Cultural Status* (Routledge, 2012); Lynn Spigel, *TV by Design: Modern Art and the Rise of Network Television* (University of Chicago Press, 2008).

27. Claire Bishop, *Artificial Hells: Participatory Art and the Politics of Spectatorship* (Verso, 2012), 2.

28. Stephanie Smith, ed. *Institutions and Imaginaries* (University of Chicago Press. 2014), 1.

29. Participatory video has existed since the dawn of TV, emerging in full force in the 1960s, though this history is largely white and connected to elite art world circles. Still, some scholars find roots for popular contemporary genres like reality TV and YouTube in midcentury participatory television. See Daniel Marcus, "From Participatory Video to Reality Television," in *A Companion to Reality Television*, ed. Laurie Ouellette (Wiley, 2014); Marita Sturken, "TV as a Creative Medium," *Afterimage* 11, no. 10 (May 1984): 5–9; Stephanie Tripp, "From TVTV to YouTube: A Genealogy of Participatory Practices in Video," *Journal of Film and Video* 64, no. 1–2 (2012): 5–16.

30. K. J. Greene, "Copyright, Culture & (and) Black Music: A Legacy of Unequal Protection," *Hastings Communications and Entertainment Law Journal* 21, no. 2 (1998): 364.

31. Greene, "Copyright, Culture & (and) Black Music," 368. Siva Vaidhyanathan writes that the relationship between blues composers and their labels was "blatantly exploitative," though Chicago had a thriving independent distribution system that served artists for decades. See Siva Vaidhyanathan, *Copyrights and Copywrongs: The Rise of Intellectual Property and How It Threatens Creativity* (NYU Press, 2001), 218; Pruter, *Chicago Soul.*

32. Jacqueline Stewart, *Migrating to the Movies: Cinema and Black Urban Modernity* (University of California Press, 2005), 194.

33. Allyson Field, "The Ambitions of William Foster: Entrepreneurial Filmmaking at the Limits of Uplift Cinema," in *Early Race Filmmaking in America*, ed. Barbara Lupack (Routledge, 2016), 54.

34. Christine Acham, "Subverting the System: The Politics and Production of *The Spook Who Sat by the Door*," in *Race and the Revolutionary Impulse in "The Spook Who Sat by the Door,"* ed. Michael T. Martin, David C. Wall, and Marilyn Yaquinto (Indiana University Press, 2018).

35. Sonya Williams, *Word Warrior: Richard Durham, Radio, and Freedom* (University of Illinois Press, 2015).

36. Williams, *Word Warrior*; see also "*Bird of the Iron Feather*," Television Academy, interview with Newton Minow, posted March 9, 2011, YouTube, https://interviews.televisionacademy.com/shows/bird-iron-feather.

37. Christopher Anderson and Michael Curtin, "Mapping the Ethereal City: Chicago Television, the FCC, and the Politics of Place," *Quarterly Review of Film & Video* 16, no. 3–4 (1999): 289–305.

38. Joel Sternberg, "Chicago Television: A History," *Quarterly Review of Film & Video* 16, no. 3–4 (1999): 229.

39. Chad Raphael, "Utopia Out of Place: Studs' Place, Popular Front Culture and the Blacklist in Chicago Television," *Quarterly Review of Film & Video* 16, no. 3–4 (1999): 253.

40. Raphael, "Utopia Out of Place," 255.

41. Raphael, "Utopia Out of Place," 256–257.

42. Sternberg, "Chicago Television," 240.

43. Ayana Contreras, *Energy Never Dies: Afro-Optimism and Creativity in Chicago* (University of Illinois Press, 2021).

44. Christopher P. Lehman, *A Critical History of Soul Train on Television* (McFarland, 2008).

45. Aymar Jèan Christian, "The OTV Artist and Community 2015–2019," OTV, accessed September 26, 2024, https://www.weareo.tv/research//the-otv-artist-amp-community-2015-2019.

46. It is important to note that one of Lear's writers and the show's cocreator Eric Monte, a Chicagoan, accused Lear's company of denying him the many millions of dollars it made from the show. See Nina Metz, "The Complicated Legacy of Norman Lear and 'Good Times,'" *Chicago Tribune*, December 6, 2023.

47. For more on intersectionality as a concept not "owned" by people who survive racism and sexism daily, see Jennifer Nash, *Black Feminism Reimagined: After Intersectionality* (Duke University Press, 2018).

48. William T. Bielby and Denise D. Bielby, "'All Hits Are Flukes': Institutionalized Decision Making and the Rhetoric of Network Prime-Time Program Development," *American Journal of Sociology* 99, no. 5 (1994): 1287–1313.

49. Kara Keeling, *The Witch's Flight: The Cinematic, the Black Femme, and the Image of Common Sense* (Duke University Press, 2007).

50. Alfred Martin, "Surplus Blackness," *Flow* 27, no. 2 (2021), https://www.flowjournal.org/2021/04/surplus-blackness.

51. Devorah Heitner, *Black Power TV* (Duke University Press, 2013).

52. Laurie Ouellette writes that PBS was designed to challenge commercial media's mass audience and represent minority populations but ended up "culturally tied to 'influential' professionals with disproportionately high incomes and education levels." See Laurie Ouellette, "Reinventing PBS: Public Television in the Post-Network, Post-Welfare Era," in *Beyond Prime Time: Television Programming in the Post-Network Era*, ed. Amanda D. Lotz (Routledge, 2009).

53. Deirdre Boyle, *Subject to Change: Guerrilla Television Revisited* (Oxford University Press, 1997); John Downing, *Radical Media: Rebellious Communication and Social Movements* (SAGE, 2001); DeeDee Halleck, *Hand-Held Visions: The Impossible Possibilities of Community Media* (Fordham University Press, 2002).

54. Though this moment was also preceded by Maya Angelou's TV series, *Blues, Blacks, Black!* See Adrien Sebro, "Once Lost, Painfully Present: Maya Angelou's *Blacks, Blues, Black!* (1968)," *International Journal of Communication* 16 (2022): 4724–4738.

55. Gayle Wald's book on *Soul!* is the definitive case study and peels back the curtain on how Haizlip elevated Black women as producers and hosts cultivated an intimate relationship with the Black audience in the studio and in New York City. See Gayle Wald, *It's Been Beautiful: "Soul!" and Black Power Television* (Duke University Press, 2015).

56. Keeling, *The Witch's Flight*; Douglas Crimp, *"Our Kind of Movie": The Films of Andy Warhol* (MIT Press, 2012); Samuel R. Delany, *Times Square Red, Times Square Blue* (NYU Press, 1999); Stephane Dunn, *"Baad Bitches" and Sassy Supermamas: Black Power Action Films* (University of Illinois Press, 2010); Chon Noriega, "Imagined Borders: Locating Chicano Cinema in America/América," in *The Ethnic Eye: Latino Media Arts*, ed. Chon A. Noriega and Ana M. López (University of Minnesota Press, 1996), 4; Chon Noriega, *Shot in America: Television, the State, and the Rise of Chicano Cinema* (University of Minnesota Press, 2000); Juan A. Suarez, *Bike Boys, Drag Queens, and Superstars: Avant-Garde, Mass Culture, and Gay Identities in the 1960s Underground Cinema* (Indiana University Press, 1996); Matthew Tinkcom, *Working Like a Homosexual: Camp, Capital, Cinema* (Duke University Press, 2002).

57. Beretta Smith-Shomade's work on BET and Arlene Dávila's exploration of the emergence of the Latino market (and the many blindnesses and elisions marketers had in response) are two one of the most robust case studies of how media marketing misrepresents communities. See Arlene Dávila, *Latinos, Inc.: The Marketing and Making of a People* (University of California Press, 2012); Beretta E. Smith-Shomade, *Pimpin' Ain't Easy: Selling Black Entertainment Television* (Routledge, 2012).

58. Joseph Turow, *Niche Envy: Marketing Discrimination in the Digital Age* (MIT Press, 2008).

59. Boyle, *Subject to Change*; Alexandra Juhasz, *AIDS TV: Identity, Community, and Alternative Video* (Duke University Press, 1995); Laura Stein, "Access Television and Grassroots Political Communication in the United States," in *Radical Media: Rebellious Communication and Social Movements*, ed. John Downing (SAGE, 2001).

60. Writing about the legacy of the Independent Television Service (ITVS), created by Congress in 1988, Pat Aufderheide writes that "public television post-1967 has suffered dramatically from incursions from both government and economic interests" (174). Aufderheide quotes Marlon Riggs's Senate testimony that public TV should represent the underserved but that it "had made its lowest priority 'emerging independent producers, producers of color, producers with voices and visions that risk upsetting the status quo, that challenge not only what public television says but how it says it'" (178). See Pat Aufderheide, "Public TV and the Public Sphere," *Critical Studies in Media Communication* 8, no. 2 (1991): 168–183.

61. Charlotte Howell, "Symbolic Capital and the Production Discourse of *The American Music Show*: A Microhistory of Atlanta Cable Access," *Cinema Journal* 57, no. 1 (2017): 1–24.

62. Lauren Herold, "Cable Comes Out: LGBTQ Community Television on New York Public Access Stations" (PhD diss., Northwestern University, 2021), ProQuest (28644151); Juhasz, *AIDS TV*; Frances Negron-Muntaner, "Drama Queens: Latino Gay and Lesbian Independent Film/Video," in *The Ethnic Eye: Latino Media Arts*, Chon A. Noriega and Ana M. López (University of Minnesota Press, 1996), 61.

63. Herman Gray, *Watching Race: Television and the Struggle for Blackness* (University of Minnesota Press, 1995); Kristal Brent Zook, *Color by Fox: The Fox Network and the Revolution in Black Television* (Oxford University Press, 1999).

64. Phillip Lamarr Cunningham, "Color by the CW," in *CW Comes of Age: Essays on Programming, Branding and Evolution*, ed. Ashley Lynn Carlson and Lisa K. Perdigao (McFarland & Co., 2022).

65. Jennifer Fuller, "Branding Blackness on US Cable Television," *Media, Culture & Society* 32, no. 2 (2010): 287.

66. Curiously, Lotz misses the clear racial/racist dynamics of peak white male antihero programming on cable, but the corpus of her sample tells the tale. See Amanda D. Lotz, *Cable Guys: Television and Masculinities in the 21st Century* (NYU Press, 2014).

67. Nigel Coutinho, "Awkward Black Girl's Next Misadventure: Her Own Studio," Blavity, September 23, 2014, https://shadowandact.com/awkward-black-girls-next-misadventure-her-own-studio.

68. *Preserving an Open Internet for Consumers, Small Businesses, and Free Speech: Hearing Before the House Subcommittee on Communications and Technology of the Committee on Energy and Commerce*, 116th Congress, February 7, 2019 (testimony of Ruth Livier).

69. Christopher Ali, "Telecommunications Localism: The Fight for Control over Local Communication Networks in the United States," *Media International Australia* 190, no. 1 (2024): 7–22.

70. Stefania Marghitu, "*Broad City* and *Insecure*'s Millennial Showrunners: From Indie Web Series to Cable and Streaming Crossovers," *Feminist Media Studies* 19, no. 7 (2019): 1–4.

71. Marlon Rachquel Moore, "Between Women TV: Toward the Mainstreaming of Black Lesbian Masculinity and Black Queer Women in Community," *Black Camera* 6, no. 2 (2015): 201–216.

72. For a study of the first generation of indie distributors around the concept of intersectionality, see Aymar Jèan Christian, "Beyond Branding: The Value of Intersectionality on Streaming TV Channels," *Television & New Media* 21, no. 5 (2020): 457–474.

73. Christian, "Beyond Branding."

74. For more on how racial politics of the publishing industry relate to other culture industries like TV, music, film, and online production, see Anamik Saha, *Race and the Cultural Industries* (John Wiley & Sons, 2018).

75. Kristen J. Warner, *The Cultural Politics of Colorblind TV Casting* (Routledge, 2015).

76. Racquel J. Gates, *Double Negative: The Black Image and Popular Culture* (Duke University Press, 2018); Jack Halberstam, *Trans: A Quick and Quirky Account of Gender Variability* (University of California Press, 2018); Cáel M. Keegan, "On the Necessity of Bad Trans Objects," *Film Quarterly* 75, no. 3 (2022): 26–37.

77. Warner, *The Cultural Politics of Colorblind TV Casting*, 33.

78. Warner, *The Cultural Politics of Colorblind TV Casting*, 35; see also Mary Beltran, "Meaningful Diversity: Exploring Questions of Equitable Representation on Diverse Ensemble Cast Shows," *Flow* 12, no. 7 (August 2010), https://www.flowjournal.org/2010/08/meaningful-diversity.

79. See "organic representation": Aymar Jèan Christian and Khadijah Costley White, "Organic Representation as Cultural Reparation," *Journal of Cinema and Media Studies* 60, no. 1 (2020): 143–147.

80. Isabel Molina-Guzmán, "#OscarsSoWhite: How Stuart Hall Explains Why Nothing Changes in Hollywood and Everything Is Changing," *Critical Studies in Media Communication* 33, no. 5 (2016): 438–454.

81. The diversity within *Latinidad* is a consistent theme in Latina/o/é media studies. In this context, I have found that indie TV creators tend to fill in gaps that exist in both the "mainstream" and "Spanish-language" US markets. See Aymar Jèan Christian, *Open TV: Innovation Beyond Hollywood and the Rise of Web Television* (NYU Press, 2018), 143–153; Arlene Dávila, *Latinos Inc.: The Making and Marketing of a People* (University of California Press, 2001); Frances Negrón-Muntaner, *The Latino Media Gap: A Report on the State of Latinos in US Media* (Center for the Study of Ethnicity and Race, Columbia University, 2014); Angharad N. Valdivia, *Latino/as in the Media* (Polity, 2010).

82. Much of performance studies argues this, which we can see specifically in E. Patrick Johnson's notion of "quare" performance, or generally in Jon McKenzie's review of the discipline in monograph that combines an analysis of cultural performance with organizational and technological performance. See E. Patrick Johnson, "'Quare' Studies, or (Almost) Everything I Know About Queer Studies I Learned from My Grandmother," *Text and Performance Quarterly* 21, no. 1 (2001): 1–25; Jon McKenzie, *Perform or Else: From Discipline to Performance* (Routledge, 2002).

83. Bielby and Bielby, "'All Hits Are Flukes.'"

84. Amy Chozick, "The Math of a Hit TV Show," *Wall Street Journal*, May 12, 2011, https://www.wsj.com/articles/SB10001424052748703864204576315240324571266.

85. Todd Gitlin, *Inside Prime Time*, 2nd ed. (Routledge, 2017).

86. We can think of the deepening history of branding as a capitalist practice to scale markets for agricultural goods and, of course, slaves to reflect on how Hollywood's focus on branding turns complex beings—people, stories, communities—into commodities to be bought and sold.

87. Indeed, years after I handed OTV to a full-time staff, I still received regular texts and emails from artists looking for advice or support; it is very difficult to place borders on an organic, reparative practice.

88. Adrian Miller, *Soul Food: The Surprising Story of an American Cuisine, One Plate at a Time* (University of North Carolina Press, 2013), 2.

89. Tony L. Whitehead, "In Search of Soul Food and Meaning: Culture, Food, and Health," in *African Americans in the South: Issues of Race, Class, and Gender*, ed. Hans A. Baer and Yvonne Jones (University of Georgia Press, 1992), 101.

90. kimberly d. nettles, "'Saving' Soul Food," *Gastronomica* 7, no. 3 (2007): 106–113.

91. John Jackson Jr., *Thin Description* (Harvard University Press, 2013).

92. Writers Guild of America West, *Inclusion & Equity Report 2022* (Writers Guild of America West, 2022), https://www.wga.org/uploadedfiles/the-guild/inclusion-and-equity/Inclusion-Report-2022.pdf.

93. For more on worker stories, see Aymar Jèan Christian and Chelsea Peterson-Salahuddin, "Rage Against the Streaming Studio System: Worker Resistance to Hollywood's Networked Era," *Information, Communication & Society* 26, no. 5 (2023): 923–940.

94. For the full survey results, see Media and Data Equity (MADE) Lab, *Creativity and Wellness in the Chicago Film/TV Industry* (MADE, 2022), https://www.madelab.org/research/the-health-of-chicago-film-tv; Christian and Peterson-Salahuddin, "Rage Against the Streaming Studio System."

95. Christian, *Open TV*.

96. Kevito Clark, "'Brown Girls' Producer Sam Bailey Talks Post-#OscarsSoWhite Vibes + Budding Show Hype [Interview]," Okayplayer, November 16, 2016, https://web.archive.org/web/20161121234245/https://www.okayplayer.com/news/brown-girls-series-sam-q-bailey-interview.html.

97. "Dream Bigger: An Interview with the Brilliance Behind Brown Girls," Black Nerd Problems, February 24, 2017, https://blacknerdproblems.com/dream-bigger-an-interview-with-the-brilliance-behind-brown-girls.

98. John Caldwell, *Production Culture: Industrial Reflexivity and Critical Practice in Film and Television* (Duke University Press, 2008), 194.

99. Michael Z. Newman and Elana Levine, *Legitimating Television: Media Convergence and Cultural Status* (Routledge, 2012), 3.

100. Ien Ang, *Watching "Dallas": Soap Opera and the Melodramatic Imagination* (Routledge, 1985); Jacqueline Bobo, *Black Women as Cultural Readers* (Columbia University Press, 1995); Henry Jenkins, *Textual Poachers: Television Fans and Participatory Culture* (Routledge, 1996); Tamar Liebes and Elihu Katz, *The Export of Meaning: Cross-Cultural Readings of "Dallas"* (Oxford University Press, 1990); Jan A. Radway, *Reading*

the Romance: Women, Patriarchy, and Popular Literature (University of North Carolina Press, 2009).

101. Ted Magder, "Television 2.0: The Business of American Television in Transition," in *Reality TV: Remaking Television Culture*, ed. Sarah Murray and Laurie Ouellette (NYU Press, 2009).

102. Felicia D. Henderson, "It's Your Own Fault: How Post-Strike Hollywood Continues to Punish Writers for Striking," *Popular Communication* 8, no. 3 (2010): 232–239; Vicki Mayer, "Little Hollywoods: The Cultural Impacts of Runaway Production," in *The Routledge Companion to Global Popular Culture*, ed. Toby Miller (Routledge, 2014).

103. King, *Inclusive Screenwriting for Film and Television*, 10.

104. Coya Paz, *Ensemble-Made Chicago: A Guide to Devised Theater* (Northwestern University Press, 2019), 91.

105. William Orchard, "Bruja Theory: Latinidad Without Latinos in Popular Narratives of Brujería," in *Posthumanism and Latin(x) American Science Fiction*, ed. Antonio Córdoba and Emily A. Maguire (Palgrave Macmillan, 2023), 213.

106. Diane Bou Khalil, "'Code-Switched' Director Karan Sunil on His New South Asian Sitcom," *Borderless*, November 13, 2020, https://borderlessmag.org/2020/11/13/code-switched-director-karan-sunil-on-his-new-south-asian-sitcom.

107. Khalil, "'Code-Switched' Director Karan Sunil."

108. Al-Baab Khan, Katherine Pieper, Stacy L. Smith, Ariana Case, and Sam Wheeler, *Erased or Extremists: The Stereotypical View of Muslims in Popular Episodic Series* (USC Annenberg Inclusion Initiative, 2022), https://assets.uscannenberg.org/docs/aii-study-muslim-erased-or-extremists-20220901.pdf.

109. TV's core business practices show queer possibilities, as Lynne Joyrich and Taylor Cole Miller have found. See Lynne Joyrich, "Queer Television Studies: Currents, Flows, and (Main) Streams," *Cinema Journal* 53, no. 2 (2014): 133–139; Taylor Cole Miller, "Syndicated Queerness: Television Talk Shows, Rerun Syndication, and the Serials of Norman Lear" (PhD diss., University of Wisconsin–Madison, 2017).

110. See http://weareo.tv/submit.

CHAPTER 4

1. Angèle Christin and Yingdan Lu, "The Influencer Pay Gap: Platform Labor Meets Racial Capitalism," *New Media and Society*, ahead of print April 29, 2023, https://doi.org/10.1177/14614448231116499. For the many other issues that creators of color face, see Jalessa Rosario Turner and Julie Hui, "Racial Capitalism Online: Navigating Race Among Creative Professionals of Color," *Proceedings of the ACM on Human-Computer Interaction* 7, no. CSCW1 (2023): 1–23, https://doi.org/10.1145/3579518.

2. Tressie McMillan Cottom, "Where Platform Capitalism and Racial Capitalism Meet: The Sociology of Race and Racism in the Digital Society," *Sociology of Race and Ethnicity* 6, no. 4 (2020): 443.

3. Thomas Poell, David Nieborg, and Brooke Duffy, *Platforms and Cultural Production* (Polity, 2022), 4.

4. See the section on YouTube in Aymar Jèan Christian, "Scaling Open TV: The Challenges of Big Data Television," in *Open TV: Innovation Beyond Hollywood and the Rise of Web Television* (NYU Press, 2018), 226–240; see also Aymar Jèan Christian, "How YouTube Blew It," *Los Angeles Review of Books*, January 19, 2018, https://lareviewofbooks.org/article/how-youtube-blew-it.

5. Esther Newton, *Mother Camp: Female Impersonators in America* (University of Chicago Press, 1972).

6. Jenn Jackson, "Black Feminisms, Queer Feminisms, Trans Feminisms," in *Routledge Companion to Black Women's Cultural Histories*, ed. Janell Hobson (Routledge, 2021).

7. The TRiiBE, Tiffany Walden, and Morgan Elise Johnson, "The Vixen Revisits the Starting Line of Her Personal Drag Race," *Chicago Reader*, May 17, 2018, https://chicagoreader.com/music/the-vixen-revisits-the-starting-line-of-her-personal-drag-race.

8. T. L. Taylor, *Watch Me Play: Twitch and the Rise of Game Live Streaming* (Princeton University Press, 2018), 22.

9. Nathan Grayson, "How Twitch Lost Its Way," *Washington Post*, March 23, 2023, https://www.washingtonpost.com/video-games/2023/03/23/twitch-subs-ads-layoffs-kai-cenat

10. Grayson, "How Twitch Lost Its Way."

11. Brooke Duffy, Kate Miltner, and Amanda Wahlstedt, "Policing 'Fake' Femininity: Authenticity, Accountability, and Influencer Antifandom," *New Media & Society* 24, no. 7 (2022): 1657–1676; Lei Guo and Summer Harlow, "User-Generated Racism: An Analysis of Stereotypes of African Americans, Latinos, and Asians in YouTube Videos," *Howard Journal of Communications* 25, no. 3 (2014): 281–302; Oliver L. Haimson, Daniel Delmonaco, Peipei Nie, and Andrea Wegner, "Disproportionate Removals and Differing Content Moderation Experiences for Conservative, Transgender, and Black Social Media Users: Marginalization and Moderation Gray Areas," *Proceedings of the ACM on Human-Computer Interaction* 5, no. CSCW2 (2021): 1–35, https://doi.org/10.1145/3479610; Brianna January, "The Right Is Dominating Facebook Engagement on Content About Trans Issues," Media Matters, July 20, 2020, https://www.mediamatters.org/facebook/right-dominating-facebook-engagement-content-about-trans-issues; Amber Johnson, "Antoine Dodson and the (Mis)Appropriation of the Homo Coon: An Intersectional Approach to the Performative Possibilities of Social Media," *Critical Studies in Media Communication* 30, no. 2 (2013): 1–19; Harris

Kornstein, "Under Her Eye: Digital Drag as Obfuscation and Countersurveillance," *Surveillance & Society* 17, no. 5 (2019): 681–698.

12. World of Wonder ignored the problem for years before finally producing a public service announcement in 2020 after a summer of Black Lives Matter protests. See Daniel Reynolds, "Black *Drag Race* Stars Urge Fans to 'Stop the Racism' in PSA," *The Advocate*, September 22, 2020, https://www.advocate.com/race/2020/9/21/black-drag-race-stars-urge-fans-stop-racism-psa.

13. GLAAD, *Social Media Safety Index 2023* (GLAAD, 2023), https://assets.glaad.org/m/7adb1180448da194/original/Social-Media-Safety-Index-2023.pdf.

14. Raven Maragh-Lloyd, *Black Networked Resistance: Strategic Articulations in the Digital Age* (University of California Press, 2024), 112.

15. Meredith D. Clark, "DRAG THEM: A Brief Etymology of So-Called 'Cancel Culture,'" *Communication and the Public* 5, no. 3–4 (2020): 88–92.

16. Brooke Erin Duffy, *(Not) Getting Paid to Do What You Love: Gender, Social Media, and Aspirational Work* (Yale University Press, 2017).

17. André Brock Jr., *Distributed Blackness: African American Cybercultures* (NYU Press, 2020).

18. Chun, "Homophily," 81–138.

19. Chun, "Homophily," 85.

20. Chun, "Homophily," 85–86.

21. We see this in one of the earliest studies of drag performance culture. See Newton, *Mother Camp*.

22. Henry Chu, "Issa Rae Talks About Her White Audience, Shonda Rhimes, and Male Nudity," *Variety*, October 17, 2018, https://variety.com/2018/tv/news/issa-rae-insecure-hbo-shonda-rhimes-male-nudity-1202982674; Alexander Riley, "The Rebirth of Tragedy Out of the Spirit of Hip Hop: A Cultural Sociology of Gangsta Rap Music," *Journal of Youth Studies* 8, no. 3 (2005): 297–311; Charles Scruggs, "'All Dressed Up but No Place to Go': The Black Writer and His Audience During the Harlem Renaissance," *American Literature* 48, no. 4 (1977): 543–563.

23. Rebecca Lewis, "'This Is What the News Won't Show You': YouTube Creators and the Reactionary Politics of Micro-Celebrity," *Television & New Media* 21, no. 2 (2019): 201–217; Rebecca Lewis, *Alternative Influence: Broadcasting the Reactionary Right on YouTube* (Data & Society Research Institute, September 2018), https://apo.org.au/sites/default/files/resource-files/2018-09/apo-nid193281.pdf

24. Catherine Knight Steele, *Digital Black Feminism* (NYU Press, 2021), 17.

25. Maragh-Lloyd, *Black Networked Resistance*, 116.

26. Ferdinand Tönnies, *Community and Society* (1887; Dover Publications, 2002), 33–34.

27. Nancy K. Baym, *Tune In, Log On: Soaps, Fandom, and Online Community* (Sage, 2000); Henry Jenkins, *Fans, Bloggers, and Gamers: Exploring Participatory Culture* (NYU Press, 2006); Barry Wellman, *Networks in the Global Village* (Routledge, 1999).

28. Ted K. Bradshaw, "The Post-Place Community: Contributions to the Debate About the Definition of Community," *Community Development: Journal of the Community Development Society* 39, no. 1 (2008): 5.

29. Diane Carol Fujino, *Heartbeat of Struggle: The Revolutionary Life of Yuri Kochiyama* (University of Minnesota Press, 2005), xxvi; Audre Lorde, "Age, Race, Class and Sex: Women Redefining Difference," in *Sister Outsider: Essays and Speeches* (Crossing Press, 1984).

30. Kelly Hayes and Mariame Kaba, *Let This Radicalize You: Organizing and the Revolution of Reciprocal Care* (Haymarket Books, 2023).

31. Talia Stroud, Caroline Murray, and Emily Graham, *Front Porch Forum: Fostering Civic Engagement and Building Community in Vermont* (New_Public/Center for Media Engagement, University of Texas–Austin, 2024), https://mediaengagement.org/wp-content/uploads/2024/08/Front-Porch-Forum-report.pdf.

32. Poell, Nieborg, and Duffy, *Platforms and Cultural Production*, 8, 80; see also debates on revising Section 230 of the Communications Decency Act of 1996, which insulates platforms from liability: Jaron Lanier and Allison Stanger, "The One Internet Hack That Could Save Everything," *Wired*, February 13, 2024, https://www.wired.com/story/the-one-internet-hack-that-could-save-everything-section-230.

33. Tarleton Gillespie, *Custodians of the Internet: Platforms, Content Moderation, and the Hidden Decisions That Shape Social Media* (Yale University Press, 2018), 5.

34. Gillespie, *Custodians of the Internet*, 82.

35. Gillespie, *Custodians of the Internet*, 11.

36. Siva Vaidhyanathan, *Anti-Social Media: How Facebook Disconnects Us and Undermines Democracy* (Oxford University Press, 2018), 199.

37. Sarah Roberts, *Behind the Screen: Content Moderation in the Shadows of Social Media* (Yale University Press, 2021).

38. Taina Bucher, *If . . . Then: Algorithmic Power and Politics* (Oxford University Press, 2018).

39. Phillip Napoli, "Automated Media: An Institutional Theory Perspective on Algorithmic Media Production and Consumption," *Communication Theory* 24, no. 3 (2014): 343.

40. Joseph Turow, *The Daily You: How the New Advertising Industry Is Defining Your Identity and Your Worth* (Yale University Press, 2012).

41. Nick Couldry, "Social Media: Human Life," *Social Media + Society* 1, no. 1–2 (2015); Lisa Nakamura, "Race in/for Cyberspace: Identity Tourism and Racial Passing on the Internet," *Works and Days* 13, no. 1–2 (1995): 181–193.

42. Anna Everett, "The Revolution Will Be Digitized: Afrocentricity and the Digital Public Sphere," *Social Text* 20, no. 2 (2002): 125–146; Kara Keeling, "Queer OS," *Cinema Journal* 53, no. 2 (2014): 152–157; Anamik Saha, *Race and the Cultural Industries* (Polity Press, 2018).

43. Ruha Benjamin, *Race After Technology: Abolitionist Tools for the New Jim Code* (Polity, 2019), 36.

44. Katherine Sender, "The Gay Market Is Dead, Long Live the Gay Market: From Identity to Algorithm in Predicting Consumer Behavior," *Advertising & Society Quarterly* 18, no. 4 (2017), https://doi.org/10.1353/asr.2018.0001.

45. Simone Browne, *Dark Matters: On the Surveillance of Blackness* (Duke University Press, 2015).

46. danah boyd, "Why Youth (Heart) Social Network Sites: The Role of Networked Publics in Teenage Social Life," in *Youth, Identity, and Digital Media*, ed. David Buckingham (MIT Press, 2008); Chelsea Peterson-Salahuddin, "'Pose': Examining Moments of 'Digital' Dark Sousveillance on TikTok," *New Media & Society* 26, no. 5 (2024): 2387–2406.

47. John Cheney-Lippold, *We Are Data* (NYU Press, 2017); Nick Couldry and Ulises A. Mejias, *The Costs of Connection: How Data Is Colonizing Human Life and Appropriating It for Capitalism* (Stanford University Press, 2019).

48. Oscar Gandy, *The Panoptic Sort: A Political Economy of Personal Information*, 2nd ed.(Oxford University Press, 2021).

49. Kate Crawford, *Atlas of AI* (Yale University Press, 2021), 5.

50. Crawford, *Atlas of AI*, 15.

51. Mary L. Gray and Siddharth Suri, *Ghost Work: How to Stop Silicon Valley from Building a New Global Underclass* (Houghton Mifflin, 2019); Billy Perrigo, "Exclusive: OpenAI Used Kenyan Workers on Less Than $2 Per Hour to Make ChatGPT Less Toxic," *Time*, January 18, 2023, https://time.com/6247678/openai-chatgpt-kenya-workers.

52. Seeta Peña Gangadharan and Jędrzej Niklas, "Decentering Technology in Discourse on Discrimination," *Information, Community & Society* 22, no. 7 (2019): 882–899.

53. Lucas Shaw, "For Every Hit TV Show, There Are More Than 100 Misses," Bloomberg, November 5, 2023, https://www.bloomberg.com/news/newsletters/2023-11-06/what-are-netflix-s-most-popular-tv-shows-these-are-the-top-10.

54. Sam Gutelle, "Here's What We Can Learn from the Reactions to YouTube's Demonetization Controversy," Tubefilter, September 7, 2016, https://www.tubefilter.com/2016/09/07/youtube-demonetization-controversy.

55. Arturo Arriagada and Sophie Bishop, "Between Commerciality and Authenticity: The Imaginary of Social Media Influencers in the Platform Economy,"

Communication, Culture and Critique 14, no. 4 (December 2021): 568–586, https://doi.org/10.1093/ccc/tcab050; Brooke Erin Duffy and Elizabeth Wissinger, "Mythologies of Creative Work in the Social Media Age: Fun, Free, and 'Just Being Me,'" *International Journal of Communication* 11 (2017): 20, https://ijoc.org/index.php/ijoc/article/view/7322/2185; Stuart Cunningham and David Craig, "Being 'Really Real' on YouTube: Authenticity, Community and Brand Culture in Social Media Entertainment," *Media International Australia* 164, no. 1 (2017): 71–81.

56. Much of the literature about branding online focuses on individual influencers who can effectively brand because they embody *one* identity as opposed to multiple ones; corporate brands designed to sell one specific product with a unique aesthetic; or mega-brands that spend billions serving global constituencies. I found evidence for the challenge of branding for small, intersectional channels in this piece: Aymar Jèan Christian, "Beyond Branding: The Value of Intersectionality on Streaming TV Channels," *Television & New Media* 21, no. 5 (2020): 457–474.

57. Margaret Kovach, *Indigenous Methodologies: Characteristics, Conversations, and Contexts* (University of Toronto Press, 2010), 10.

58. Kemi Adeyemi, who supported OTV briefly while a PhD candidate at Northwestern, has an extensive analysis of Slo' Mo and its space at the Whistler in the gentrifying neighborhood of Logan Square in her book, which argues that "slowness is an optic through which we can sense other ways that people negotiate the very real pressures of making-do in environments where we are at times slowly and subtly, and sometimes quickly violently, removed" (42). See Kemi Adeyemi, *Feels Right: Black Queer Women and the Politics of Partying in Chicago* (Duke University Press, 2022), 42.

59. Wendy Chun, *Discriminating Data: Correlation, Neighborhoods, and the New Politics of Recognition* (MIT Press, 2021).

60. Pablo Boczkowski and Eugenia Mitchelstein, *The Digital Environment: How We Live, Learn, Work, and Play Now* (MIT Press, 2021), 8.

61. Nancy Baym, *Playing to the Crowd: Musicians, Audiences, and the Intimate Work of Connection* (NYU Press, 2018), 157.

62. We understand that this segmentation of identity is contrary to the core aims of an intersectional framework, as "questions should be intersectional in design; that is they ought to tap the interdependence and mutuality of identities rather than imply . . . that identities are independent, separate, and able to be ranked" (Lisa Bowleg, "When Black + Lesbian + Woman ≠ Black Lesbian Woman: The Methodological Challenges of Qualitative and Quantitative Intersectionality Research," *Sex Roles* 59, no. 5 (2008): 316). However, Bowleg concedes that the separation of variables is inevitable in any quantitative research design: "It is virtually impossible, particularly in quantitative research, to ask questions about intersectionality that are not inherently additive" (314). The dangers of this is the presumption that "social inequality increases with each additional stigmatized identity" (314). However,

because our research design is organic and led by intersectional artists, we have found the exact opposite. Moreover, we have segmented identities but included "intersectional" to specify which platforms specifically focus on complex identifications and will discuss these categories in relation to each other as much as feasible.

63. It is my suspicion that most of the loads marked as "Vimeo" in the *Brown Girls* data set actually come from "browngirlswebseries.com," as a plurality of the "views" come from that site.

64. Dayna Chatman, "Black Twitter and the Politics of Viewing Scandal," in *Fandom: Identities and Communities in a Mediated World,* 2nd ed., ed. Jonathan Gray, Cornell Sandvoss, and C. Lee Harrington (NYU Press, 2017).

65. Sarah J. Jackson, Moya Bailey, and Brooke Foucault Welles, *#HashtagActivism: Networks of Race and Gender Justice* (MIT Press, 2020), xxxviii.

66. Machines struggle to learn how to decode the ways that diverse peoples self-express and how to prioritize human over automated communication. For one, many of the *Brown Girls* retweets on premiere nights came from Twitter bots or spam accounts. In another part of the experiment, we ran an automated sentiment analysis on a sample of 1,049 *Brown Girls* tweets from 2017 to 2019 and found that overall engagement was positive. However, the research team also found that the sample was more positive than the machine estimated. Our recoding of the data, by researchers who identified with the communities represented, revealed many positive tweets rated negative by the machine, presumably for use of vulgarity or sarcasm. This shows the importance of community-engaged practitioners in the platform management. See Desmond U. Patton, William R. Frey, Kyle A. McGregor, Fei-Tzin Lee, Kathleen McKeown, and Emanuel Moss, "Contextual Analysis of Social Media: The Promise and Challenge of Eliciting Context in Social Media Posts with Natural Language Processing," in *AIES '20: Proceedings of the AAAI/ACM Conference on AI, Ethics, and Society* (ACM, 2020).

67. D. Soyini Madison, "Performing Theory/Embodied Writing," *Text and Performance Quarterly* 19, no. 2 (1999): 108.

68. Omi Osun Joni L. Jones, "Performance Ethnography: The Role of Embodiment in Cultural Authenticity," *Theatre Topics* 12, no. 1 (2002): 7, 10.

69. For the full report, see Chelsea Peterson-Salahuddin, "Chicago Community on OTV (2017–18)," OTV, September 3, 2019, https://www.weareo.tv/research//chicago-community-on-otv-2017-18.

70. Elizabeth Ellcessor, *Restricted Access: Media, Disability, and the Politics of Participation* (NYU Press, 2016), 4.

71. Ellcessor, *Restricted Access*, 5.

72. Kerry Cardoza, "'The Long Dream' and a Labor Nightmare," *Chicago Reader*, March 3, 2021, https://chicagoreader.com/arts-culture/the-long-dream-and-a-labor-nightmare.

73. "MCA Chicago x OTV Partnership Engagement Letter," OTV, March 24, 2021, https://www.weareo.tv/community//otv-x-mca-partnership-engagement-letter.

CHAPTER 5

1. For more on the difference, see M. Kay Harris, "Transformative Justice: The Transformation of Restorative Justice," in *Handbook of Restorative Justice: A Global Perspective*, ed. Dennis Sullivan and Larry Tifft (Routledge, 2005).

2. Shira Hassan, "Harm Reduction Is Our Shared Root: Interview with Mariame Kaba," in *Saving Our Own Lives: A Liberatory Practice of Harm Reduction* (Haymarket Books, 2022).

3. Cam Awkward-Rich, *The Terrible We: Thinking with Trans Maladjustment* (Duke University Press, 2022), 4.

4. Hil Malatino, "The Promise of Repair: Trans Rage and the Limits of Feminist Coalition," *Signs* 46, no. 4 (2021): 845–846.

5. Rebecca Wanzo, "An Ethics of Uncare: Coalition Politics After the Turn of the Century," in *Routledge Companion to Intersectionalities*, ed. Jennifer C. Nash and Samantha Pinto (Routledge, 2023), 14.

6. Ray Pride, "Aymar Jean Christian: 25 New Faces of Indie Film," *Filmmaker*, September 14, 2018, https://filmmakermagazine.com/people/aymar-jean-christian.

7. Aymar Jèan Christian, "Open TV Production," in *Open TV: Innovation Beyond Hollywood and the Rise of Web Television* (NYU Press, 2018).

8. It was also motivated by a trademark lawsuit from Open TV, Inc., a tech company defending its brand as required by trademark law. As a project of Northwestern not owned by the university, the university's lawyers would not defend me. I hired my own lawyers, pro bono, who recommended that we rebrand, eventually as OTV | Open Television, and incorporate as an entity so liability would not fall on me personally.

9. adrienne maree brown, *Emergent Strategy: Shaping Change, Changing Worlds* (AK Press, 2017).

10. Rebecca Alter, "Every Blackface Episode and Scene That's Been Pulled from Streaming so Far," *Vulture*, June 29, 2020, https://www.vulture.com/2020/06/blackface-tv-episodes-scenes-removed-streaming.html.

11. In anthropology there is more awareness of this, starting with the work of Ruth Behar. See Ruth Behar, *The Vulnerable Observer: Anthropology That Breaks Your Heart* (Beacon Press, 1997).

12. "A Public Call to Support Restorative Justice for Sol Cabrini," OTV, January 13, 2021, https://www.weareo.tv/community//a-public-call-to-support-restorative-justice-for-sol-cabrini.

13. Tourmaline, introduction to Hassan, *Saving Our Own Live*, xviii–xix.

14. Sol Cabrini, ".JPG," in *Tgirl.jpg* (Roof Books, 2024).

15. Founder's syndrome has been defined as "the influential powers and privileges that the founder exercises. . . . The use of the word *syndrome* further suggests unhealthy organizational situations in which founders are more heavy-handed and indifferent about the imbalance of their control over organizations." See Stephen R. Block and Steven Rosenberg, "Toward an Understanding of Founder's Syndrome: An Assessment of Power and Privilege Among Founders of Nonprofit Organizations," *Nonprofit Management & Leadership* 12, no. 4 (2002): 354.

16. Media Impact Funders, *Foundation Maps for Media Funding: Introducing a New Tool for Unlocking the Power of Media Grants Data* (Media Impact Funders, 2016), https://mediaimpactfunders.org/wp-content/uploads/2016/06/Map-Report_final-to-print.pdf.

17. Edgar Villanueva, *Decolonizing Wealth: Indigenous Wisdom to Heal Divides and Restore Balance* (Berrett-Koehler, 2018).

18. John Palfrey, "Examining Demographics, Changing Our Status Quo," MacArthur Foundation Perspectives, October 29, 2020, https://www.macfound.org/press/perspectives/examining-demographics-changing-our-status-quo.

19. I never profited from OTV Studio, and only once was I paid by the OTV nonprofit: during the leadership transition from 2020 to 2021, when the organization needed over two dozen grants written at the same time I had to redevelop five classes for Zoom during the pandemic.

INDEX

Page numbers in italics indicate figures.

Publisher contact:
The MIT Press
Massachusetts Institute of Technology
77 Massachusetts Avenue, Cambridge, MA 02139
mitpress.mit.edu

EU Authorised Representative:
Easy Access System Europe, Mustamäe tee 50,
10621 Tallinn, Estonia
gpsr.requests@easproject.com

Printed by Integrated Books International,
United States of America